Speaking Chicana

Speaking Chicana

Voice, Power, and Identity

◆ ◆

Edited by

D. Letticia Galindo

◆

María Dolores Gonzales

◆ ◆ ◆

THE UNIVERSITY OF ARIZONA PRESS

TUCSON

The University of Arizona Press
© 1999 The Arizona Board of Regents
First Printing

⊖ This book is printed on acid-free, archival-quality paper.
Manufactured in the United States of America

04   03   02   01   00   99   6   5   4   3   2   1

Library of Congress Cataloging-in-Publication Data
Speaking Chicana : voice, power, and identity
/ edited by D. Letticia Galindo and María Dolores Gonzales.
p. cm.
Includes bibliographical references (p.) and index.
ISBN 0-8165-1814-9 (acid-free, archival-quality paper)
ISBN 0-8165-1815-7 (pbk. : acid-free, archival-quality paper)
1. Mexican American women—Language. 2. Sociolinguistics—
United States. I. Galindo, D. Letticia (Delma Letticia), 1952–
II. Gonzales, María Dolores, 1946–
P40.45.U5 S68 1999   98-40147
306.44'6'0820973—dc21   CIP

British Cataloguing-in-Publication Data
A catalogue record for this book is available from the British Library.

Publication of this book is made possible in part by the proceeds of a
permanent endowment created with the assistance of a Challenge Grant
from the National Endowment for the Humanities, a federal agency.

In Memory of

D. Letticia Galindo

1952–1998

◆

Para mi abuela, Juanita Pérez Mejía (1903–1993),

and mi mamá, Lydia Mejía Galindo, with great love,

respeto, and admiration

◆

To my sisters, Consuelo, Erlinda, Cecilia, y Gloria,

con amor y cariño

CONTENTS

◆ ◆ ◆

Acknowledgments ix

List of Abbreviations xi

Introduction 3

PART ONE   Reconstruction:
Language Varieties, Language Use, and Language Attitudes

1 Crossing Social and Cultural Borders: The Road to Language
    Hybridity
  María Dolores Gonzales 13

2 Fighting Words: Latina Girls, Gangs, and Language Attitudes
  Norma Mendoza-Denton 39

PART TWO   Reflection: Testimonios

3 Speaking as a Chicana: Tracing Cultural Heritage through
    Silence and Betrayal
  Jacqueline M. Martínez 59

4 The Power of Language: From the Back of the Bus to the Ivory
    Tower
  Christine Marín 85

5 Challenging Tradition: Opening the Headgate
  Ida M. Luján 98

6 Mexican Blood Runs through My Veins
   Aurora E. Orozco 106

PART THREE   Innovation:
Speaking Creatively/Creatively Speaking

 7 Searching for a Voice: Ambiguities and Possibilities
   Erlinda Gonzales-Berry 123

 8 Sacred Cults, Subversive Icons: Chicanas and the Pictorial
      Language of Catholicism
   Charlene Villaseñor Black 134

 9 Caló and Taboo Language Use among Chicanas: A Description of
      Linguistic Appropriation and Innovation
   D. Letticia Galindo 175

10 *Máscaras, Trenzas, y Greñas:* Un/Masking the Self While
      Un/Braiding Latina Stories and Legal Discourse
   Margaret E. Montoya 194

About the Contributors 213
Index 217

Acknowledgments

The editors would like to take this opportunity to thank those individuals and institutions that made this volume possible. This volume would not have taken shape without our contributors—*las mujeres*—who hail from diverse academic and personal backgrounds. This is a truly eclectic effort in the transmission of myriad Chicana voices. *¡Muchas gracias!*

I, Letticia Galindo, would like to take this opportunity to thank the Hispanic Research Center at Arizona State University for their continuing research support and the staff at the Humanities Computing Lab, who assisted me in computer-related matters as I formatted and edited this volume. My thanks also to María Dolores y familia, who have treated me kindly during my many trips to Albuquerque and Embudo. Gracias for the hospitality, New Mexican cuisine, and ambiance that facilitated the conceptualization and termination of this volume.

I, María Dolores, thank the Southwest Hispanic Research Institute at the University of New Mexico for its assistance and in-kind services, which made this volume a reality. To Tey Diana Rebolledo, who listened to my ideas and gave me valuable feedback; to Ricardo, for helping me with the Embudo summits; and to my family—Damián, Juliana and Alejandro, Rafael and Geraldine. And special thanks to my dear friend and colega, Letticia, who shared my dream.

My thanks also to Letticia's students, friends, and colegas for the financial assistance they provided to complete the indexing of this book.

ABBREVIATIONS

ASU	Arizona State University (Tempe)
CARA	*Chicano Art: Resistance and Affirmation, 1965–1985*
CCC	Civilian Conservation Corps
CSU	California State University
ESL	English as a Second Language
FEP	Fluent English Proficient
LEP	Limited English Proficient
LULAC	League of United Latin American Citizens
MASO	Mexican American Students Organization
MECHA	Movimiento Estudiantil Chicano de Aztlán
SJHS	Sor Juana High School (northern California)
SUNY	State University of New York
UC	University of California
UCLA	University of California at Los Angeles
UCSB	University of California at Santa Barbara

SPEAKING CHICANA

INTRODUCTION

In 1992, María Dolores and I attended and participated in the Second Berkeley Women & Language Conference as presenters. Given the fact that there are not many Chicana sociolinguists as a whole and, more specifically, who conduct research on women and language, we decided to jointly showcase our empirical scholarship that examined language use among Tejanas and Nuevo Mexicanas in a paper entitled "A Sociolinguistic Description of Linguistic Self-expression, Innovativeness, and Power among Chicanas in Texas and New Mexico." We made several observations at this conference, the most salient being the paucity of Women of Color as presenters, more specifically Chicanas/Latinas. Our academic voices were heard by an audience composed mainly of Euro-American, educated women who represented a cross section of disciplines beyond sociolinguistics. Being junior faculty members, it was important for us to have our work published in volume 1 of the *Proceedings* (Hall, Bucholtz & Moonwomon 1992) from an institution such as UC Berkeley. What also struck a chord was the fact that these volumes were being edited by graduate students, not tenured or tenure-track scholars. This conference was the spark and impetus we needed. María Dolores and I came to the realization that we could do the same thing with our scholarship and with the scholarship of other Chicanas inside and outside the academy.

Consequently, since 1992 we have been discussing the idea of doing our own volume. Through a series of "summits" held in Embudo, New Mexico—early morning walks along the Río Grande and many late-night discussions under a starlit sky—the rationale for and contents of this volume were conceptualized. Within this introduction we will provide an overview of the reasons why this volume is necessary, along with a description of the contents of each section.

Much of the current research across a variety of disciplines, including linguistics (e.g., Foster 1992; Galindo 1992; Farr 1994; Gonzales Velásquez 1995; Smitherman 1995), anthropology (e.g., Medicine 1987; Harness Goodwin 1990; Gal 1995; Menchaca 1995), Women's/Feminist

Studies (e.g., Anzaldúa 1987, 1990; Trujillo 1991; Moraga 1993), literature (e.g., Alarcón et al. 1993; Rebolledo & Rivero 1993; Herrera-Sobek &
Viramontes 1995), education (e.g., McKenna & Ortiz 1988; Valdés 1996),
and the social sciences (e.g., Harris 1988; Pérez 1990; Cuadraz 1992),
appears to address the silenced, marginalized, and often-ignored voices
of women—be they ethnic minorities, linguistic minorities, lesbians, or
immigrants.

Despite this proliferation of scholarly works—those mentioned here
and countless others that remain unmentioned—a tremendous lacuna remains in works *about* Chicanas, *for* Chicanas, and *by* Chicanas as they
pertain to language-related issues. This muting and omission of the voices
of marginalized women has meant a lack of knowledge and understanding of the realities they live. Because there is a dialectic between voice and
reality, the way in which we use language serves to construct, define, and
reshape this reality in the same way that it helps shape and construct our
language. However, past linguistic research on Chicanas has often reflected etic (outsider) perspectives that may lead to wrong assumptions or
sweeping generalizations about the cultural and linguistic norms of the
communities under study. Therefore, it is our contention that the emic
(insider) perspective is needed here in order to provide a more holistic,
nativist understanding of Chicanas' language experiences (Hymes 1989)
and to address this gap.

For the purposes of this book, "Chicana" is defined as someone
born in the United States or who migrated to the United States; someone
who has cultural and linguistic contact with two cultures and who may
have experienced the "crossing of borders" as described by Anzaldúa
(1987.) The uniqueness of this volume lies in its format, because it includes both empirical studies and personal narratives in the form of *testimonios* on language use, as well as in its content, which transcends the
discipline of linguistics to include works from art, law, Women's Studies,
and literature.

Like many other Chicanas, we have experienced exclusion and silencing in our respective speech communities of rural west Texas and
rural northern New Mexico. Not only were these done through punitive
measures by Anglo teachers for speaking Spanish in educational contexts, but also in institutions of higher learning by Latin American and
Spanish professors or fellow students who criticized and ridiculed our
varieties of Chicano Spanish. This silencing was not confined to educa-

tional domains but also occurred within our own speech communities and families. Beyond these familiar parameters exist outside hegemonic forces that continue to silence, exclude, and disempower Chicanas. Because of this repression and discrimination, we as sociolinguists believe that a volume such as this one is vital to the empowerment of the diverse Chicana voices that transcend age, socioeconomic status, education, sexual orientation, nativity, residence, and geography.

The title of this book is *Speaking Chicana: Voice, Power, and Identity.* It is divided into three parts: "Reconstruction: Language Varieties, Language Use, and Language Attitudes"; "Reflection: Testimonios"; and "Innovation: Speaking Creatively/Creatively Speaking." Underlying part 1's theme of reconstruction is the idea of "re-creating" a voice that has been dormant and undocumented. Empirical descriptions of language varieties, language uses, and language attitudes are virtually nonexistent as they pertain to Chicanas. Apparently women were never the subjects of serious linguistic investigation until the 1980s. Two empirical studies grounded in sociolinguistics, the sociology of language, and ethnographic field methods that explore women's language use in New Mexico and in northern California compose the first part of the book.

"Crossing Social and Cultural Borders: The Road to Language Hybridity" by María Dolores Gonzales discusses and describes the linguistic varieties—Spanish, English, codeswitching—that New Mexican Chicanas across three generations have at their disposal, as well as their functions and uses across private and public domains in intergroup and intragroup situations. By viewing the amalgam of two linguistic codes (Spanish and English) as one code, namely codeswitching, the author argues for this to be viewed as a linguistic hybrid that has become an accepted form of communication, especially among second- and third-generation Chicanas.

The setting for the essay "Fighting Words: Latina Girls, Gangs, and Language Attitudes" by Norma Mendoza-Denton is a northern California high school and community. On the basis of intensive and extensive ethnographic fieldwork among Latina girls, the author gives us a glimpse of their culture and the dichotomy that exists between recent arrivals and U.S.-born Latinas in terms of dress, self-identification, even language. Issues impacting language policy and programs, including English as a Second Language and its impact on these Latino/a students, are also examined.

Part 2 comprises autobiographical accounts, referred to as *testi-*

monios (Sánchez 1995), that reflect and capture the social, cultural, emotional, and linguistic ethos of the Chicana. These essays also reflect the geographic diversity of these testimonios provided by California, Arizona, New Mexico, and Texas women.

In "Speaking as a Chicana: Tracing Cultural Heritage through Silence and Betrayal," Jacqueline M. Martínez meshes her academic voice with her personal voice to convey her story of coming-to-consciousness as a Chicana. She discusses her experience of growing up in dual cultures—Anglo and Mexican—and her attempts to sort out why her Mexican-American father was silent in sharing aspects of his culture and language with her as she was growing up in southern California. In her quest to gain knowledge of what it means to be Chicana and mestiza, Martínez has embraced the writings and teachings of Chicana feminist-lesbian scholars such as Gloria Anzaldúa, Emma Pérez, and Cherríe Moraga.

A native Arizonan, Christine Marín describes growing up in a small mining town in her essay "The Power of Language: From the Back of the Bus to the Ivory Tower," and how she first experienced discrimination on a school bus during a high school band trip. Her Spanish voice had been repressed and silenced, but soon afterward, as she joined the workforce in metropolitan Phoenix, she discovered how important it was to speak two languages instead of just one. She describes other salient events in her life—her rise to becoming the curator/archivist of the Chicano Collection at Arizona State University and her involvement in MECHA as a student leader—that helped create other voices.

Northern New Mexico is the setting for the essay by Ida M. Luján, "Challenging Tradition: Opening the Headgate." Through her description of the *acequia* tradition, the reader sees how such a tradition is couched in strict gender role demarcations and how women's voices are stifled and ostracized through such a process. She describes her empowerment from these interactions and how today she has taken the chairmanship, once a male-only enterprise.

The voice of the Chicana activist can be heard in the essay, "Mexican Blood Runs Through my Veins" by Aurora E. Orozco. She describes her experiences growing up in Mexico and migrating to the Río Grande Valley. One can distinctly hear the voices of our own *madres* and *abuelas* who were strong and determined women, survivors of the Great Depression and world wars. La señora Orozco tells of her experiences with school segregation, punishment for speaking Spanish, and her role as a community activist in a south Texas city that was economically dominated by the Anglo.

Part 3 illustrates the different ways in which its authors utilize and manipulate different voices—be they Chicano Spanish, New Mexican Spanish, caló, or codeswitching—and languages—be they pictorial/visual language, taboo language, or legal language. Why do some women opt to write or speak in Spanish, English, or a combination of these as they convey their literary voice? Erlinda Gonzales-Berry's essay "Searching for a Voice: Ambiguities and Possibilities" explores this topic. As the author of *Paletitas de guayaba,* a novel written in Spanish, she discusses what led her to select these codes to be transmitted by her protagonists and why she used elements of New Mexican Spanish as well as male-dominated caló.

The semantic extension of language beyond words to pictures on canvas, what Charlene Villaseñor Black refers to as pictorial language or visual language, is captured in the essay "Sacred Cults, Subversive Icons: Chicanas and the Pictorial Language of Catholicism." Similar to the multidialectal repertoire Chicanas possess and manipulate as they transcend cultural borders as described by Anzaldúa (1987) are the pictorial discourses—including North American, Spanish/Spanish Colonial, Mexican, Chicano, Native American, and Mesoamerican—that four New Mexican artists use. This visual language of Catholicism serves as a means of articulating their cultural and ethnic identities as Chicanas.

Language used by *pachucas/pintas* is documented through the use of specialized jargons and registers. Also, the use of taboo language in the form of expletives within speech events, including challenging, insulting, and boasting, further defines the innovativeness, creativity, and agility to handle one or various linguistic codes in intra- and intergroup settings. This is the topic of D. Letticia Galindo's essay, "Caló and Taboo Language Use among Chicanas: A Description of Linguistic Appropriation and Innovation."

Margaret E. Montoya uses the motif of braids and weaves together the personal and the academic voice, legal scholarship, and scholarship from other disciplines in her essay *"Máscaras, Trenzas, y Greñas:* Un/Masking the Self While Un/Braiding Latina Stories and Legal Discourse." Though untidy *(greñas),* these linguistic and conceptual braids *(trenzas)* challenge conventional paradigms within the legal academy and subvert the dominant discourse.

We believe this volume truly offers a multifaceted perspective on what we refer to as the Chicana voice, and hope that it will penetrate the walls of the academy across disciplines, as well as reach *nuestras hermanas* outside the academy. That is our vision, our *sueño*.

REFERENCES

Alarcón, N., et al. (eds.) (1993). *Chicana Critical Issues.* Berkeley, CA: Third Woman Press.

Anzaldúa, G. (1987). *Borderlands/La Frontera: The New Mestiza.* San Francisco: Aunt Lute Books.

—— (ed.). (1990). *Making Face, Making Soul: Haciendo Caras.* San Francisco: Aunt Lute Books.

Cuadraz, G. (1992). Experiences in multiple marginality: A case study of Chicana scholarship women. Special issue: "Chicanos in Higher Education 1992." *Journal of the Association of Mexican American Educators,* 31–43.

Farr, M. (1994). Echando relajo: Verbal art and gender among Mexicanas in Chicago. In M. Bucholtz et al. (eds.), *Cultural Performances: Proceedings of the Third Berkeley Women & Language Conference* (pp. 168–186). Berkeley, CA: Berkeley Women & Language Group.

Foster, M. (1992). Are you with me? Power, solidarity and community in the discourse of African American women. In K. Hall et al. (eds.), *Locating Power: Proceedings of the Second Berkeley Women & Language Conference,* Volume 1 (pp. 132–144). Berkeley, CA: Berkeley Women & Language Group.

Gal, S. (1995). Language, gender, and power: An anthropological review. In K. Hall & M. Bucholtz (eds.), *Gender Articulated: Language and the Socially Constructed Self* (pp. 169–182). New York: Routledge.

Galindo, D. L. (1992). Dispelling the male-only myth: Chicanas and caló. *Bilingual Review/La Revista Bilingüe* 17 (1), 3–35.

Gonzales Velásquez, M. D. (1995). Sometimes Spanish, sometimes English: Language use among rural New Mexican Chicanas. In K. Hall & M. Bucholtz (eds.), *Gender Articulated: Language and the Socially Constructed Self* (pp. 421–446). New York: Routledge.

Hall, K., M. Bucholtz, & B. Moonwomon (eds.) (1992). *Locating Power: Proceedings of the Second Berkeley Women & Language Conference,* Volume 1. Berkeley, CA: Berkeley Women & Language Group.

Harness Goodwin, M. (1990). *He-Said-She-Said: Talk as Social Organization among Black Children.* Bloomington: Indiana University Press.

Harris, M. (1988). *Cholas: Latino Girls and Gangs.* New York: AMS Press.

Herrera-Sobek, M., & H. M. Viramontes. (1995). *Chicana (W)rites: On Word and Film*. Berkeley, CA: Third Woman Press.

Hymes, D. (1989). Models of the interaction of language and social life. In J. Gumperz & D. Hymes (eds.), *Directions in Sociolinguistics* (pp. 35–71). New York: Basil Blackwell.

McKenna, T., & F. I. Ortiz. (1988). *The Broken Web: The Educational Experiences of Hispanic American Women*. Berkeley, CA: Floricanto Press.

Medicine, B. (1987). The role of American Indian women in cultural continuity and transition. In J. Penfield (ed.), *Women and Language in Transition* (pp. 159–165). New York: SUNY Press.

Menchaca, M. (1995). *The Mexican Outsiders: A Community History of Marginalization and Discrimination in California*. Austin: University of Texas Press.

Moraga, C. (1993). *The Last Generation*. Boston: South End Press.

Pérez, E. (1990). A la mujer: A critique of the Mexican Liberal Party's ideology on women. In A. Del Castillo (ed.), *Between Borders: Essays on Mexicana/Chicana History* (pp. 459–482). Encino, CA: Floricanto Press.

Rebolledo, T. D., & E. Rivero (eds.). (1993). *Infinite Divisions: An Anthology of Chicana Literature*. Tucson: University of Arizona Press.

Sánchez, R. (1995). *Telling Identities: The Californio Testimonios*. Minneapolis: University of Minnesota Press.

Smitherman, G. (1995). *African American Women Speak Out on Anita Hill–Clarence Thomas*. Detroit: Wayne State University Press.

Trujillo, C. (ed.). (1991). *Chicana Lesbians: The Girls Our Mothers Warned Us About*. Berkeley, CA: Third Woman Press.

Valdés, G. (1996). *Con Respeto: Bridging Distances between Culturally Diverse Families and Schools—An Ethnographic Portrait*. New York: Columbia University, Teachers College Press.

ONE

RECONSTRUCTION

LANGUAGE VARIETIES, LANGUAGE USE, AND LANGUAGE ATTITUDES

1

•••

CROSSING SOCIAL AND CULTURAL BORDERS

The Road to Language Hybridity

María Dolores Gonzales

The words "crossing borders" conjure up visions of individuals traversing from one country to another. In the Southwest, "crossing borders" suggests individuals coming into the United States at one of many entry points: from Juárez to El Paso, from Tijuana to San Diego, or from Reynosa to McAllen. And as for those individuals who move across these borders, we think of monolingual Spanish-speakers coming to a country where English is the superordinate language. Rarely do we think of crossing social and cultural borders within the already established speech communities in which different languages and cultures have been in contact over long periods of time—since 1848 in the Southwest. What occurs in situations of language and cultural contact is not a new phenomenon; in fact, it has been a subject of repeated study. However, most of the research conducted here in Nuevo México, as well as throughout the Southwest, has focused either on the maintenance of Spanish or on the shift toward English (Ortiz 1975; Hudson-Edwards & Bills 1982; Chávez 1984). Seldom have studies focused on women's language use. Since women have historically been the guardians of language and culture (Zentella 1987), it would seem appropriate that studies focus on women's linguistic behavior. Such studies would provide a better understanding of the mechanics and implications of language use and language choice when Chicanas' social networks are extended beyond the private domains and across generations.[1]

In this study, I illustrate how three generations of women from Córdova, New Mexico, extend their social networks and, in doing so, readily cross social, cultural, and linguistic borders vis-à-vis various domains. By grounding my work within the concepts of language choice and border culture in a Spanish/English context of various speech communities, this study reveals that women have at their disposal various linguistic codes that they deem appropriate to use across private and public domains and with select interlocutors.[2] Furthermore, the variables of ethnicity, identity, solidarity, accommodation, age, respect, and social networks are taken into account in describing the linguistic interactions in both in-group and transcultural interactions by Cordovan women.[3]

HISTORICAL BACKGROUND

I include a brief historical synopsis inasmuch as it provides us with information about what transpired linguistically after the United States conquest of 1848, and how these factors influenced the present linguistic situation in Córdova, New Mexico. The northern New Mexico dialect, brought in by the early Spanish and Mexican settlers, was established by the profound and prolonged isolation experienced by Nuevo Mexicanos from 1598 to 1848. The first sustained contact the northern New Mexican Spanish-speaking people had with the English-speaking Anglo Americans occurred with the conquest and occupation in 1848. The conquest brought about many changes. The proliferation of the Anglo population left the Spanish-speaking people vulnerable to an intrusive language and culture. By the end of the nineteenth century, complete economic, social, and political subjugation had occurred in spite of the fact that the Treaty of Guadalupe Hidalgo had provided formal guarantees to preserve language, property and political rights for the new Spanish-speaking citizens (Acuña 1972).

The need to "Americanize" the native population was first and foremost on the minds of the Anglo colonizers, and education was seen as the means to accomplish this. However, according to Milk (1980), there were several reasons why the public education system did not go into effect immediately. Besides the limited resources as a result of the tax base and the role of the Catholic Church in education, the native population was skeptical about the establishment of public education. They were not as willing to sacrifice traditional values in the name of "progress" as were the Anglo newcomers and some of the elite Hispanos. In fact, one Mexicano perspective was that "a common school system for all children, aside from being alien to their cultural tradition, was an idea that symbolized a covert attempt on the part of Anglo outsiders to subvert their culture through the inculcation of alien values in their children" (Milk 1980:214). The native population was not wrong in suspecting that a public education system would mean the loss of the mother tongue and cultural domination by the Anglos. The language question was at the heart of the school issue.

Although the language issue was not dealt with explicitly by the organizers of the educational proposals, "It was assumed that any public education system established in a territory in the United States would use English as a medium of instruction, especially since the strongest rationale for providing schooling in the first place (at least among those who saw a public school system as a precondition for statehood) was to provide English instruction for those children who came from non-English speaking homes" (Milk 1980:215). Resistance to public education on the part of many Mexicanos during the territorial period contributed not only to the confrontation between the two groups but also helped strengthen group solidarity and unity because of the threat to the native language and cultural traditions.

SETTING

Córdova is a rural community of seven hundred inhabitants, only two of whom are Anglos. The uniqueness of this speech community is its tight-knit social structure, which has survived since the mid-eighteenth century and which continues to function as a norm-enforcement mechanism for the maintenance of the vernacular, Spanish. The stability of the dense and multiplex social structure has created a strong sense of in-group cohesiveness and linguistic security. Although the community language is Spanish, Córdova is a fairly stable bilingual community in that despite its rural and isolated nature, residents across generations are fluent in English because of schooling and social contact with English-speaking individuals in the public domain.

DESIGN

The design of this study was based on the assumption that the linguistic patterns of the respondents could not be understood independently of social and cultural patterns, and vice versa. Thus, an ethnographic approach was used to examine the use of Spanish, English, and codeswitching among Cordovan women. This ethnographic approach involved living in Córdova for ten weeks to gain entry and ultimately become a participant rather than a mere observer in women's social interactions. Respondent 3B, who was my student at the University of New Mexico, introduced me to the respondents who participated in this study as well as to other community members. To gain an overall perspective of language use within this speech community, general observations of the language behavior of all members—both male and female, adults and children—were documented. However, the focus remained on same-sex linguistic interactions.

DATA COLLECTION

Data collection took place over a ten-week period. Formal interviews and observations of language use of the nine respondents were conducted in two contexts: intragroup and intergroup (transcultural) situations. These events included an anniversary party, a bridal shower, a family reunion, and a wedding. "Intragroup interaction" is defined as the linguistic interaction that takes place among those individuals belonging to a specific speech community or ethnic group, the in-group (Sherif 1966). "In-group" is defined as those individuals belonging to an ethnic group who share the same language and cultural identity (Sherif 1966). When speaking Spanish, these women identify themselves as Mexicanas who speak Mexicano. "Intergroup interaction" is defined as the interaction that occurs, collectively or individually, between members of two distinct groups (Sherif 1966). In this case, persons not residing in Córdova are considered outgroup members, regardless of their ethnic background. The formal interview was based on twenty-six questions that were divided into three categories: (1) demographic information; (2) uses of Spanish and English; and (3) attitudes related to the use and maintenance of both Spanish and English. These open-ended questions produced a vast and dynamic range of responses that helped in explaining women's use of English and/or Spanish in different settings.

The formal interview lasted between one and two hours and was tape-recorded in the respondents' homes, as was the informal discourse that occurred between women. The self-reported and self-evaluation in-

Table 1.1 Three Cordovan Families: Ages of Women by Generation

Generation	Family A	Family B	Family C
1	79	96	46
2	52	65	26
3	25	23	3

formation pertaining to language use was compared with observed linguistic interactions so as to confirm the general speech patterns and language use of the respondents.

To obtain these linguistic interviews, it was possible to draw on my own experiences and memories of having been a resident of a small village in northern New Mexico. I knew that the most important task was not to be viewed as an "outsider." I was aware that being an urban, middle-class, educated Chicana could create unfriendliness, distrust, and rejection. Nevertheless, my cultural, ethnic, and linguistic background permitted me to establish rapport with the women in the community. Rather than employing a traditional interview primarily as a device for obtaining information in the least amount of time and with the least amount of personal contact, I concentrated on the interview process as a communicative event; that is, I functioned as a coparticipant in the dialogue and discourse that transpired between the respondents and other women. This participation contributed to rapport-building speech events that helped decrease the distance between cultural and communicative norms of the researcher and those of the respondents. This friendly atmosphere prevented a hiatus that could have generated interpersonal tensions and misinterpretation in the interviewing process (Briggs 1986).

CORDOVAN WOMEN: A DESCRIPTION

The respondents were chosen on the basis of their interest in participating and their availability. The most important factor was the presence in the community of three generations of the family: daughter, mother, and grandmother. The ages of the respondents ranged from three to ninety-six, as shown in table 1.1. The families are identified as Family A, Family B, and Family C, and within each family the individual women are identified by generational number only.

Because there was information on four generations available in Family C, I included second-generation Respondent 1C as part of the first generation, rather than her mother (age seventy-five), in order to observe linguistic interaction with and by a three-year-old, Respondent 3C. Observing the three-year-old's linguistic behavior allowed me to determine whether Spanish was being transmitted to the younger generation.

Linguistic Characteristics

Language competence and use of the women varied. Respondents 1A and 1B are both monolingual in Spanish. The remaining seven respondents are proficient in both Spanish and English. Respondents 3A and 3B are English-dominant, and Respondents 2A, 2B, 1C, 2C, and 3C are Spanish-dominant.

Domain

The language patterns summarized above suggest that domain is an important means of predicting language choice in bilingual/bicultural settings. The concept of domain follows closely that elaborated by Fishman (1966:980), who identifies family, friendship, employment, education, government, and religion as typical and appropriate clusters of settings and relationships affecting language choice for most bilinguals. "Domains are defined, regardless of their number, in terms of institutional contexts and the congruent behavioral co-occurrences. They attempt to summate the major clusters of interaction that occur in clusters of multilingual settings and involving clusters of interlocutors." Congruent behavior is that which occurs when individuals interact in appropriate role relationships with each other, in appropriate locales for those relationships, and discuss topics appropriate to their role relationships. In keeping with Fishman's paradigm, interactions that occur in the intimate setting, the home, and the informal intragroup interactions that take place with family members, friends, neighbors, and community are classified in this study as belonging to the private domain. The clusters of interaction within the public domain take place in settings outside of the community, such as government, educational, and employment locales. In view of the isolation and the tight-knit social structures present in Córdova, I have included the community setting as a component of the private domain.

Language Varieties and Their Uses in Córdova

With the parameters of "domain" well defined, it is necessary to point out that the language options available to the respondents within their speech community were English, Spanish, and codeswitching. In some situations only English was used, in others only Spanish was used, and in others all three (Spanish, English and codeswitching) were utilized. Having these three codes available produced other patterns of language use. These involved the use of both languages but with clear separation of the two codes depending on the domain. Some speakers used equal amounts of Spanish and English, while others used primarily English with some Spanish, or primarily Spanish with some English, but without alternation of the two languages in a single situation.[4] Finally, speakers could separate by domain the use of Spanish, English, and codeswitching.

As expected, given their minimal contact with English-speakers, Respondents 1A and 1B spoke only Spanish in both the private and the public domain. Language choice among the second generation was more varied. Respondent 2A spoke only Spanish in the private domain, and in the public domain she spoke Spanish with some English. For example, if she interacted with English-speaking individuals in the public domain, she would speak English, but at her place of employment she spoke mostly Spanish because her coworkers were also Spanish-speakers. By contrast, her daughter, Respondent 3A, used both English and Spanish in the private domain, and especially Spanish when speaking with the elderly. When interacting with her peer group, she used mostly English. This pattern was much the same in the public domain.

Respondent 2B used Spanish, codeswitching, and some English in the private domain, and all three varieties in the public domain; her language use in both domains was determined by her interlocutors' language use. Respondent 3B, on the other hand, used mostly Spanish with some English in the private domain, and in the public domain, mostly English with some Spanish.

Although the increasing use of English over generations often points to linguistic assimilation (Sánchez 1983), speakers may consciously resist such a tendency. For this reason Respondents 1C's and 2C's language use was somewhat identical. They used Spanish, codeswitching, and some English in both the private domain and the public domain. Respondent

1C explained, "I prefer Spanish, and if I don't have to use English, I don't." Respondent 3C also used Spanish with some English in both domains. Her language proficiency can be best explained by the fact that she is only three years old and Spanish is her mother tongue. She is being reared by her grandparents and does not attend day care. The English she knows is limited, but she does watch *Sesame Street* and other television programs in English.

Another important option available to most of the respondents is codeswitching. Although codeswitching is often misinterpreted as evidence of a lack of linguistic ability or deterioration of one or both languages, recent research confirms that codeswitching plays an important role in social and discourse functions (Sánchez 1983; Zentella 1987). Not only are some of the respondents proficient in two languages, English and Spanish, but they are also adept in codeswitching. Respondents 2B, 1C, and 2C, who displayed the highest rates of codeswitching, have contact with the three (Spanish, English, and codeswitching) speech communities. These encounters influence them to accommodate their interlocutors in different linguistic situations (Valdés 1982). Viewing codeswitching within a style/strategy framework, we can say that these three respondents alternate strategically between English and Spanish when interacting with individuals who may codeswitch, or they switch for stylistic purposes (Giles 1978).[5] This linguistic behavior can also be considered as a strategy for crossing borders.

Education

The Public Education Act was introduced in the Territory of New Mexico in 1891 but did not impact Córdova until the 1930s, when the first public school was established (Milk 1980). Eventually, a standardized curriculum and textbooks in English became mandatory. Bilingual teachers were hired, and classroom instruction was conducted in both Spanish and English until the early 1940s; thereafter, primarily English was used. The paving of roads in 1953 improved accessibility to public and private junior high and high schools in neighboring communities, permitting the isolated villagers to have greater contact with outside groups, including Anglos and more urbanized Chicanos (Briggs 1986).

Reflecting the diversity of educational attainment, respondents 1A and 1B did not attend school beyond the third grade, whereas the women of the second and third generations received high school diplomas. Respondent 3B, the only college graduate, was in the process of finishing her master's degree in communication disorders at the University of New Mexico, and Respondent 3C was just beginning Head Start, a federally funded program for low-income children.

Educational experiences were not always positive. For example, Respondent 2A dropped out of the mission boarding school after her sophomore year in 1952 and later received her high school equivalency degree. She had always used Spanish until she left the community as an eighth grader. When she arrived at the boarding school, she was expected to use English; however, she chose to speak Spanish whenever she could. She recalled, "I was always given demerits for speaking Spanish." Her behavior was considered a sign of defiance. Despite the strong pressures to give up her native language, Respondent 2A remained loyal to Spanish.

This language behavior was influenced by her need for identity and solidarity with her ethnic group. Respondent 2A's experiences have analogies in the history of government educational policy for Native Americans in the early 1900s. According to Adams (1988), this policy was based on "Americanizing" the children by removing native customs, manners, and language. Consequently, English was imposed on students in boarding schools and use of the native language was punished. Medicine (1987:159) argues that "the introduction of the majority language—English—placed and continues to place a heavy burden on Indian women because adopting the English language often has meant losing linguistic symbols of culture." It is precisely this kind of loss that Respondent 2A prevented in her refusal to abandon Spanish.

Family Size

Because women's lives are greatly influenced by their ability or inability to control their fertility, it is important to consider the outcomes in women's lives if they choose to limit the size of their families. The smaller the family, the greater the options—social, economic, and educational. This pattern was evident in the contrast of family size between the first and second generations of women. Respondent 1A had eight children; her daughter, respondent 2A, had one daughter. Respondent 1B had ten children and her daughter, respondent 2B, had five children. Respondent 1C's mother had six children and she had three. For the younger generations, exercising more control over their fertility meant having more control over their own lives thereby increasing their feelings of efficaciousness in helping determine their family's future (Whiteford 1980).

The social changes occurring during the 1940s in Córdova propelled the second generation of women toward innovation. Innovation is "the recombination or redefinition of options, invention of new options, or taking advantage of new options" (Whiteford 1980:120). The Cordovan women now had access to the educational system that would eventually affect their lifestyles through employment outside the home, social mobility, and a decrease in family size. In the process of adapting to these new changes, the women became more adept in participating in the public domain, the dominant society, which included the use of English.

Thus, the second-generation women functioned as the "cultural brokers" defined by Bea Medicine (1987) as women who have the role of mediator between their own community and white society: "they are often vested with this role because of their facility with the English language" (162). This new role for the second generation required the "crossing of borders" (Anzaldúa 1987), both linguistically and culturally. Their educational achievement and knowledge of English permitted them to become gainfully employed outside the community. However, to maintain their ethnic identity, they countered the rapid current of these cultural and linguistic changes by performing a balancing act in two separate realities. Functioning in the dominant society did not interfere with maintaining the traditional role of wife and mother or the transmitting of traditional values, culture, and language to their children. For example, Respondent 2B had a variety of jobs such as cosmetologist, social worker, and emergency medical technician. She received an associate's degree in social work through a correspondence course from a nearby college, yet she still managed to raise her five children traditionally and to pass on the Spanish language.

Employment

The inhabitants of Córdova, like those of other Hispano villages in northern New Mexico that began with community grants, survived for two centuries by living off the land and depending on a barter system, a cooperative exchange of goods and services meeting most needs. Today the majority of Cordovans are employed in Los Alamos, Española, or Santa Fe. Those employed at Los Alamos work at the National Laboratory, the branch campus of the University of New Mexico, and the Pan Am Corporation, which provides maintenance, construction, and security services for government housing. First-generation women primarily worked in the home and community in the production, preparation, and distribution of food, as well as in communal labor such as plastering, adobe-making, sewing, and mattress-making (Deutsch 1985). Prior to becoming a *santera* [a wood-carver of saints], Respondent 1C worked as a housekeeper in Los Alamos. She then devoted herself full-time to wood carving, a skill she had learned as a child from her parents and grandparents. Her workshop is next to her home, and she works there on a daily basis.

The women of the second and third generation are or have been employed in their homes and outside the community, primarily in service and blue-collar jobs. Respondent 2A is employed at Los Alamos National Laboratory as a custodian and works the evening shift. Her daughter, Respondent 3A, is employed outside of Córdova as a bank teller. Respondent 2B is now retired, but her work experience included working with the elderly and the disabled as a mediator and interpreter between community members and government agencies. Respondent 3B now has an M.A. degree from the University of New Mexico and is presently employed in Albuquerque as a speech pathologist. Respondent 2C has been employed in blue-collar jobs outside of the community. As is evident, Cordovan women have been on the cutting edge. They have played the role of innovator and cultural broker; crossing borders by working outside the home and having contact with the larger society while playing the role of enforcers of tradition and guardians of culture (Zentella 1987).

Drawing from the language maintenance and language shift frameworks (Fishman 1966, 1972; Stevens 1986), we are able to correlate Cordovan women's language use with their educational and employment status as well as their residence. Studies (Lewis 1971; Myers 1973; Spolsky 1969; Thompson 1974) have shown that residents in rural areas, with greater isolation and less contact with the English-speaking community, have a tendency to retain the mother tongue to a greater extent and for more generations. Córdova was settled between 1725 and 1743, and for many generations this village was isolated from the dominant society; hence, Spanish was maintained as the community language. For employment and educational achievement, more knowledge of English was required. The acquisition of the English language became the vehicle for upward mobility for some of the women, whereas the maintenance of Spanish restricted socioeconomic movement for others. Sánchez (1983) states that in most situations where language contact exists, the structural (labor process) and cultural (social process) institutions can be instrumental in the maintenance or the loss of the mother tongue: "Social contact is of course determined by the class factor, by the labor process and the relations of production. Participation in the labor process with a given income and occupation in turn determines the area of residence, the people with whom one socializes, educational goals, consumption of commodities and ideology, all factors which determine one's continued use or non-use of the Spanish language" (64).

It is obvious that social and economic factors have determined the functions of Spanish and English in this speech community as well as the domains in which they are used. Geographic and social isolation from the dominant group, however, has limited the contact with the English-speaking society and English-based institutions, thereby contributing to the retention of the mother tongue in intimate and informal functions. Nonetheless, many individuals have enough contact with English to acquire some degree of bilingualism.

Consequently, two questions emerge regarding the linguistic behavior of these Cordovan women. Why do they choose to speak Spanish rather than English or vice versa in certain linguistic interactions? What factors influence their linguistic choice in both intragroup and intergroup situations? The variables considered—ethnicity and identity, solidarity, accommodation, age, respect, and social networks—were constrained by the community status of interlocutors (in-group versus out-group) and the location of interaction. These factors yielded four different interaction types: (1) interaction among community members in Córdova (intragroup interaction in the private domain); (2) interaction among community members away from Córdova (intragroup interaction in the public domain); (3) interaction with noncommunity members in Córdova (intergroup interaction in a noncongruous domain situation, the private-cum-public domain); and (4) interaction with noncommunity members away from Córdova (intergroup interaction in the public domain). Discussion regarding these categories follows.

INTERACTION AMONG COMMUNITY MEMBERS IN CÓRDOVA

When the respondents interacted with each other or with other women of the community in the private domain, Spanish was almost always used.

The wide use of Spanish may be explained by the social network frame-work (Milroy 1992). Leslie Milroy maintains that network participation, rather than external social variables, is the pertinent element in language use. Within a close-knit network structure, speakers are able to create solidarity that strengthens their resistance to linguistic and social pres-sure from the dominant group. In Milroy's terms, the number of social contacts among various members of a community is its density. Contacts can occur through the personal networks of friends, relatives, and neigh-bors, and through participation in religious activities and specific group membership (e.g., clubs or choirs).

In the case of Córdova, such density factors as the size of the village, its historical background, and the social networks such as *compadrazgo* and church-related functions, established during the agricultural era, have contributed to the transmission of cultural and linguistic patterns from one generation to another.[6] An example of the social networks in Córdova is as follows: Family A is related to Family B because the hus-band of Respondent 1A is the uncle of Respondent 1B's husband, and these respondents are also neighbors.

Four exceptions to the dominant use of Spanish surfaced in in-group situations within the community. These exceptions involved Re-spondents 3A, 3B, 1C, and 2C. Respondents 3A and 3B belong to the same generation and are identified as English-dominant bilinguals. English has become the primary language for Respondent 3B since she began living in Albuquerque and attending the university, and Respondent 3A has daily contact with English-speaking institutions through her employment. When Respondents 3A and 3B interacted with each other, they used mostly English and some Spanish. Respondent 3B was observed speaking with younger teenage cousins in English, but she used Spanish with two older cousins, approximately thirty-five and forty years old. English was probably used because the younger generation is bilingual and more com-fortable speaking both languages, whereas the older generation is gener-ally Spanish dominant and more at ease speaking Spanish.

This linguistic behavior among the younger generation may be at-tributed to a weakened network structure (not having as much contact with Spanish-dominant speakers) and to the amount of contact both of these respondents have with English. Sánchez (1983:63) suggests that "the more contact with the English-speaking community, the more likeli-hood there is of bilingualism or monolingualism in English. The greater the social distance and the more limited the contact with English institutions, the more probability that Spanish will retain intimate and informal functions."

Two other exceptions involved codeswitching by Respondents 1C and 2C. Their codeswitching is best explained by the notion of accommodation, which is a process whereby individuals adapt or converge to one another's speech (Giles 1978). In this case both respondents converged toward the speech style of the interlocutors, who, according to the respondents, always codeswitch. The first interaction was observed between Respondent 1C and her cousin. The cousin is the same age and is a social worker in Española, where codeswitching is widely used. In the other instance, the interlocutor of Respondent 2C was a twenty-four-year-old female from a nearby community where codeswitching is always used. Consequently, codeswitching dominated in these interactions.

Codeswitching is a practical linguistic option available to these Cordovan women because of their bilingual skills in Spanish and English. Codeswitching functions as part of their verbal repertoire, as do English and Spanish. The women have acquired these three codes, and use them appropriately in different interactions and social and linguistic settings. This strategy can be interpreted as innovative behavior by Cordovan women, although codeswitching has been explained as the beginning of language shift toward English (Sánchez 1983). In my observations of their language use, the respondents were cognizant of a need to change speech styles in different situations with different interlocutors. Their codeswitching is correlated to language contact; when the borders of certain speech communities become blurred, the blending of Spanish and English follows. A third code—a hybrid or by-product of Spanish and English—is created and becomes integrated as a viable and socially accepted language code among its speakers and hearers. I refer to this process as language hybridity.

INTERACTION AMONG COMMUNITY MEMBERS
AWAY FROM CÓRDOVA

In almost all (fifteen of eighteen) linguistic interactions between the respondents and community members in public domains, Spanish dominated and language choice was most heavily influenced by identity and ethnicity. Of the remaining three interactions, English was utilized in one, Spanish and English in another, and codeswitching in the third. The observations of the in-group behavior indicate that the sense of solidarity and identity functions equally outside and within the community. Spanish is used among in-group members. The best example of this linguistic and social behavior was observed during wedding activities held in Albuquerque. Although the women were not in their community environment, they continued to function as if they were. The presence and number of family and community members (approximately one hundred) contributed to the creation of a private domain within a public domain. The need to identify as a speech community as well as an ethnic group influenced the language choice of Cordovan women in this setting.

Ninety percent of guests at this wedding were from Córdova and neighboring communities and were predominantly bilingual. The priest, the choir, the musicians, the food, and the women who helped with the reception came from the Córdova area. Because the wedding took place in a public domain, I expected that English would be the language of choice. However, the respondents' role of cultural brokers was evident in this situation and influenced language use.

After the Mass, a receiving line was formed outside the church. The bride's employers and colleagues were all Anglos. Respondent 2B, the mother of the bride, converged toward the speech behavior of these guests, who spoke English. With the first-generation guests from Córdova and other villages who were monolingual Spanish-speakers, she converged and used Spanish. Many of the second-generation women codeswitched; thus respondent 2B converged toward their speech style. Respondent 3B spoke Spanish with the elderly guests from Córdova and other communities. With all other guests she converged to their language choice.

The use of Spanish by Cordovan women at this event reveals how they interact with one another in public domains. The women adhered to community norms by not deviating from the use of Spanish. This linguistic behavior may be explained within the intergroup-distinctiveness framework. Tajfel (1974) suggests that when members of different groups are in contact, they compare themselves on dimensions that are important to them (such as personal attributes, abilities, and material possessions), and that will lead them to differentiate themselves favorably from the out-group: "Interpersonal social comparisons will lead individuals to search for and even create, dimensions on which they can make them-

selves positively distinct from the outgroup"(68). All observed noncon-
vergent linguistic behavior at the wedding was in reaction to an interlocutor's use of English. This pattern may be interpreted as a powerful symbol
whereby the Cordovan women displayed their intention of maintaining
their identity, cultural distinctiveness and group solidarity. Divergence
by the women of this speech community can also be interpreted as a
means of resistance or as a means of expressing pride in their language
and their ethnic identity. By distancing themselves linguistically, they
are able to resist assimilation and at the same time maintain their group
distinctiveness. It is also plausible that the respondents wanted not
merely to maintain their own speech style but to emphasize it in interaction with others. This in-group behavior reinforces their positive social
identity as well as satisfaction with in-group membership by affirming
their competence in community norms (Tajfel 1974).

INTERACTION WITH NONCOMMUNITY MEMBERS IN CÓRDOVA

When communicating with speakers who were not members of this
speech community, the Cordovan women tended to use more English. An
example of this took place in Respondent 2B's home with an Anglo nun
from Santa Cruz who works with the parish priest. Because Respondent
2B and her husband were the *mayordomos* [overseers] of the community
church and also choir members, the discussion centered on religious
activities. Although the nun knew some Spanish, this conversation was
conducted entirely in English. The reason for the visitor's choice of English may have been that she was aware that she was an outsider, and as
an English-dominant speaker was uncomfortable speaking in Spanish
with the respondent and her husband. An alternative explanation may be
that English was already the established language of their interactions
when in the public domain. In support of this second explanation, I observed the nun interacting with Respondent 1B in both the private and
the public domain, and in both situations she used Spanish with this
respondent.

English with an equal amount of Spanish was used in four other
interactions. The first observation occurred when I first met Respondent
3A at her grandmother's home. At first she spoke primarily in English
with me, yet she spoke to her grandmother only in Spanish. After two
hours of becoming acquainted, she began to use Spanish with me as well,

although she kept both codes separate. It seemed that certain topics related to the community or the elderly precipitated the use of Spanish.

Other interactions that included equal amounts of Spanish, English, and codeswitching involved respondents 2B and 3B. They took place in Córdova on a Sunday afternoon in the front yard of Respondent 2B's home. Her three daughters had been home for the weekend and were preparing to leave for Albuquerque. Respondent 2B used only Spanish with her oldest daughter, codeswitched with the other two daughters, and used English with her seventeen-year-old granddaughter. When respondent 3B spoke with her older sister, she used English. She later explained that English is her usual language in the city with her older sister, whereas with her other sister, she tends to codeswitch or uses both English and Spanish.[7] Although this linguistic interaction took place in the community, Respondents 2B and 3B accommodated the speech styles of their noncommunity relatives.

In all of the above examples, although the respondents were in their speech community, they did not adhere to its norms by using only Spanish. To understand the linguistic behavior, it is important and relevant to make some broader distinctions related to the notion of speech community. I use the Hymesian definition "a community sharing rules for the conduct and interpretation of speech, and rules for the interpretation of at least one linguistic variety" (Hymes 1972:54). These rules permit speakers to associate particular modes of speaking, topics, or message forms with particular settings and activities. Second and more important is this question: Who are the members of a speech community? Members are those who have knowledge of those varieties and those speaking rules that potentially enable them to move communicatively within that speech community.

In this study three speech communities are distinguished: (1) the local village; (2) the surrounding Hispano community of northern New Mexico; and (3) the broader population of New Mexico. Some women participate only in the local community or treat it and the Hispano community as the same speech community. But for some, the Hispano community is developing its own distinctive identity. And while Spanish is de rigueur in the local community and English in the larger New Mexican community, it appears that codeswitching is developing as the appropriate code for the Hispano community. This became apparent after visiting various communities with Respondents 3B and 2C during my stay in

Córdova, as well as after taking care of business matters, such as paying electric and gas bills, banking, and buying groceries in Española. Code-switching was the preferred variety and was quite evident in all the linguistic interactions that I observed. It is my opinion that codeswitching used in this community reflects strategies that unfold within the parameters of border culture. Recent social theory (Anzaldúa 1987; García-Canclini 1989) recognizes that in border settings, two worlds merge to form a third world, thus creating a border culture. This culture evolves as the result of the transculturation of the individuals belonging to the Córdova speech community. The latter find themselves straddling the Chicano and Anglo cultures, urban and rural cultures, thereby establishing a new border culture, a new border identity, and a new border language, the alternation of Spanish and English.

Recognizing the existence of these three speech communities, we must conclude that one of the most salient criteria in deciding which code to use is this: What speech community do(es) this (these) interlocutor(s) belong to? Furthermore, a major constraint on actual language behavior of an individual is her network of communication: With which members of which speech communities does this individual interact?

The data presented above also suggest that the respondent's language choice—English, Spanish, or codeswitching—in intergroup interaction in Córdova was principally motivated by accommodation. Convergence in code selection may be attributed to various reasons. On the one hand, it is possible that a speech community, consciously or unconsciously, perceives its variety as less prestigious. Thus, when speakers interact with out-group members, this attitude may influence their choice of the more prestigious code, English. However, many of the noncommunity women with whom the respondents interacted used codeswitching, a variety that is also perceived, at least within the dominant society, as less prestigious. This would lead us to believe that convergence to English did not result from a need for approval or for the potential rewards for adopting English, but because of the speaker's verbal repertoire as well as her capacity to innovate. The role of "cultural broker" is activated and implemented, hence the choice of the appropriate code.

This capacity to innovate can be influenced by the attitudes that exist in other communities toward the Spanish spoken by Cordovans. Respondent 3B mentioned that during her first year in junior high school, her classmates would comment, "The people from Córdova speak very fast and you can't understand them" or "I can tell you are from Córdova because your Spanish is different." In addition to her becoming aware of the linguistic differences between Córdova and the Española Valley and the attitudes toward the Cordovan speech styles, it was apparent to Respondent 3B that the children from Córdova had a higher level of proficiency in Spanish than did the children from the other communities. Consequently, every time Cordovan women leave their community, they cross borders, an act that prompts innovative behavior; in this situation innovation means adapting a gap-bridging linguistic strategy—a border language—codeswitching.

INTERACTION WITH NONCOMMUNITY MEMBERS
AWAY FROM CÓRDOVA

A total of thirty-four interactions between the respondents and noncommunity members were observed in the public domain (that is, all interactions occurring away from the community with out-group members). Of these, twenty-four included the use of English. The dominance of English in these interactions was expected because they occurred in the public domain. Most of these interactions were between the respondents and monolingual English speakers or third-generation women who were dominant in English. Respondents 1A and 1B used Spanish only in all of their interactions, and the women from the second and third generations used Spanish when interacting with the older generation. Codeswitching was used by respondent 2B and 2C primarily when interacting with friends who codeswitched.

The most salient variable influencing language choice in the public domain is age, which results in accommodation due to the adherence to the cultural norm of *respeto* toward the elderly. Within the Chicano culture, courtesy and respect for members of the older generation are often demonstrated by accommodating to their language preferences, that is, convergence to Spanish. Individuals belonging to the younger generations are expected to adhere to this social norm. Respondent 2C commented on the social norm of using Spanish with the older generation:

> *El Español se me hace importante por los viejitos si uno va a platicar con ellos. Pues, si tú les dices algo en inglés, ellos no te van a entender que les estás diciendo. Como cuando va uno*

*a misa, primero teníanos un padre, la primera vez que vino,
les dió misa en inglés, y allí estaban los viejitos; nomás se
miraban uno al otro, no sabían que estaba pasando.*

[I think Spanish is important for the elderly if one is going to
speak with them. Well, if you tell them something in English,
they are not going to understand. For example, when one goes
to Mass, first we used to have a priest, the first time he came,
he gave Mass in English, and the elderly sat there looking at
each other, they didn't know what was happening.]

A final and more detailed example of cross-generational linguistic
interaction that leads to accommodation and respect is the bridal shower
given in honor of Respondent 2B's daughter. It was held at a public hall
in Española (population forty-five thousand). Approximately seventy-
five women attended, and of those attending, the majority were aunts,
cousins, in-laws, friends, and neighbors. Most came from the surrounding smaller villages, and a few were from Santa Fe and Albuquerque.
There were approximately twenty-five first-generation women (ages 55–
96), thirty second-generation women (ages 30–54), and twenty third-
generation women (ages 2–29).

The linguistic interaction among the guests varied. Members of the
first generation spoke to each other in Spanish. The second generation
spoke Spanish with the first generation, either codeswitched or used
Spanish or English among themselves, and used English with some of
the third generation. The third generation tended to speak only English
among themselves, English with some Spanish to the second generation,
and Spanish with the first generation.

Prior to the beginning of the activities of this event, Respondent 2B,
the bride-to-be (twenty-seven years old), and the matron of honor (thirty-
five years old) greeted the guests as they arrived. Both mother and daughter greeted those belonging to the first generation in Spanish. The women
of the second and third generations were typically greeted in English
with some codeswitching, and the guests from Córdova were invariably
greeted in Spanish. After the guests had gone through the receiving line,
Respondent 2B introduced the bride-to-be and the matron of honor, who
were both from the city. English was used by the matron of honor, and
Spanish and English were used by the bride-to-be. Although the bride-
to-be has lived in Albuquerque for ten years, she still follows the rules of

discourse of her native speech community. The matron of honor, who is an urban Chicana, did not speak Spanish although she understands it; when spoken to by Spanish-speakers, she responded in English. The language behavior of the bride-to-be and the matron of honor reveals how language use during the childhood years will influence language choice in the adult years. An important factor is where a person spent her childhood rather than where she currently lives (Peñalosa 1980). The bride-to-be was reared in Córdova; to deviate from the norm would mark her as an outsider or one who did not respect communal norms. There is obviously a need for the bride-to-be to continue to identify with the community, and she does so by adhering to the community norms although she has been gone for ten years.

The shower took place one week after my arrival in Córdova, prior to any interviews, and I wondered why so much English was being spoken. I had anticipated more Spanish since so many women attending were Spanish-speakers. However, by the end of the shower I concluded that English was primarily used to accommodate the out-of-town guests from the city, and furthermore, the setting was in the public domain, which determined the language choice of the majority of the women. I observed the mother of the bride-to-be, Respondent 2B, accommodating to the English spoken by her *comadres* from Albuquerque who also spoke Spanish. To have spoken Spanish with these women who were not members of the Cordovan in-group might have denied the importance of Spanish as a marker of intragroup solidarity. It is interesting to speculate whether these same women would have used Spanish with their city comadres had the shower been held in Córdova. On the one hand, I believe they would have, for setting is an exceedingly important variable in language choice for Cordovans. However, on the other hand, if the city comadres initiated the use of English, then the Cordovan women most likely would have accommodated them linguistically.

Once the introductions and the acknowledgments were completed, Respondent 2B announced in English that the first game was about to begin. She then switched to Spanish and said, *"¡Voy a usar inglés y español porque sé que hay algunas mujeres aquí que no entienden inglés o prefieren español, incluyendo yo misma! Entonces usaré las dos idiomas. Quiero dar la bienvenida y vamos a jugar un game."* ["I am going to use English and Spanish because I know there are some women here who do not understand English or prefer Spanish, myself included. So I will use both languages. I want to welcome you and let's play a game."] She proceeded to give the instructions, codeswitching intrasententially. This received a warm response, some applause, and comments in Spanish such as *"¡Ah, qué bien!"* and *"No entiendo el inglés muy bien."* ["Oh, good!" and "I don't understand English very well."]

The first game was *consejos para la novia* [advice for the bride]. This advice was to be given at random on a voluntary basis. Here are a few examples of the consejos given:

1st woman:	Always be ready to go with him.
2nd woman:	*Hazle frijoles todos los días, que es la mejor comida.* [Make him beans every day, it is the best food.]
Mother:	(Repeats the consejo in Spanish in case it was not heard the first time. There is applause from the guests.)
Bride:	He likes frijoles. *Le gustan los frijoles y las tortillas.* We're on our way.
4th woman:	Give him three hugs and three kisses a day.
Bride:	That's a good one. I like that one.
5th woman:	*Que no deje su marido ir solo para dondequiera; que se esté junto de ella* (laughter, cheers, and loud applause). [Don't let your husband go anywhere by himself, he should stay by her.]
Bride:	I already . . . *Ese sí me acuerdo.* [That one I'll remember.]
Mother:	*Ese sí te gustó.* [You liked that one.]
Bride:	*Ese me gusta mucho.* [That one I like a lot.]
5th woman:	You better believe it.

As we can see, these consejos were given in Spanish and English. Other consejos given in Spanish and English by the first and second generation were religious and traditional. The advice given in English by the third generation focused on themes of equality. The use of religious and traditional themes by certain women can imply that these women are conserving the mother tongue more than the younger generation. Although the themes of younger women's consejos seem to indicate that they are being innovative in their views of female-male relationships, the form of the consejos, with greater use of English, suggests that the women are innovative in their language behavior as well.

The interaction at this women-only event bears out that the networks within this speech community established throughout the generations are not only dense and multiplex but stable. This stability gives Cordovan women confidence to cross borders; as they do so, they expand their networks and are forced to engage in innovative language behavior. For example, Respondent 1C, as a santera, crosses borders on a daily basis when she interacts with a variety of individuals: international tourists, museum curators, business associates. When she does this, she uses English without hesitation. I attribute this innovative behavior to the strong sense of in-group cohesiveness and security that permits the respondents to cross social, cultural, and linguistic borders and to enter new social networks. In the process they alter their communal language behavior without feeling a threat to their sense of identity.

CONCLUSION

The results of this study indicate that a variety of social changes since the 1940s—change from agricultural subsistence to wage labor, greater educational opportunities, decrease in family size, and increasing linguistic and cultural contact with the dominant society—have influenced the language choices of Cordovan women. More important, these changes have affected their role as both innovators and conservators in language use as well as their economic empowerment and educational and social mobility. It is apparent that *cordoveñas* have not relinquished their use of Spanish in favor of English, but have devised linguistic strategies that allow them to participate effectively in the broader communities—northern New Mexico Chicano and dominant Anglo—that surround them. These strategies have not only assisted in the maintenance of their mother tongue but possibly have decelerated language shift toward English. Furthermore, there are indications that the Cordovan women have not resisted the innovations that have impinged on their personal and social networks, but have instead used them as strategies in order to adapt to their new environments. In other words, Cordovan women have been exceedingly successful as "cultural brokers" as they mediate between separate realities—the Cordovan speech community and the broader Chicano and English-speaking community. They have also succeeded in surviving the potentially hemorrhaging effects of the *herida abierta* [open wound] underscored by Anzaldúa (1987), where the Third World grates against the First World and bleeds rather than succumbing to what she calls "linguistic terrorism," or the suppression of the mother tongue that accompanies crossing cultural and linguistic borders. In fact, the Cordovan women may be viewed as trailblazers on this road to language hybridity.

ACKNOWLEDGMENTS

I would like to thank the women from Córdova, New Mexico who opened up their hearts and their homes to me. Without their generosity I would not have been able to complete this project.

NOTES

1. The terms Chicana, Nuevo Mexicana, and Mexicana are used interchangeably in this chapter.
2. In *Borderlands/La Frontera: The New Mestiza,* Gloria Anzaldúa (1987:3) discusses the merging of two worlds that form a third country. She defines this concept as border culture: "The U.S.-Mexican border *es una herida abierta* where the Third World grates against the first and bleeds. And before the scab forms, it hemorrhages again, the lifeblood of two worlds merging to form a third country—a border culture. Borders are set up to define the places that are safe and unsafe, to distinguish *us* from *them.* A borderland is a vague and undetermined place created by the emotional residue of an unnatural boundary. It is in a constant state of transition."
3. Transculturation is encompassing or extending across two or more cultures. In this study transculturation is correlated with Cordovan women going beyond the already established Hispano and Anglo cultures and establishing a new border culture, a new border identity, and even a new border language.
4. Equal amounts of Spanish and English use by respondents is different from codeswitching in that the respondent would speak about a certain theme in Spanish for ten minutes to half an hour or more. Then the conversation could change, with English being used in the same manner. And depending on the interlocutor, the respondent might also codeswitch, using both Spanish and English with more frequency—intrasententially or intersententially.
5. The speech style/strategy framework provides a valuable approach for studying and explaining linguistic behavior of women and men as members of subordinate and dominant groups. The social identity of group members is enhanced by

the knowledge of their own membership in particular groups and the value that the individual gives to this membership. It is not uncommon for people to emphasize their in-group identity and psychological distinctiveness from others in certain situations by accentuating certain linguistic features.

6. *Compadrazgo* is a social structure in which *people* assume symbolic positions of kinship through religious rituals. The godparents of a baptized child become the *compadres* [literally "coparents"] of the parents. The godfather is the compadre and the godmother is the *comadre*. This linkage can also occur through marriage and confirmation, and the compadres are then considered part of the extended family.

7. Respondent 3B was living in Córdova for the summer.

REFERENCES

Acuña, R. (1972). *Occupied America: The Chicano's Struggle for Liberation*. San Francisco: Canfield Press.

Adams, D. W. (1988). Fundamental considerations: The deep meaning of Native American schooling, 1880–1900. *Harvard Educational Review* 59 (1), 1–28.

Anzaldúa, G. (1987). *Borderlands/La Frontera: The New Mestiza*. San Francisco: Aunt Lute Books.

Briggs, C. (1986). *Learning How to Ask: A Sociolinguistic Appraisal of the Role of the Interview in Social Science Research*. Cambridge: Cambridge University Press.

Chávez, E. (1984). *Sexual differentiation in bilingual language proficiency*. Ph.D. dissertation, University of New Mexico.

Deutsch, S. J. (1985). *Culture, class, and gender: Chicanas in Colorado and New Mexico 1900–1940*. Ph.D. dissertation, University of New Mexico.

Fishman, J. A. (1966). *Language Loyalty in the United States*. The Hague: Mouton.

——. (1972). *Language in Sociocultural Change*. Stanford: Stanford University Press.

García-Canclini, N. (1989). *Culturas hibridas: Estrategias para entrar y salir de la modernidad*. México, D.F.: Grijalbo Consejo Nacional para la Cultura y las Artes.

Giles, H. (1978). Linguistic difference in ethnic groups. In H. Tajfel (ed.), *Differentiation Between Social Groups* (pp. 361–393). London: Academic Press.

Hudson-Edwards, A., & G. D. Bills. (1982). Intergenerational language shift in an Albuquerque barrio. In J. Amastae & L. Elías-Olivares (eds.), *Spanish in the United States: Sociolinguistic Aspects* (pp. 135–154). Cambridge: Cambridge University Press.

Hymes, D. (1972). Models of the interaction of language and social life. In J. J.

Gumperz & D. Hymes (eds.), *Directions in Sociolinguistics* (pp. 35–71). New York: Holt, Rinehart & Winston.

Lewis, G. E. (1971). Migration and language in the USSR. *International Migration Review* 5 (2), 147–179.

Medicine, B. (1987). The role of American Indian women in cultural continuity and transition. In J. Penfield (ed.), *Women and Language in Transition* (pp. 159–165). Albany: SUNY Press.

Milk, R. (1980). The issue of language in education in territorial New Mexico. *Bilingual Review/Revista Bilingüe* 7 (3), 212–222.

Milroy, L. (1992). *Language and Social Networks.* Oxford: Basil Blackwell.

Myers, S. K. (1973). *Language Shift among Migrants to Lima, Perú.* Chicago: University of Chicago Press.

Ortiz, L. I. (1975). *A sociolinguistic study of language maintenance in the northern New Mexico community of Arroyo Seco.* Ph.D. dissertation, University of New Mexico.

Peñalosa, F. (1980). *Chicano Sociolinguistics: An Introduction.* Rowley, MA: Newbury House.

Sánchez, R. (1983). *Chicano Discourse: Socio-historic Perspectives.* Rowley, MA: Newbury House.

Sherif, M. (1966). *Group Conflict and Cooperation: Their Social Psychology.* London: Routledge & Kegan Paul.

Spolsky, B. (1969). Attitudinal aspects of second language learning. *Language Learning* 19, 271–285.

Stevens, G. (1986). Sex differences in language shift in the United States. *Sociology and Social Research* 71 (1), 31–34.

Tajfel, H. (1974). Social identity and intergroup behavior. *Social Science Information* 13 (2), 65–93.

Thompson, R. M. (1974). Mexican language loyalty and the validity of the 1970 census. *Linguistics* 128, 7–18.

Valdés, G. (1982). Social interaction and code-switching patterns: A case study of Spanish/English alternation. In J. Amastae & L. Elías-Olivares (eds.), *Spanish in the United States: Sociolinguistic Aspects* (pp. 209–230). Cambridge: Cambridge University Press.

Whiteford, L. (1980). Mexican American women as innovators. In M. B. Melville (ed.), *Twice a Minority: Mexican American Women* (pp. 109–126). London: C. V. Mosby.

Zentella, A. C. (1987). Language and the female identity in the Puerto Rican community. In J. Penfield (ed.), *Women and Language in Transition* (pp. 167–179). Albany: SUNY Press.

2

•••

FIGHTING WORDS

Latina Girls, Gangs, and Language Attitudes

Norma Mendoza-Denton

In this chapter I examine the sociology of language and the educational situation of a group of gang-affiliated Latina high school girls, and explore how larger social pressures play an important role in determining their community's attitudes toward Spanish and English, as well as individual community members' eventual position along a Spanish-English linguistic continuum.

The polar extremes of the Latinas in this community primarily consist of a group of recent immigrants who identify with a Mexican identity and call themselves *Sureñas,* and another group of Latinas, the majority U.S.-born, who identify with a bilingual/bicultural Chicana identity and call themselves *Norteñas.* Although Sureñas and Norteñas technically share the same ethnicity (sometimes their parents are from the same towns in Mexico), they are in deep conflict over the politics of identity in their community. This conflict is reflected in their language attitudes toward Spanish and English and, as a consequence, in their eventual success in the American educational system.

In a northern California high school that I will refer to as Sor Juana High School (SJHS), I conducted over two years of ethnographic fieldwork and community service. The ethnographic fieldwork consisted of (a) sociolinguistic interviews with students at school during their free time and in classes with the consent of students, parents, and instructors; (b) audio recordings of naturally occurring interactions among students and between students and myself; and (c) my extensive participant observation of various aspects of community life. In the domain of community service, I participated as a volunteer, often teaching and tutoring as well as providing general in-kind community assistance such as rides, baby-sitting, chaperoning, godmothering [being a *madrina*], or any other task for which the community expressed a need.

I will ask the reader to suspend knowledge of ethnicity- and race-related terms for the rest of the chapter and allow me to introduce some new terminological distinctions. In an effort to be ethnographically accurate and to capture the attitudes of the members of the community, I want to use the members' own categories. This will allow us to probe into distinctions that the community members make but that the matrix society does not. Thus I will use the term Chicana/o to refer to the Mexican-origin population that has lived in the United States for a longer period of time and is more acculturated and linguistically flexible than recent immigrants, whom I will refer to as Mexican. Latina/o will be an umbrella term referring to any person of Latin American origin, whether acculturated to U.S. culture or not.

CHICANAS AND MEXICANAS IN THE UNITED STATES

By the end of the twentieth century, Spanish-speakers will be the largest minority in the United States, and according to population statistics, sometime in the twenty-first century, people of Mexican descent will constitute the majority of the population in California. Between 1970 and 1980 the Hispanic population of California nearly doubled, according to U.S. Census figures. In California, Hispanics make up over 20 percent of the state's total population, and almost 42 percent of all persons of Mexican descent in the United States live in California (Camarillo 1985).

Chicanas and Chicanos have a distinct culture within the United States, with their own cultural traditions, history, expressive culture, celebrations, and language. Their linguistic varieties—composed of Chicano Spanish and Chicano English and their variants—differ from both the Mexican and the American standard varieties. The coexistence of two languages and cultures within a single community is not without conflict, however, as feminist philosopher and writer Gloria Anzaldúa (1987: 58–59) explains:

> Chicanas who grew up speaking Chicano Spanish have internalized the belief that we speak poor Spanish. It is illegitimate, a bastard language. And because we internalize how our

language has been used against us by the dominant culture, we use our language differences to oppress each other. . . . Chicanas feel uncomfortable talking in Spanish to Latinas, afraid of their censure. Their language was not outlawed in their countries. They had a whole lifetime of being immersed in their native tongue; generations, centuries in which Spanish was a first language, taught in school, heard on radio and T.V., and read in the newspaper. If a person, Chicana or Latina, has a low estimation of my mother tongue, she has a low estimation of me. Often with Mexicanas and Latinas we'll speak English as a neutral language. Even among Chicanas, we tend to speak English at parties or conferences. Yet, at the same time, we're afraid the other will think we're agringadas because we don't speak Chicano Spanish.

Anzaldúa's reflections portray the rupture of a community in transition. In California, the setting of a Chicana/Chicano community with great historical depth, the arrival and settling in of Mexican immigrants within these ethnic enclaves has often resulted in conflicting and oppositional relationships between the "native" Chicanas and the "recently arrived" Mexicanas. I argue that, for some Latina girls in California, Spanish and English are not neutral media of communication but symbols of social allegiance and identity. The use of different languages or dialects as symbolic of identity has been repeatedly observed in many different communities (Gal 1993). I focus on how, in their role as symbolic markers of identity in this community, Spanish and English evoke different cultural, national, and ideological orientations. Consequently, young people may embrace or resist a language based on its symbolic connotations. For some of these young people, a decision to disidentify with Standard English affects not only their educational attainment but also their opportunities in the United States, where great emphasis is placed by the school system on the acquisition of Standard English and the knowledge of other languages is devalued through repeated suggestions to outlaw the use of languages other than English.

In the context of this high school where transitional English as a Second Language (ESL) is taught to all non–Standard-English–speaking immigrant students, attitudes toward Standard English are influenced by the students' entrance into the already opposed symbolic discourses of different groups of Latinas in the United States. Different groups of Latinas are polarized at opposite ends of a continuum that ranges from Chicana identity to Mexican identity. In the next section I focus on these oppositions and how they are enacted and maintained in school.

SAME SCHOOL, SEPARATE LIVES

Sor Juana High School is located in one of the wealthy suburbs of Silicon Valley in northern California. Until about ten years ago, it was almost exclusively Euro-American. Since then, the demographics of the area have changed, mostly due to an influx of immigrants from Mexico, Central America, and Southeast Asia that has drastically altered the ethnic complexion of the school. Today, Sor Juana High School has a majority of "minority" students, many of whom are Latina/o. This seemingly monolithic Latina/o group consists of Chicanas, Mexicanas, and recent immigrants from other Latin American countries, including a significant number of Salvadorans. Within these groups, there are crosscutting allegiances of varying strengths; students divide themselves along national, ethnic, class, and Chicana/Mexican lines.

I do not wish to claim that all or even a majority of the Latinas at this school are involved with gangs or gang-influenced groups, nor that gang activity is the most prominent aspect of any of their lives. As with any broad spectrum of individuals, it is hard to find a "typical" representative of any group, especially in a community as large and diverse as that of Latinas. One of my principal research objectives was to explore the linguistic correlates of peer-group identification of these students; my special interest in gangs is a reflection of the powerful linguistic dynamics that crystallize in these groups. A thorough understanding of Latina youth gang culture and its sociolinguistic issues not only would benefit schools in northern California but also would shed light on the larger sociocultural processes operating in immigrant communities like this one.

NORTE AND SUR

Although the gangs trace their history to the Nuestra Familia and Mexican Mafia gangs that evolved in southern California prisons as far back as 1958 (Donovan 1993), the connection between prison gangs and street youth gangs is weak. In this particular geographic area, the street youth gangs have evolved far from the original northern/southern California split that characterized prison gangs. Norte and Sur today have come to signify Chicana and Mexican, respectively, and the strength of this dichotomy often overrides other things that these groups of students may have in common.

At SJHS, the concept of a gang as a small, close-knit group does not apply. Official gang membership is restricted to a small group inducted through a ritual beating, but many more students participate in the oppositional dynamics of gang identity than are actual members of the gangs. Often the official members are indistinguishable from the unofficial wanna-bes. The best analogy I can think of is that of rival soccer teams. On the one hand there are the actual players who are officially on the team, who have had to pass some sort of qualifying test to be on that team, and on the other hand are their fans, who wear the team colors and team insignia, and occasionally participate in team-oriented activities. Often what school officials and the police see as "gang fights" would be more aptly described as "fan fights."

Unlike gangs that are organized around concepts of territory (Moore 1991) and profit (Padilla 1992), the Norteñas and Sureñas (and their wanna-bes) at SJHS are organized around ideology. Issues of "Mexicanness," authenticity (Who is the real Mexican?), representation (Who can call themselves Mexican?), and the question of whether linguistic competence determines group membership (Do you have to speak Spanish to be Mexican?) are at the heart of the conflict between Norte and Sur.

Norte and Sur organize themselves around concepts and displays of cultural identity. By virture of their Chicana or Mexican background, newly arrived students are recruited by one or the other of the gangs, or are asked where they stand in relation to the social structure by wanna-bes and neutral observers. Gang members utilize the diverse cultural resources around them to construct oppositional identities. Norteñas and Sureñas are associated with a color (red and blue, respectively); a number (14 and 13, often seen as XIV and XIII in graffiti and originally referring to the alphabetical order of the letters *N* (Nuestra Familia) and *M* (Mexican Mafia); a language (English and Spanish); different ways of dressing and wearing makeup and hair; and, according to some students, even different ways of walking (Mendoza-Denton 1996). In this setting, everything

Table 2.1 Symbolic Markers of Chicana and Mexicana Identity

Marker	Norteñas	Sureñas
Color	red, burgundy	blue, navy
Language	English	Spanish
Numbers	XIV, 14, 4	XIII, 13, 3
Music	Motown oldies	*banda* music
Hairdo	feathered hair	vertical ponytail
Makeup	deep red lipstick	brown lipstick

from the color of one's lipstick to the brand of one's sneakers becomes a symbolic statement. Table 2.1 displays a few of the symbolic markers that each group has adopted.

Along with these outward markers of allegiance come attitudes that the group members hold toward each other. Norteñas see Sureñas as poor, unsophisticated newcomers who, according to one Norteña, "remind me of all the things I'm embarrassed of." Sureñas, on the other hand, see Norteñas as overly Americanized and hopelessly losing sight of what it means to be authentic, even to the degree that they no longer speak good Spanish. In fights (and in passing, to provoke fights), the gangs draw on the racist discursive practices of their respective countries of orientation: Norteñas call Sureñas "wetbacks" and "scraps," and tell them, of all things, to "go back to Mexico."

In many cases girls who consider themselves Sureñas overwhelmingly disidentify with English because they view it as symbolic of Americanization, assimilation, and loss of Mexicanness. Although many of the Sureñas are native Chicano English-speakers, within their peer group they are dominant Spanish users. Many of the girls I interviewed have expressed that dominant English use *no es chido* [it's not cool], and consider their fluent, fast Spanish (incomprehensible to language-shifted Norteñas) a symbol of "Mexican pride." Sureñas' attitudes run directly counter to larger social expectations that immigrants will learn English and are especially in conflict with ESL programs, which most of them attend.

Norteñas, on the other hand, identify with a Chicana ideology that stresses their bilingual ability and bicultural identity. Since the majority of them were born in the United States or immigrated as young children, they are native English-speakers. The dialect of English that they speak—

Chicano English—is markedly different from Standard English in areas of phonology (pronunciation) and lexicon (vocabulary). These differences, which sound to mainstream Euro-American interlocutors like a "Spanish accent," are in fact new patterns of an emerging ethnic dialect (Santa Ana 1991).

Young people I spoke to repeatedly pointed out the connection between language use and group identity. For instance, while I was talking on the phone to a Norteña whom I will call Sad Eyes, she asked me if I had noticed that a newly arrived girl named Ana was looking more like a *chola* [gang-identified girl] every day. "Yes," I replied. Indeed, Ana had been wearing darker lipstick and baggier pants as the school year progressed. "She wants to be jumped into Norte," reported Sad Eyes. "Oh, yeah," I said, "how do you know that?" She matter-of-factly replied: "Her eyeliner's all the way out and the other day I sat around and talked to her and she was talking to me in English the whole time, you know." "Is that a sign, that she's talking to you in English?" " Hell, yeah," retorted Sad Eyes, "she just got here, too."

Gang girls of both groups continuously create alliances that establish and reinforce their individual and group social identity. Both Norteñas and Sureñas have distinctive creative pastimes, linguistic codes, and routinized patterns of behavior. But because of the educational structure described above and its emphasis not only on transitioning students away from Spanish but also on accepting only a narrow range of Standard English competency, both groups of girls are in many ways cut off from opportunities for economic advancement.

In studying language attitudes and linguistic resistance among Latinas, I seek to address issues in the language politics of Latina identity as well as to add to our knowledge of the linguistic display of identity in high school settings much as Eckert (1989) did.

ETHNIC DIVERSITY, LINGUISTIC DIVERSITY, AND EDUCATIONAL POSSIBILITY

Sor Juana High School is a microcosm of the demographic situation that faces schools across the country where rising immigrant populations have created diversity that challenges teachers, exceeds school capacities, and provides students with opportunities for learning about new cultures. Sor Juana High School—with a total student body of 1,162 students—is 32 percent European-American, 22 percent Asian/Asian-American, 20 percent Latina/o, 14 percent African-American, 7 percent Pacific Islander, and 5 percent Other. It boasts student populations numerous enough to sustain cultural activities such as Mexican, Filipino, and Vietnamese classical dance troupes and African-American steppers.

The diversity of the student body, though usually depicted idealistically as a sort of mini-United Nations, brings its share of challenges, especially when it comes to providing instruction for students who speak languages other than English. In a few cases, immigrant students are absorbed into the educational system if their country of origin has English as its sole official language, but for the majority of immigrant students, the school undertakes a complex procedure to classify them based on their linguistic needs.

The California Education Code requires schools to determine the language(s) spoken at home by each student. Upon each student's enrollment at SJHS, parents are sent the Home Language Survey, an instrument designed by the State of California Department of Education to determine the home language background of the student. The survey consists of the following questions:

> Which language did your son or daughter learn when he or she first began to talk?
> What language does your son or daughter most frequently use at home?
> What language do you use most frequently to speak to your son or daughter?
> Name the language most often spoken by adults at home.

Based upon parents' answers to these questions, students are categorized and assigned a code corresponding to the home language. If all of the answers reflect an English-only household, the student is assigned a code of "English," but if any of the answers reflect the use of languages other than English, the student is assigned a code that identifies the language used in the home. Thus, minimal use of another language by members of the household, but not necessarily by the student, can serve to classify a student as having a non-English language background.

According to this criterion, 60 percent (695/1,162) of Sor Juana students have English as their sole home language. These are considered to be the "mainstream" students who are following the high school core curriculum and have the opportunity to take college preparatory courses. The "mainstream" student population includes most Euro-American students, most African-American students, and certain Asian-American students from long-established Asian-American communities. The remaining 40 percent (467/1,162) of Sor Juana students have a language other than English as their home language.

Each student who has been evaluated based on the aforementioned criteria to speak a language other than English in the home is assigned to one of two categories: (1) Limited English Proficient (LEP) or (2) Fluent English Proficient (FEP). Of the students who were found to have a language other than English as their home language, 61 percent (283/467) were classified as Limited English Proficient, while 40 percent were judged to be Fluent English Proficient. In effect, this means that fully one quarter of the entire student body (283/1,162) is considered to have limited English proficiency. But how does the school actually determine which students are Limited English Proficient and which are Fluent English Proficient?

When I interviewed the director of the school's English as a Second Language program, she stated that in order to be reclassified as Fluent English Proficient, a student "has to score above the 36th percentile on a standardized reading test, pass a [state-administered] competency exam, have passing grades, and be *functioning* [my emphasis] in school." If any of these four criteria are not met, the student cannot be reclassified as Fluent English Proficient.

The lockstep use of standardized testing, a legacy of the school reform movement of the 1980s, is especially treacherous for immigrant and language-minority children who are evaluated according to Standard English proficiency as well as mainstream Euro-American cultural standards (Valdés 1988). Inflexible grade placement—where grade promotion (and especially level promotion in the case of ESL students) is tied to designated cutoff scores on standardized achievement tests—can be especially discouraging for these students.

In addition to facing the hurdles of standardized testing and retainment, LEP students must additionally prove that they are "functioning." Even after having achieved FEP status, a student is still under observation by the school. A failed class (even a nonacademic class like wood shop or physical education) or complaints from a teacher that a student is not functioning ("disruptive in class," as noted on report cards) can be enough to prevent a student from achieving FEP status. In this way, one important criterion to advance to the next level of proficiency is in some cases non-linguistic. In the course of my fieldwork, I have encountered many orally fluent Chicano English-speakers who continue to be classified as LEP because of "disruptive" behavior or low test scores.

Even by the school's own measuring standards there are many students who achieve a high degree of oral language fluency but nevertheless cannot be reclassified as FEP. One additional exam that the school administers to LEP students is an individual oral proficiency examination. The examination is scored on a scale from 1 (lowest proficiency) to 5 (highest proficiency). According to this scale, 51 percent (92/181) of Latina/o Limited English Proficient students obtained the highest possible score on the oral fluency test. This examination, however, does not play a part in determining a student's Limited/Fluent status but is used to assess whether the student is eligible to be "mainstreamed" in some classes, like arts and crafts or health, that are deemed to require mostly oral/listening skills as opposed to literacy.

So here a paradox emerges: even though fully half of the Latina/o LEP students have high scores on oral proficiency examinations, it is still the case that the great majority of these students are not succeeding in school, have high dropout rates, and are placed in low-level classes because of low grades, low overall test scores, or behavioral issues.

The technical criteria by which an institution such as a school system assesses fluency would not be of such importance if LEP and FEP statuses were mere formalities, or served only internal statistics-keeping functions. In fact, these acronyms play a large role in determining and predicting a student's educational opportunities. When classified as LEP, a student may not follow the school's regular course program for college preparation, but instead must continue to take English as a Second Language courses. Although ESL courses count toward fulfilling a student's high school graduation requirements, only the most advanced ESL courses count toward fulfilling the basic four-year college entrance requirements. College preparatory curricula to enter higher education in the University of California (UC) system or the California State University (CSU) system are standardized across the state, and a student's initial placement within the high school ESL system can easily determine whether or not she/he will be able to fulfill UC/CSU requirements by the time she/he is a graduating senior.

The Sor Juana High School 1993–1994 course guide lists a total of twenty ESL courses spread over a number of areas, including not only the standard English courses but also history, mathematics, sciences, and even typing. Only four of the twenty ESL courses (advanced English, U.S. history, civics, and algebra I) count toward UC/CSU requirements. In effect, this means that for the vast majority of ESL students, the only way to have the opportunity to attend a branch of UC or CSU is to be placed in advanced ESL as incoming freshmen (ninth graders), so that they will be able to complete the four-year English course requirement for college entrance.

The vast majority of incoming ESL students at SJHS have been recommended by middle school officials for placement in beginning or intermediate sections of ESL. In fact, only five of thirty entering Latina/o LEP freshmen were placed in advanced ESL during the 1993–1994 school year. The systematic outcome of this structured level program is that many orally fluent Latina/o students do not move out of the LEP designation, and as a result are unable to attend four-year institutions. Even when they do graduate from high school and attend a community college, the remedial ESL courses that they must take in order to qualify for enrollment in regular college classes will set them back at least one year. The opportunity cost of that time is simply too high for poor families who gradually come to rely on their children for increasing financial contributions to the household (NCAS 1988).

Latina/o students come up against various types of institutional barriers that stem from this system of classification. Alejandra immigrated from Mexico when she was five years old. Now fifteen, she is a fluent Chicano English speaker and has been promoted through ten grade levels without ever being reclassified as FEP. She is just too rowdy, say the teachers. "I am bored in class," says Alejandra. " 'What is this? This is a dog. This is a cat.' Give me a break! I'd rather get kicked out of class." What seems especially ironic about Alejandra's case is that she does not speak Spanish at home with her family but displays a common pattern reflective of ongoing language shift: her parents speak Spanish to her and her siblings; she answers exclusively in English.

Annia is a student whose mother fought a bitter battle with teachers as Annia was about to enter high school. Although Annia was a stellar student in middle school, her test scores were too low to have her reclassified as FEP. After two months of fighting and showing teachers Annia's personal diary in English (much to Annia's dismay), her mother finally gave up and secretly enrolled Annia in the public high school in the next district. The family succeeded in getting Annia an FEP designation in her new school; consequently today she is an eleventh grader taking a regular college curriculum.

The last example of institutional barriers to student success comes in the form of a student article in the *Sor Juana Times,* the high school weekly newspaper. In the spring of 1994, Laurie Bexley, a half-Mexican, half-Euro-American, wrote an article entitled "Even Unintentional Racism Hurts." In this article, Laurie chronicles the experiences of her mother at an SJHS teacher-parent conference.

> When I first came to Sor Juana, I wasn't doing well in Biology, and when my mom went to [teacher-parent conference] night, she talked to my teacher about it. My mother has a very thick accent and it is clear to almost everyone that she comes from Latin America. When she asked my teacher what was wrong, he replied by telling her that students at Sor Juana come from very different schools and that my junior high probably didn't prepare me as well as others for this course. When my mom went on to say that I went to [a prestigious school] and had a 4.0 in the past, he was stupefied. "Oh, oh, oh. Laurie is your daughter, I'm so sorry I thought you were someone else's mother," my teacher replied. It was pitiful. My teacher had made an obviously racist assumption that because my mother was Hispanic I went to an inferior junior high and that was the reason for my problems in Biology. It doesn't stop there, though. I've seen it time and time again, and it all gets swept under the rug by the administration who likes to focus their efforts on the prestigious, rich, white kids at Sor Juana.

All of the aforementioned student experiences reflect the way that the curriculum is structured for Latinas/os at SJHS. But is it the case that this system of linguistic classification is reflected in the communities of Latinas/os at the school? In the following section I will describe two of the student groups at SJHS and chronicle their relationship to immigration history, socioeconomic standing, and linguistic status at SJHS.

EFFECTS OF LINGUISTIC DISIDENTIFICATION

Within this system of oppositional discursive practices, the linguistic resources of the students are polarized and politicized so that speaking a particular variety of Spanish or English is an act of identity that displays one's position vis-à-vis the social dynamics of the groups at school.

Research on the language attitudes of Mexican Americans has shown that academic achievement is often closely tied to language attitudes. Positive correlations have been found in the attitudes of pupils toward Standard English and their achievement in reading and English. On the other hand, negative attitudes toward the students' codeswitching varieties on the part of the teachers resulted in lower gains in reading (Ramírez 1978). SJHS students who affiliate with the Sureña cultural identity display negative language attitudes toward English that undoubtedly affect their performance in such crucial areas as reading and writing. Furthermore, the students' identification with Mexicanness is such that they retard their own entry into mainstream English classes because of their unwillingness to enter classes with Norteñas and mainstream students.

The following is a sample interview with a Sureña whom I will call Thalia. Thalia is a high school junior in the transitional ESL program who is currently attending Beginning II level classes. She is sixteen years old and was born in Los Angeles. She is a very interesting student because, like many people of Mexican descent residing in the United States, she has had a history of traversing between the two countries. She was born in Los Angeles and lived there until she was about five. At that point her family moved to Mexico and she spent the next eight years there. She returned within the past three years. Because she spent her early childhood here, and because some of her relatives speak English, Thalia's pronunciation is quite good and she can carry on a colloquial conversation without any problems. What struck me about her, and the reason why I was interested in following her progress, is that she has poor reading and writing skills despite her excellent listening comprehension and the long time that has elapsed since her return. Currently Thalia is in danger of failing Beginning II. Although she is U.S.-born, Thalia considers herself to have grown up in Mexico and identifies as a Sureña. She dresses mostly in blue, the gang color, and wears a Sureña hairdo, clothes, and makeup. All of her boyfriends and crushes until now have been Sureños. In the transcript (G.47.94), Norma is the interviewer.

10 Thalia: *A mí me gustan, morenitos me gustan, porque los gringos . . . ¡ay, no, no me gustan!* [I like, I like dark-skinned guys, because gringos, oh, no, I don't like them!]

11 Norma: *¿Por qué?* [Why?]

12 Thalia: *No sé, no me gustan.* [I don't know, I don't like them.]

13 Norma: *¿No te gustan por güeros o por gringos?* [You don't like them because they're blond or because they're gringos?]

14 Thalia: *No sé, pero creo que porque estan muy güeros, y luego no me gusta como . . . su forma de ser de ellos.* [I don't know, but I think it's because they're very blond, and also I don't like their personalities.]

15 Norma: *Aha, aha. ¿Qué tienen? ¿Son aburridos o algo?* [Aha, aha. What's wrong? Are they boring or something?]

16 Thalia: *Sí, casi los únicos que echan desmadre son los mexicanos, ¿no ves? Los mexicanos son divertidos.* [Yeah, just about the only ones that raise a ruckus are the Mexicans, you know? Mexicans are fun.]

17 Norma: *Mhmm. Relajientos.* [Mhmm. Fun-loving individuals who create a relaxed/fun mood.]

18 Thalia: *Ellos no, como en las clases, yo, mira, ese tiempo que tomé Health en el sexto período, había casi puros gringos y nada de desmadre, ahí bien callados, como topos.* [They (gringos) don't, like in classes, remember when I had Health 6th period, there were just about all gringos there and there was no ruckus or activity, they were all quiet like moles.]

19 Thalia: *No, una clase con un gringo, no, no me gustaría con ellos.* [No, having a class with gringos, no, I wouldn't like it with them.]

In the interview, Thalia expresses her attitudes toward gringos and *güeros* [blondes]. It is worth mentioning here that Thalia herself has white-blond hair and is very pale because she is from Jalisco, a region in Mexico that experienced massive immigration from France. Interestingly, she prefers the darker skin tone that is considered normative and symbolic by the group that she aligns with. She even makes disparaging remarks about people whose skin tone is similar to hers. (It is also clear from other conversations I've had with her that she does not think of herself as ethnically or racially white.) Thalia expresses a general dislike for the learning style and social interaction style of mainstream white students. She later admitted to dropping out of the health class because there were only mainstream Euro-American students there. Her language attitudes are also quite strong, and they come through in the following excerpt:

43 Norma: *Aha. Y este, ¿a tí que te gusta más hablar, inglés o español?* [So what do you prefer to speak, Spanish or English?]

44 Thalia: *Español.* [Spanish.]

45 Norma: *Español, ¿por qué?* [Spanish, why?]

46 Thalia: *No sé. Me gusta más español.* [I don't know. I like Spanish better.]

47 Norma: *Lo que se me hace interesante es que, pues tú teniendo ya tanto tiempo aquí, acostumbrada al idioma de acá, no, que te juntas mucho con mex-icanos y que hablas mucho español.* [What I think is interesting is that you, having been here so long, and being used to the language here, you associate mostly with Mexicans and speak a lot of Spanish.]

48 Thalia: *Yo pienso que aunque hablara mucho inglés, yo hablaría siempre español. . . . Algunos dicen, no, que nomás 'ta aprendiendo inglés, y ya no, habla español. ¡Porque de muchas (toca la mesa) aquí, nomás aprenden el inglés y ya no quieren hablar español y eso a mi me cae gordo!* [I think that even if I spoke a lot of English, I would only speak Span-ish. . . . Some say, no, that she's just learning En-glish and that she doesn't speak Spanish anymore. Because there are a lot (of girls) here (taps the table) that as soon as they learn English, they don't want to speak Spanish anymore, and I really hate that!]

49 Norma: Mhmm.

50 Thalia: *Y tú les hablas español y ellas te . . . te contestan en inglés, eso me cae gordo a mí.* [And you speak in Spanish to them and they answer you in English, I really hate that.]

In this excerpt exploring Thalia's language attitudes, she declares a preference for Spanish. I remark to her that her insistence on Spanish is remarkable since she speaks English well and is very much accustomed to life in the United States. This question is implicitly one of membership as well. Since her English is so good, why shouldn't she be a Norteña? Certainly she has everything that could enable her to join that group if she wished. Her answer is very revealing. She denies being able to speak a lot of English and states that even if she did, she would still choose to speak Spanish. This dramatically illustrates not only her rhetorical position with respect to the language question but also her self-perception that, despite her near-native pronunciation, does not allow her to "construct" herself as an English-speaker. Thalia looks down on people who refuse to speak Spanish after having learned English (an indirect reference to Norteñas), implying that they shun much more than a linguistic code by opting for English. She even disapproves of interspeaker codeswitching, one of the linguistic devices most often used by Norteñas.

Thalia is an example of the effect that language attitudes can have on educational outcomes. I believe that her socially precipitated disidentification with English has severely affected her ability to acquire reading and writing skills in English at an important learning period, and since the school's support for Spanish language instruction is limited (the main goal being for all nonnative speakers to learn English), this may be affecting her literacy skills in Spanish as well.

CONCLUSION

This study, grounded in the sociology of language framework and ethnographic field methods, has traced the complex interrelationships between language attitudes, gang ideology, educational programs, and curricula as they are formulated in the context of a community of high-school Latinas in northern California. We have seen how the implementation of educational policies and programs interlocks with minority intragroup identity to give rise to a phenomenon of linguistic resistance and oppositional disidentification with English. I hope that by bringing this problem to the surface we will contribute as researchers and educators in addressing this and similar situations affecting immigrant communities across the United States.

ACKNOWLEDGMENTS

When I did my fieldwork, many people helped me in my research, gave of their time, their energies, and accepted me into their communities. Thanks most of all to the girls who participated in my study and with whom I shared amazing conversations on language and ethnicity: Babygirl, Raisa, Sadgirl, Reina, Yadira, Veronica, Mariana, Cati, Jackie, Tina, Jill, and Yolanda (though pseudonymed, you know who you are). There are many more kids whom I would acknowledge and thank by name were it not for confidentiality agreements. I extend my warmest thanks also to the editors of this volume and to Penny Eckert, John Rickford, Elizabeth Traugott, Candy Goodwin, and Guadalupe Valdés for their comments and support. Any flaws in this study remain my own, of course. This research was supported in part by the Spencer Foundation, the Institute for Research on Learning, and Stanford University.

REFERENCES

Anzaldúa, G. (1987). *Borderlands/La Frontera: The New Mestiza.* San Francisco: Aunt Lute Books.

Camarillo, A. (1985). *Chicanos in California: A History of Mexican Americans in California.* San Francisco: Boyd & Fraser.

Donovan, J. (1993). An introduction to street gangs. In Northern California Gang Investigators Association (ed.), *1993 Gang Training Seminar Handbook* (pp. 1–4). Sacramento: NCGIA.

Eckert, P. (1989). *Jocks and Burnouts: Social Categories and Identity in the High School.* New York: Teachers College Press.

Gal, S. (1993). Diversity and contestation in linguistic ideologies: German speakers in Hungary. *Language in Society,* 22 (3), 337–359.

Mendoza-Denton, N. (1996). "Muy macha": Gender and ideology in gang girls' discourse about makeup. *Ethnos,* 61 (1–2), 47–63.

Moore, J. (1991). *Going Down to the Barrio: Homeboys and Homegirls in Change.* Philadelphia: Temple University Press.

National Coalition of Advocates for Students (1988). *New Voices: Immigrant Students in U.S. Public Schools.* Boston: NCAS.

Padilla, F. (1992). *The Gang as an American Enterprise.* New Brunswick, NJ: Rutgers University Press.

Ramírez, Arnulfo. (1978). Language attitudes and the achievement of bilingual (Spanish-English) pupils. Paper read at the National Conference on Chicano and Latino Discourse Behavior, Princeton, April 17–19.

Santa Ana, O. (1991). *Phonetic simplification processes in the English of the barrio.* Ph.D. dissertation, University of Pennsylvania.

Valdés, G. (1988). The language situation of Mexican Americans. In S. L. McKay & S. C. Wong (eds.), *Language Diversity: Problem or Resource?: A Social and Educational Perspective on Language Minorities in the United States* (pp. 111–139). New York: Newbury.

TWO

REFLECTION

TESTIMONIOS

SPEAKING AS A CHICANA

Tracing Cultural Heritage through Silence and Betrayal

Jacqueline M. Martínez

> I knew that then, sitting in the Oakland auditorium (as I know in my poetry), that the only thing worth writing about is what seems to be unknown and, therefore, fearful.
> —CHERRÍE MORAGA

> In our self-reflectivity and in our active participation with the issues that confront us, whether it be through writing, front-line activism, or individual self-development, we are also uncovering the inter-faces, the very spaces and places where our multiple-surfaced, colored, racially gendered bodies intersect and interconnect.
> —GLORIA ANZALDÚA[1]

IDENTIFYING MODES OF ETHNIC CONSCIOUSNESS

Coming to speak as a Chicana has been, for me, a long and very personal struggle. It is a struggle that seeps deeply into my professional life as an academic; my academic work has been, in fact, the primary avenue through which I have taken up the very personal issue of my identity as a Chicana. Reflecting on the processes involved in my coming to speak as a Chicana, I can identify three distinct modes of consciousness that define major shifts in my thinking, feeling, and acting in relation to myself, my family, and the many students and colleagues of color (both gay and straight) in the academy whom I have had the privilege of knowing and working with over the course of my academic career. These three

modes of consciousness are not discrete, but share overlapping boundaries. My movement between and among them is not linear, though it is
progressive and spiraling. This chapter is an account of that progressive
and spiraling movement between and among these three modes of consciousness. Originally written in 1992 and rewritten in 1997, it takes
account of the very terrain upon which I have come to consciousness as a
Chicana.[2]

What, then, are these modes of consciousness? I call the first mode
of consciousness an *unknowing-knowing.*[3] This consciousness was dominant throughout my childhood and up until the age of twenty-three, when
I began attending California State University at Northridge. It was at Cal.
State Northridge that I first sought out connection with a group of Chicano
students. Prior to seeking out those students, I *knew* I had Mexican-
American ancestry from my father, but my family's fairly affluent southern California lifestyle made the knowledge of my Mexican-American
heritage, something *unknown,* become seemingly not relevant—a message I got from my father. This unknowing-knowing consciousness encouraged assimilation.

The second mode of consciousness emerged as I began asking *barely
conscious questions,* entirely of myself, about what, exactly, my relationship was to Chicanos/as, Mexican Americans, and Spanish-speaking people generally.[4] When I began broaching these questions to myself, I had no
clear idea of where to go to find answers. Showing up at the Chicano Students Association meeting at the university had not yet involved me in
asking explicit questions about my family's history or our ethnic heritage.
But as soon as I began participating, I did ask myself if I belonged there.
The only way I knew to answer such a question was to see if the Chicano
students seemed to think I belonged there. Despite the fact that I spoke
only English and that I was very middle-class white American in my gestures and speech patterns, I felt welcomed. Feeling welcomed, yet seeing
the differences carried in my economic class standing and lacking the
language (I heard the students use a lot of Spanglish), left me feeling like
a fake, a phony, someone who really didn't belong with Chicanos. This
mode of consciousness, then, has a particular precariousness about it; it is
situated in the realm of the preconscious, where there is a reverberation
back and forth between the *unknown-known* and the *known-knowing.* It
is a mode of consciousness marked by ambiguity and uncertainty (and,
therefore, possibility and danger).

The third mode of consciousness regarding my Chicana identity involved an *explicit asking of questions,* first of myself and my family history, then of the history of the Chicano people—especially those whose histories lie upon the land of the southwestern United States. It is upon this land that acts of oppression and blatant racism have defined the struggle for survival of the native and mestizo people. Entering this mode of consciousness coincided with efforts at formal and informal education where I began reading about the histories of various sorts of oppressions and efforts at liberation. I also began seeking out other Chicanas and women of color in an effort to find common points of identification.

My effort in what follows is to detail the overlapping contours of consciousness and experience that have defined my coming to identity as a Chicana, lesbian, and feminist academic. I begin with some theoretical and experiential considerations about the conjunctions and disjunctions between my coming to awareness as a Chicana and as a lesbian. Then I shift to concrete descriptions of my ethnic heritage and consider how it was carried in the unknowing-knowing of my young adult and childhood experiences. I shift back and forth between theory and experience in an effort to evoke the movements through which I have come to speak as a Chicana. I conclude the chapter by focusing primarily on the third mode of consciousness identified above. Here I connect my own family history to the history of Chicanas, Chicana lesbians, and the Chicano people.

ENTERING INTO A CHICANA LESBIAN WORLD

Coming into consciousness as a Chicana has been, for me, intricately connected with my coming to consciousness as a lesbian.[5] The knowledge produced by coming out to myself as a lesbian was transformative for me personally; it also revealed to me the ways in which culture and social discourse can literally preclude knowledge and understanding (as unknowing) that is central to our very existence as particular human beings. Coming out as a lesbian at the age of twenty-two revealed to me the ways in which culture can directly oppress people deep within their own psychic being.

Like many other gay and lesbian people, once I came out, I could look back on the whole of my life and see the ways in which I had always been a lesbian but had never been allowed the space to actually live and consciously experience that part of myself. So I began to broach barely conscious questions to myself: If the oppressions of culture have prevented me from seeing important aspects of sexuality, then how have the oppressions of culture prevented me from seeing important aspects of my ethnicity?

My explorations into feminist theory had allowed me to understand that because cultural norms made heterosexuality compulsory (Rich 1980), certain power relations between men and women were reinforced within culture. So I knew that by presenting ethnic heritage as secondary to "American" (white) identity, certain power relations between darkness and lightness were maintained. I just didn't know what those power relations were because I had lived the privileges of white identification. Identifying as "white" as I was growing up created an important difference for me between coming to consciousness as a lesbian and coming to consciousness as a Chicana: whereas there was very little ambiguity for me about my lesbian self, I was filled with nothing but ambiguity about my Chicana self. The ambiguities of my Chicana identity situated me firmly within the second mode of consciousness identified above: a mode of asking barely conscious questions entirely to myself about the ambiguities of my situation.[6]

Entering into a new consciousness-of-self via certitude versus ambiguity makes an important difference. It makes a difference because having certitude generally discourages asking questions about that which is certain. Having ambiguity, on the other hand, provokes questions. The ambiguities of my Chicana identity propelled me, first and foremost, into questions about my father and his life; second, into the relationship between social location and ethnic identity, and the circumstances of sociocultural powers and privileges that are distributed according to the perceptible signs of a person's ethnic identity. Because my father kept his own life history largely inaccessible to me, my development of Chicana identity was very much occupied with concerns about my own privilege and how that militated against my ability to enter into a Chicana world. The description I offer below illustrates how I processed this concern by separating out my lesbian certainty from my Chicana ambiguity. I illustrate this point concretely by comparing my experiences coming to consciousness as a lesbian and as a Chicana, first theoretically and then with a description of experience.

Although I have always been entrenched within the heterosexist discourses of culture, there was a certain point (around the age of twenty-two) at which a number of circumstances converged to create an explosion of certainty whereby I knew that the people and the world were wrong in assuming I was heterosexual and that I was at varying degrees of risk in revealing the error of heterosexual presumption. Thus began a struggle in which, as a normal feature of my daily life, I had to consciously consider how, when, and to what degree to control my expressions as a lesbian. Early in the coming-out process, simple things like switching pronouns so that it was obvious I was talking about a female-female intimate couple were major markers of being out. With heterosexual friends, topics about couples, dating, or the attractiveness of a member of the opposite sex presented particular challenges. Simply to go along with the conversation would make one tacitly pass as heterosexual. In these cases, commenting on the attractiveness of another woman or the predicaments of a lesbian relationship constituted a coming out. As I became more comfortable with my lesbian identity among heterosexuals, it became easier to initiate "lesbian" topics for conversation, comment on homophobic remarks, or say simply, "as a lesbian. . . ." Yet, for every choice made there was always the knowledge that such acts of coming out involved very real risks. These risks ranged from simple rejection to outward disdain and even outright violence. I began what is a lifelong predicament of dealing with the gay closet in a heterosexist culture.

My conscious struggles with ethnic identity have been, like my conscious struggles with sexual identity, a feature primarily of my adult life. I am not sure what prompted me to seek out Chicano students as a twenty-three-year-old undergraduate. Perhaps it was that in coming out as a lesbian I sensed vast areas of discovery waiting out there for me. Perhaps coming out as a lesbian emboldened me enough to seek out other aspects of myself and chart my own way in life. I don't remember consciously deciding to seek out Chicanos/as. I do remember attending their meetings and their dances, feeling terribly excited and a little out of place. But I must say that in the twelve or so years since I first began tentatively seeking out Chicanos/as and other people of color, I have felt entirely welcomed and have never been questioned about the "authenticity" of my ethnic standing. No, over time I came to realize that it was primarily among Anglos that I could fail the ethnic test. In the beginning, however, I didn't need others to question my ethnic identity because I was very busy questioning it myself.

I sought out feminist theory primarily to help me understand more about what I knew was my lesbian self. As I studied feminist texts, I encountered discussions of racism and classism. Works by Baca Zinn et al. (1986), Gonzales (1977), Zavella (1989), and Moraga and Anzaldúa (1983) were especially important during this time. Moraga and Anzaldúa's work, along with Audre Lorde's work (1984), was crucially important in helping me make connections between the experiences of Chicanas and other women of color. García's (1989) essay was important in helping me to make connections with African-American, Asian-American, and Native American women. I began to see these questions of racism and classism within feminist theory as having relevance to my own life. I was already in graduate school by this time, studying the philosophy of communication.[7] It was 1986, I was twenty-six years old, and I was in the Department of Speech Communication at Southern Illinois University. Moving to the Midwest from southern California was a culture shock, to say the least. Adjusting to life in the Midwest provided another layer of experiences and feelings for me to grapple with. I went to graduate school because I felt it would allow me to continue to pursue the journey of self-discovery that was initiated by my coming out as a lesbian.

During the initial stages of finding relevance in issues of race and ethnicity, I generally maintained silence regarding my developing ethnic identity: I did not seek out other Chicanas, other Chicana lesbians, or other women of color. Being a graduate student and living in southern Illinois made it difficult for me to actively pursue connections with Chicanas, Latinas, and other people of color. There were no other Chicanas or Latinas in my graduate program.[8] I did participate in the black students' protest against the downsizing of battered women's shelters, but whatever Chicana or Latina community was there was beyond my perception as I struggled to figure out how graduate school worked, how to form new relationships, and how to be "out" as a lesbian. Whereas I could carry my lesbian self fairly openly, I didn't feel any openness about my ethnic self. I felt that absence of ethnic self because of my comparative class privilege and my entirely Anglo speech patterns, and because I had been raised to pass. I could move about in my everyday world without having questions about my ethnic identity provoked by myself or others.

Unlike my experience as a lesbian, I rarely felt myself in a position of having to consciously consider how, when, and to what degree to control any conscious expression of my ethnic identity. If there were any cases where persons stereotyped me on the basis of my dark hair and facial features (on light-brown skin), almond-shaped eyes, and high "Indian" cheekbones, I was oblivious to it. Unlike my sexual identity, I did not, at this time, experience my ethnic identity as problematic within the dominant discourses of culture. My recognition of racism within feminism fueled my own questions about my ethnic identity and helped create conditions that moved me more consciously into my own ambiguities regarding my ethnic identity. My internal questions about my ethnic identity came more and more to occupy my thinking and feeling. But still, it wasn't until I received my doctoral degree and had my first tenure-track position on the east coast that I wrote about my Chicana identity.

The difference between the certitude I carry within my sexual identity and the ambiguity I carry within my ethnic identity has a lot to do with the concreteness of the human body and the way it carries out perception and expression. Once I came out to myself as a lesbian, I realized that I had been ignorant about my sexuality. But after having come out, I never again felt ignorant about my sexual identity. I have often, on the other hand, felt an ignorance about my ethnic identity—although I have, ironically, come to know more about Mexican-American history than gay history. The difference, I think, lies in the fact that I experience my lesbian sexuality concretely in my own body. My ethnic body, in contrast, has never been tied to the concreteness of speaking Spanish—a fact that I regret immensely but over which I had no control as a child. Since coming out as a lesbian I have often looked in the mirror and wondered how people looking at me could not know that I'm a dyke. I've always carried myself in a fairly butch way and prefer masculine to feminine clothing. Living as an "out" lesbian meant seeing the butchiness that I present to the world as revealing my lesbian self. In this way, the human body is a sign that signifies both to myself and to others (and as my perception of their perception of me). Coming out as a lesbian allowed me to see the code of my lesbian self as it had organized much of my bodily style throughout my life. Once I came out as a lesbian, I knew that my body spoke the language of lesbian sexuality; there was absolutely no question about my standing as a lesbian.

There is, of course, an important parallel to the process of coming to see the ethnicness one presents to the world. For Mexican Americans, Spanish is a primary code through which ethnicness is carried out. A young child growing up in Texas during the 1930s, for example, might have received the message that the Spanish language through which his body communicated naturally to the world was a "bad" language that signified ignorance and low social standing. If Spanish was the home language, the child must then distance himself from the linguistic code that had been most intimately connected to the self. As the child internalizes the racist message about his home language, he seeks to distance himself from the formal linguistic code (Spanish) and all the tonalities, rhythms, and corporealities carried out in speaking the language that is his most intimate contact with the world. Should the child continue down this road in developing his capacity for human expression, the tonalities, rhythms, and corporealities of spoken English will come to dominate, and thus the child's connection to cultural patterns carried out in the Spanish language diminishes. Assimilation becomes inevitable. Should the child, at some later point in his life, consciously reject the dominant culture's message about his home language, he may embrace Spanish and come to see his speaking in Spanish as a way of embracing an ethnic self that the dominant culture would have preferred to remain assimilated. In the moment of embracing the language he had learned to distance himself from, a new possibility for seeing one's self and body as an ethnic self and body emerges. Such a person might look in the mirror, or listen to himself speaking in Spanish, and wonder how anyone, including himself, could deny the ethnicness of his body.

It has taken a long time for me to come to see and feel my own body as an ethnic body. Absent the capacity to express myself in Spanish, I am left to reach for less tangible traces of an ethnic self that have been buried under layers of assimilation into Anglo culture and practice. The fact that I have spent so much of my adult and professional life occupied with questions about my ethnic self and my familial-cultural heritage becomes the primary signifier of this ethnic self of mine. It is a signifier that, although it lacks the obvious concreteness of experiencing one's own sexuality or speaking Spanish, retains the general concreteness of human perception. There is, for example, the experience of looking into the mirror and the faces of others. I remember when I first began speaking about my struggles with my ethnic identity. Linda Alcoff, a Latina colleague, reminded me about "the politics of the visible," and suggested that I looked more ethnic than she did—a fact that certainly made a difference in others' perception of me. The next time I looked in the mirror, I saw dark features and wondered what I had been seeing when I looked in the mirror previously. Thus began a process in which I have learned to see myself seeing into my own face and the faces of others and seeing more than white or black; it is a searching for subtleties and complexities that Anglo cultural perception denies. Yet, still, there is a profoundly important way in which, until this body of mine can speak in Spanish, gesture in a "Spanishly" way, and be immersed in Spanish-speaking communities, there will remain questions about its ethnic identification.[9] There is a crucially important difference, it seems, between rebuking Anglo culture from within the linguistic code of that culture, and being immersed within the fundamentally different cultural codes carried with the language of the different and subjugated culture.

In developing my Chicana identity I have been very aware of the degree to which I embody all of the signs of a white, middle-class U.S. American. The fact that I embody those signs gave me an advantage but also presented a danger. The advantage is that I have been able within my professional life to represent the concerns of Chicanas/os and other students of color within the predominantly white institution of higher education. During my three years as a member of the faculty at a private liberal arts and business college just outside of Boston, I found that administrators seemed quick to listen to what I had to say about "diversity issues." I often wondered if those same administrators would have been as quick to listen if I had not embodied so many of the signs of mainstream Anglo culture (although, in the end, I felt that even though they did listen to me, they never really heard what I was saying).

It took me a long time to be comfortable with the role of speaker on behalf of "diversity" or "students of color" because of the degree to which I recognized ignorances in my own experience and understanding about what it means to be discriminated against or stereotyped on the basis of one's ethnic identity. The danger is that I might, in the name of speaking for marginalized groups within the academy, actually perpetuate prejudices because of my own ignorances. Or, worse, that my speaking on behalf of "diversity" might lead others (white people) to falsely believe that by feeling comfortable with the Angloness in me, they have pushed themselves to examine their own stereotypes and prejudices.

My struggles with ethnic identity and my social privilege during graduate school were informed by how I saw privilege working in the context of hetero/homosexual identification. I came to understand something about the dangers of one's privileges and ignorances when claiming a marginalized identity because of experiences I had had as a lesbian. I came to know what it's like to have to endure another level of silencing and marginalization as a result of a heterosexually privileged other's self-serving and willfully ignorant assertions. The example below illustrates this point.

During a graduate seminar on rhetorical theory and criticism, a white female peer and I were giving a presentation on feminist rhetorical criticism. As we began our presentation, my peer quickly proclaimed that she considered herself a lesbian (citing Adrienne Rich's [1980] concept of "lesbian continuum"). She did not make this proclamation as a way of illustrating how Adrienne Rich develops her notion of a "lesbian continuum," how it is designed to bring visibility and understanding about a human experience that has been systematically silenced, or how it is indebted to a long history of oppression endured by practicing lesbians. This peer was an openly married and practicing heterosexual. Her husband had been a regular visitor to the department, was part of our Sunday softball games, and showed up with his wife at all of our social gatherings. By simply declaring that she was a lesbian and then going on with some nondirectly related point about feminist rhetorical criticism, she erased the concrete experiences of struggle faced by sexually practicing lesbians. Everyone in that classroom knew both her and her husband. In claiming an identity as a lesbian she erased the particularities and risks that I faced as someone who could not carry the heterosexual privilege she took for granted.

Without contextualizing her claim with an understanding of the differences between her identification as a lesbian and sexually practicing lesbians, she sought to gain status by virtue of her "lesbian" connections to the women in her life. When I spoke next, I alerted our audience to the difference between claiming an identification on the basis of being emotionally connected to women, and actually living a life and engaging in practices that put one at risk within a concrete social world. I saw my peer as seeking to benefit from the status of "being a lesbian" without ever having engaged the emotionally difficult and socially threatening circumstance of being at risk because of her lesbian identification.

I didn't have a problem with her identifying herself as a lesbian as a way to gain visibility for the importance of her relationships with women. But her failure to identify the privileges and comforts of being a clearly identifiable heterosexual in her daily life erased the concrete risks experienced by lesbians who cannot carry her heterosexual privilege. In this case, her speaking "as a lesbian" benefited only herself in claiming a status unavailable to our mostly male—and, as far as I was aware, heterosexual—audience. The selfish ends of her discursive strategy were confirmed for me months later at a social gathering when she told me how "angry" she was with me for "discrediting" her in front of our peers. Her priorities were clearly aligned with the authority and power entailed within the discourses of the graduate classroom. She stood willfully ignorant regarding the extent to which her utterances silenced and erased the experiences of those whose sexuality could not be lived so unselfconsciously as her own.

This experience, during a crucial period of my developing ethnic identity, led me to consider very seriously the kinds of social discriminations that get perpetuated when someone like myself, a Mexican American who passes easily, speaks on behalf of or represents a marginalized group such as Chicanas.[10] It also led me to think back, very carefully, about my family life when I was growing up and the extent to which I lived with traces of a Mexican-American cultural heritage.

SEARCHING THROUGH MY FATHER'S BURIED PAST

There is a reason why I didn't learn Spanish as I grew up, and it has to do with my father's complex and mostly hidden life history. It has taken me a long time to be able to write with empathy and understanding about my father's life. I have, for many years, been very angry at my father—angry mostly about his profound silences and the many distances they create. As I have struggled in my adult life to understand the circumstances of my own life when I was growing up, I have looked to my father's life as a place to build understanding. The details about my father's life that I provide below have come to me only very recently. Finally, long after I had begun writing about my ethnic identity and family history, I called my father on the telephone and said, "Can I ask you some questions?" I then moved through a formal interview protocol dealing with questions about the facts of his and his parents' life; questions about Spanish, education, religion, holiday celebrations, and experiences of discrimination. He seemed willing to respond and elaborate. He answered all my questions, even encouraged me to ask again. Yet, I felt a strong twinge of anger at his encouragement because he was acting as if he was then, and had always been, open to sharing with me his experiences growing up.

Prior to that direct and formal interview, I had asked my father, on several occasions throughout my life, about his life while growing up, his father, his family, his experiences, and so on. I can never recall a time when he gave me anything more than a curt response. During my year (1990–1991) at the University of California at Santa Barbara, where I was a Chicana dissertation fellow, I saw my father and grandmother more regularly than I had since I was eleven years old. He and my grandmother lived together then, as they still do, in Simi Valley.[11] Emboldened in my effort to understand my cultural heritage, I asked my father what his father was like. I saw my father physically cringe at the question. He began telling me how his father was like my mother's father, and that was why he was always glad that we were so close to my mother's parents. On another occasion during that time, I was conversing with my father and grandmother when the issue of cultural identity and discrimination came up. My grandmother looked at me hard, yet kindly, pressed her lips tightly together, stiffened her back, and shook her head back and forth. Her body was saying, "Yes, it was bad. Life was hard. We don't talk about those things." It was also during this conversation that my father told me he was glad I was at UCSB and in the Chicano Studies department, because it meant that I could make a difference for others.

Born in McAllen, Texas, in 1928, Octavio Martínez grew up very poor. When my father was very young, the family moved. First they moved to Brownsville, but a few years later they finally settled in Houston. Both his parents were bilingual, though his father had only a third-grade education and his mother had an eighth-grade education. The family spoke Spanish inside the home and English outside the home. My father's father, Octavio Tergo Martínez, was a musically inclined common laborer who struggled to provide for his family. I never knew my grandfather. He died of a stroke in 1947, when my father was nineteen years old.

My father tells me that he saw blatant discrimination as he was growing up. As kids, he and his younger brother and sister could swim in the public swimming pool on Sunday evenings only—they cleaned the pool on Monday. Certain "Anglo only" barber shops were off limits to my father and his two siblings. But he also says that the social markers he noticed most were class markers. He says that for every Anglo kid who acted in discriminatory ways toward him, there were other Anglo kids who didn't. At the same time he saw a certain disrespect for self and others carried out in the actions of some of the people around him. He says that he felt there was more discrimination within the Mexican-American community than from the Anglo community—a perception certainly encouraged by the internalized racism that functions within a racist culture.

It seems that at a young age my father identified a certain pettiness and ignorance among the poor "Mexican" people in his neighborhood. In this respect, my father has always had a sense of class. Not in the sense of having money, but in the sense of having pride and consideration for oneself and others. In his professional life, my father has always been known as a demanding but fair executive. He supported the advancement of anyone who demonstrated ability and commitment, without regard to ethnic heritage, marital status, or gender. Growing up in the world he did, he saw the Anglo world as one where he had a greater chance of being valued and rewarded for his work and abilities than he did in the barrio, where the opportunities for social advancement were small. I get the feeling, from many years of listening to my father's brief and message-sending stories about his professional life, that he believes in equal opportunity but not affirmative action. He is very clear that *life is not fair*. It never has been, and it never will be. A staunch Republican, my father believes in the economic survival of the fittest. I am sure that he carries the memories of his own economically impoverished childhood very closely within him. I am sure that he suffered greatly during his childhood. On many occasions my father has said to me that he has achieved more in his life than he ever could have imagined, as if he could lose it all tomorrow and it would be okay.

After completing high school, my father enlisted in the Navy so that he could take advantage of the G.I. Bill and get a college education. When he finished his time in the Navy, he moved to southern California and entered the University of California at Los Angeles. It was in California that he met my mother, in church. When I asked my father why he chose to marry an Anglo woman, he said that he didn't decide to marry an Anglo woman; there was less discrimination against Mexican Americans out there. He felt that there was less discrimination against Mexican Americans in California, which gave him more of a chance to be successful on his own merits. I think that my father wanted to be successful in the Anglo world, and marrying an Anglo woman just fit with those aspirations. By the time he graduated from UCLA, he and my mother had had my older brother and sister. Education was, for him, entirely about the survival of his family. Both he and my mother worked full-time as my father took a full load of classes. He knew that little piece of paper that said "Bachelor's Degree" would open doors for him. A very intellectually curious man, my father has often said that he would have loved to study economics, but he didn't have a choice.

My father's constant refrain to me and my brothers and sisters as we were growing up was "Go to school. Go to school. Go to school." He didn't mean high school. I resisted his advice for a while. As I was growing up, I never felt connected to school or education. I was much more interested in being outside and taking in the southern California sunshine that felt like my birthright. I finally did take my father's advice, recognizing that if I wanted to do anything with my life, I needed a college education. It is ironic that education ended up giving me the space to seek out the opening of my own human horizons, and thus also the means by which to look at things that he seemed so deliberately to keep from me and my brothers and sisters.

When my father settled in California, he left his life (though not his family) behind in Texas. Because my father had grown up very poor, he had lived the pain, suffering, and injustices endured by the poor. Thinking as much as I have about my father's life and trying to understand it as deeply as I can, I get the feeling that growing up poor does something to you. "We were poor," my father says, "not 'economically deprived'; we were poor." There's a certain character and pride about my father. I think it comes from never forgetting where you come from, how hard your life was, and thus never taking for granted all the good things you have in your life. But, having accumulated all those good things—those comforts of middle-class success in the United States—the avenues he had available to him for communicating to his children the painful realities of his own childhood became fewer. My father is an assimilationist: "I'm American," he says emphatically, "not Mexican American, American." Yet I have recently begun to appreciate—despite all of his denials of his Mexican cultural heritage—how deep his commitment to *la familia* has always been. Despite all the distances he seemed to create between us, his children, and his own childhood experiences as a "poor American of Mexican descent," I have finally come to see the ways in which he has always sought to provide for us the benefits of his understanding of human suffering and dignity. But it has taken me a long time to get here.

MAKING SENSE OF GROWING UP

There were various times during my childhood when I thought that my father's father was killed in the war. At other times I thought that he had died of a heart attack while digging ditches. There are still many things that I do not know about my father and his family. There have always been glaring silences surrounding my father that have stood impenetrable to me for as long as I have lived. The descriptions I offer below are ones that were, for the most part, written five years ago, primarily out of anger and a solitary effort to understand the conditions of my own life as an American of Mexican descent.

I grew up in the comfortable and exclusively white area in the suburb of Los Angeles known as the San Fernando Valley. We were a family of five kids. My older sister and brother are seven and six years older than I, respectively. I am an identical twin and have a brother who is one year older than my twin and I. We lived in a seven-bedroom house with a three-car garage, two fireplaces, a wet bar, a swimming pool, and an outside fire pit. We moved to that house in 1965, when I was four years old. It was my father's position as an executive vice president of Teledyne that brought us to that neighborhood. As a young child I remember my parents throwing cocktail parties; we had a definitively white upper-middle-class lifestyle.

From the perspective of those Anglos encountering me in that middle-class white world of my childhood, my surname Martínez rarely signified anything other than Mexican-American. I remember being a very little girl, dressed up in Sunday clothes, standing outside the church after services, adults talking. Then one adult leaned down to me, smiled broadly, and asked me if I spoke Spanish. At the time I was an expert in playing the cute little girl and responded by smiling shyly, twisting side to side on my feet, and uttering an elongated "Noooo." Always, for as long as I can remember, the question "Do you speak Spanish?" follows the Anglo-other's recognition of my surname. I think I knew then, standing outside that church, as I have known all my life, that Spanish will never be a language through which I will be able to communicate with my father. I do remember wondering why I didn't learn Spanish as I was growing up. I knew that my father spoke it, but he never uttered a word in Spanish to my mother or us kids. I have, throughout my life, felt cheated in not having access to my father's Spanish language. But there was no way for a little girl to take up such a question with her father. I knew, even as an adult formally interviewing my father, that it was too dangerous to ask why he never spoke Spanish with us kids, or why he didn't at least speak Spanish with his mother when she visited us during my childhood. I heard my grandmother speak Spanish with her sister and my aunt. I knew *mijita* was a Spanish word of endearment toward me. But my father's Spanishly silence sent powerful messages to me that to this day I do not fully comprehend. As a child, I just learned to take the Anglos' question in stride, creating a full repertoire of responses to deal with any conversation that might ensue from such a question. I pushed the questions about speaking Spanish into the unknowing consciousness that dominated my childhood.

Yet there was a knowing to this unknowingness that also dominated my childhood. As a family we ate tacos every Friday night; on those nights our dinner featured our Mexican cookware and serving dishes. I knew that we had some special connection to the Mayan calendar on our living room wall. We lived in that house until my parents got a divorce in 1978. Six years earlier, in 1972, my father had moved out of the house and back to Texas to start up a new business with his cousin. Despite the fact that my father moved out of the house when I was eleven years old, there was some deep emotional way in which I never felt abandoned by him. As a young corporate executive my father had spent a lot of time traveling. There was something about his very quiet and determined way that communicated a lot to me, regardless of his lengthy absences. As I have gotten older, I have, more than anything else, felt angry at knowing the deep humanity in this man yet having such restricted access to it. When I was growing up, money and his role as provider were the dominant signs through which he communicated to me. As an adolescent and young adult there were many times when I felt anger churning inside of me, and I wanted to yell at him, "Your credit card is *not* a substitute for you!" But as a child I think I was more angry at him for being gone so much when he did live at home, than for being gone after he finally moved out of the house. I remember feeling a little guilty that I didn't really miss him after he moved out.

My father never really shared anything about his life growing up with me. There were only a few occasions here and there when he would tell a story about his childhood, brief and to the point, always to illustrate to me and my brothers and sisters just how fortunate we were. The recurrent theme of my father's stories was one of living on the edges of survival, in poverty, ridiculed by other Mexicans who had more. One story takes prominence in my memory. When I was a little girl, my grandmother visited us and made us beans and tortillas. As she spread the beans out on the table, carefully separating the chunks of dirt and small rocks from the beans, my father told me how he remembered her doing that when he was a little boy, except that as the family sat around that table sorting the dirt from the beans, they looked at all the food they had for the week.

Then quickly my father moved back to the present, leaving the story hanging there. He offered no more details, no discussion. The only feeling I could detect resonating from him was one of mastery and accomplishment that his children never had to experience that. I knew, in retrospect, that he was trying to teach us something about the value of having food on the table. I got that message, but it receded into the background in light of what I perceived as his self-satisfaction and achievement. His achievement was one that I could never make for myself because *he* put the food on *our* table.

A second story, related when I was an adolescent and referring to a time when I was a little girl, also takes prominence in my memory. We went to visit some relatives in Santa Ana, the occasion a wedding or birthday, I think. Everyone spoke Spanish, and there were all kinds of foods I didn't recognize but saw my father eat knowingly. Mexican music, dress, and decorations were all around. Years later, on some unknown occasion, my father told me how those people, my relatives in Santa Ana, used to laugh and make fun of him because his family was so poor. But after my father had moved to California, worked his way through UCLA, and earned a very good living as a corporate manager, then they invited him to their parties and celebrations.

Again the story was short and to the point. Again the feeling of mastery, of proving oneself better. I got the message about pettiness here—it was an important message; it was a central message in my childhood, and one that I took very much to heart. But why did he have to be so curt? I sensed traces of his own anger, and I needed more from him to understand it.

A third story, more painful to my child's ears, benign on the surface, felt to me like my father was angry at me. I'm a young girl. The context has escaped me. I only remember my father telling me about his being a young boy and sitting down with his mother, brother, and sister in a family discussion. They had seventy-five cents. Only one of the children could get a new pair of shoes. Among themselves, they decided who.

Because my brothers and sisters and I grew up in relative affluence, we never understood the value of having a new pair of shoes or a new jacket the way my father did. Somehow or another, I think I had always gotten his message about human dignity; my father has always taken it upon himself to lecture his children about honesty, integrity, and respect. His own sense of ethics, respect, and determination were a big part of what made him so successful as a corporate executive, I am sure. But this particular story about the shoes, brief and cutoff as it was, left me feeling like he was criticizing me for expecting that I would have what I needed. I realize now that when he grew up, he didn't know that he would have what he needed. In my little girl's mind I thought I was wrong for making my needs known.

Growing up, I always identified strongly with my father; perhaps his absences heightened that identification. I always listened to and watched him very carefully. His short and curt stories, combined with his profound silence about the whole of his life history, silenced my natural curiosities and left me with a deep and profound sense of something being hidden. My effort to understand my father's life experiences, in the face of his withholding of those experiences, has been a crucial aspect of my own development of Chicana identity. This silence about the past and the feeling of something bad being hidden has, to a large degree, defined what limited ethnic heritage has carried forward through the assimilated lifestyle provided by my father.[12]

Because of my father's resilient silence, I feel a profound sense of betrayal in writing about these family experiences that are so private and personal. I also feel a sense of betrayal in working so hard to understand the Mexican cultural heritage that my father seemed so determined to deny. When I first began to reflect seriously about my father's cultural heritage, I felt a faint but clear sense that to search through my father's buried past was to risk encountering demons or evils of some sort. Over time, that sense of evils to be discovered has subsided and given way to a deeper understanding of the cultural and historical context in which my father—and many other Americans of Mexican descent—made the choice to assimilate in ways big and small. Reading the work of Chicana and Chicano scholars has been crucial in allowing me to see around my father's silences and understand his own place in history, and thus the forces that led him to make the choices he did. I have come to the point now where I see my "betrayal" not as one of my father so much as of a racist culture that denies its own acts of oppression and continues to use Mexicans and Mexican Americans as scapegoats.

LOOKING TO THE HISTORY OF THE CHICANO PEOPLE

I entered into Chicano/a Studies through the work of Chicana lesbians. I felt I had some solid footing to understand the experiences of other lesbians and realized that by following the paths undertaken by Chicana lesbians, I might be able to take up the experiences of Chicanos and Mexican Americans generally. Books like *Chicana Lesbians: The Girls Our Mothers Warned Us About* (Trujillo 1991) and *Compañeras: Latina Lesbians* (Ramos 1987) gave me a wide range of experiences and perspectives from which to make my own connections.

I have used Emma Pérez's essay "Gulf Dreams" (1991) to connect the incredible passion we feel in our lesbian relationships and the social binds those passions bring for us, to the passions and struggles we feel within the context of a racist culture. The feelings and struggles that fill the pages of Pérez's brave essay allowed me to connect with the experience of having to keep our most deep and powerful feelings hidden because of social restriction. The sexual attraction between her and another young woman remains unspoken and gets sublimated as they each pursue relationships with young men, some brown, some white. In the "play" of color, a young Chicana in school sees through the "conqueror's lies in history books" (p. 104), but remains mostly silent in surviving the Anglo teacher and her racist attempts to encourage the students to be glad that "Texas is in America" (p. 104). Reading the work of Chicana lesbians, I am reminded of the profound silences that capture our histories and keep them bound to the Anglo-racist accounts; they are silences that have also captured our lesbian passion.

In following along with the work of Chicana lesbians, I have been able to recognize the ways in which I have always felt connections to and curiosities about my Indian and mestizo heritage. But because of my father's silences and our social circumstances, those connections and curiosities got sublimated as I moved through my everyday life of growing up. My father's deep humanity, it seems to me, has also developed through profound silences about his own suffering. Out of this suffering grew a great spirit and passion through which he set himself to the task of rising above that suffering and creating the circumstances so that his own family would never have to suffer the way he did. That my father's effort to achieve success and comfort for his family pushed him down a road of assimilation speaks volumes about the racist logic carried out in the legacy of colonialism. This is an issue I have taken up in another essay (Martínez 1997). In that essay I use the work of Vicki Ruiz (1993) and Deena González (1993) to argue that simply to juxtapose the notion of "loyal culturalist" with that of "complicitous assimilator" obscures our effort to understand the totality of circumstances in which Mexican Americans have—across generations—struggled to survive.

By moving beyond what seems to me to be a false binary of loyal culturalist versus complicitous assimilator, I have been able to understand the ways in which all of us "darker others" have been objects of Euro-American ethnocentrism and its self-righteous domination (Acuña 1981). It is an insight that was first provoked for me by Martha Barrera's essay "Café con Leche" (1991). In this essay, Barrera addresses issues about being "ethnic enough," and whether "hanging around anglos" makes one's own ethnic heritage "corrupted." Being a person who was raised within the Anglo world, this essay helped me to feel a connection to the varying degrees of struggle all Mexican Americans face with regard to Anglo presence. Coming to see the commonality in the struggle with Anglo presence—both within our own psyches and as part of the very structure of social relations carried in our collective histories—provided a crucial point of connection for me. With such a point of connection I have come to embrace the complex history of my family heritage—its mestizo roots from my father and the traces of American Indian heritage from my mother's mostly Anglo side. In learning about these histories I can come to terms with the confusing messages I got during my childhood, and thus also with my own identity as a Chicana. In this way I am able to move beyond the internal questions and make connections with other Chicanas, Chicanos, and people of color. With these connections it becomes possible to see generations of struggle and embrace a history that the colonizing logic of Euro-American culture would have erased.

In coming to make these connections, I am deeply indebted to the work of many Chicana scholars who have offered rereadings of history going back to the original colonization of this land of the Americas. Chicana scholars have been especially insistent on rereading what Norma Alarcón (1983) calls the "male mythology of *La Malinche*." It is through the demythifying of La Malinche that scholars such as Alarcón (1983, 1989), Anzaldúa (1987), Enríquez and Mirandé (1977), Moraga (1983, 1986), and Pérez (1993) have forced a reconsideration of the "loyalist versus betrayer" binarism, especially as it is tied to Chicanas' sexuality.

Coming to learn about the legacy of colonialism and its effects on generations of mestizo people has given me important connections to men of color. When Ana Castillo (1994) critiques the Anglo use of "machismo" by citing the Anglos' own masculine bravado inherent in their attitudes of conquest, she is exposing how the mythmaking of the dominant culture serves its hegemonic interests. In learning about the history of the southwestern United States from the perspective of Chicanas/os and considering it in the context of my father's life choices, I have come to understand something of how traces of history live in the present, how they function preconsciously and unknowingly, much in the way that my assimilated family life still carries traces of my Mexican cultural heritage. In another essay (Martínez 1996), I have tried to work through how we engage in cultural recovery despite the racist legacy of colonialism that continues to encourage assimilation of all sorts. It has been through the courageous writing by Chicanas, in which they bring to bear the most deeply lived struggles of life, that I have been able to enter into a consideration of the very life circumstances by which I have carried traces of my Mexican cultural heritage, and thus recover a heritage that would have otherwise been lost.

I began this chapter by identifying three modes of consciousness that have permitted me to come to terms with my Chicana identity. My discussion has emphasized my movement from the unknown-knowing consciousness that dominated my childhood to the mode of asking myself barely conscious questions about my own life experiences and ethnic heritage. This second mode of consciousness, lying between the unknown-knowing and the known-knowing, has dominated much of my young adulthood as I have struggled with questions about my ethnic identity. Because of my lesbianism, I have had a comparative set of experiences through which to broach these barely conscious questions about my ethnic heritage. As these questions have become more conscious, I

have looked explicitly to the work of Chicana lesbians to try and understand how my own experiences might share common points with theirs.
This effort has led me to an ongoing study of the history of colonialism as
it has borne down upon generations of darker Others. This effort has
finally allowed me to understand the context of my father's life; I have
come to see more of his struggle for survival against dominating racist
forces. Developing this kind of understanding allows me to move past the
silence and distance, pain and isolation carried in my father's buried
past. In doing so, I can now make connections to movements of liberation,
like the Chicano/a movement, where struggles against racism prevent the
internalization of racist norms.

ACKNOWLEDGMENTS

This essay owes much to many people, all of whom have provided important
dialogue, support, and encouragement: Linda Alcoff, Yolanda Broyles-González,
Sara García, Deanne Pérez-Granados, Christina González, María Herrera-Sobek,
Dorothy Leland, Jane Tumas-Serna, and Bernice Zamora. It owes a special debt to
the editors of this book, who provided critical feedback laced with great encouragement. It is rare in the academy to submit a manuscript and have the editors
write back, "Your voice as a Chicana and academic needs to come through loud
and clear." It is, to me, a reflection of the unique humanizing presence Chicanas
and other women of color bring to the academy.

NOTES

1. The epigraphs are taken from Cherríe Moraga's essay "La Güera," in Moraga
and Anzaldúa, *This Bridge Called My Back* (1983); and from Gloria Anzaldúa's
"Introduction" to *Making Face, Making Soul/Haciendo Caras* (1990).
2. My focus on "modes of consciousness" is informed by and deeply indebted to
Richard L. Lanigan (1988) and his work on the phenomenology of communication, and to Chela Sandoval (1991) and her work on the theory and method of
oppositional consciousness in a postmodern world.
3. I take this concept of an unknowing-knowing from Eve Kosofsky Sedgwick
(1990), although I've changed the second term in my usage. As Sedgwick describes a feature of coming out: "It can bring about the revelation of a powerful
unknowing *as* unknowing, not as a vacuum or as the blank it can pretend to be but
as a weighty and occupied and consequential epistemological space" (p. 77).
4. A note on tense: I am using the past tense to indicate that there were precise

moments in my life at which these second and third modes of consciousness emerged; however, it is important to note that my movement between and among these modes continues.

5. In using the word "world" in the subhead "Entering a Chicana Lesbian World," I have in mind the notion of "'world'-traveling" developed by María Lugones (1987) in a truly remarkable essay.

6. It is important for me to note that this chapter was originally produced out of the ambiguities reverberating for me within this second mode of consciousness. It was the first essay I wrote after completing my doctoral dissertation. It was also my "coming-out" essay—it marked the first time I had ever written about being a Chicana.

7. My Ph.D. course work focused heavily on existential and semiotic phenomenology, particularly the work of Maurice Merleau-Ponty, Michel Foucault, and semioticians in the European (Saussure, Hjemsleve, Jakobson, Barths, Eco) and American (Reusch, Bateson, Peirce) traditions. Because I was in a speech communication department, I was encouraged to take the concreteness of my own daily living communicative experience very seriously. There was a clearly existential feature emphasized by our graduate director, Thomas J. Pace. I am deeply indebted to Tom for creating a graduate program in which we were encouraged to take up the struggles of our own particular human existences. My sense is that too few graduate programs actually do this.

8. This is one reason why it is so important to have more people of color in graduate programs. My conversations with Norman Greer, a fellow graduate student in my department, allowed me and other graduate students to take up issues of racism more directly. Were it not for Norman's presence, it would have been harder for me to take up such questions as directly.

9. My use of "Spanishly" is taken from Merleau-Ponty's use of the word "languagely." He writes, "There is a 'languagely' *[langagière]* meaning of language which effects the mediation between my as yet unspeaking intention and words, and in such a way that my spoken words surprise me myself and teach me my thought" (1964:88). See also Merleau-Ponty (1962).

10. It was an essay by Linda Alcoff (1992) that gave me important insight into understanding my own struggle with my privileged background. Alcoff's essay provided a crucial foundation from which I was able to successfully work through the very confusing set of circumstances I had to negotiate in order to come to speak as a Chicana.

11. Symbolisms reverberate for me in the fact that my father lives in Simi Valley, across the street from the Ronald Reagan Presidential Library. Simi Valley, where the Rodney King criminal trial was held.

12. Christina González, in a very important conversation, helped me to under-

stand this point; in her own work with Native American people, she has identified some ways in which the desecration of their cultures, blatantly exacted by the forces of Anglo racism, has resulted in the carrying forward of dysfunctions as cultural heritage.

REFERENCES

Acuña, R. (1981). *Occupied America: A History of Chicanos.* New York: Harper & Row.

Alarcón, N. (1983). Chicana's feminist literature: A re-vision through malintzín/or malintzin: Putting flesh back on the object. In C. Moraga & G. Anzaldúa (eds.), *This Bridge Called My Back: Writings by Radical Women of Color* (pp. 182–190). New York: Kitchen Table/Women of Color Press.

——. (1989). Traddutora, traditora: A paradigmatic figure of Chicana feminism. *Cultural Critique,* 13 (1), 57–87.

Alcoff, L. (1992). The problem of speaking for others. *Cultural Critique,* 13 (1), 57–87.

Anzaldúa, G. (1987). *Borderlands/La Frontera: The New Mestiza.* San Francisco: Aunt Lute Books.

——. (ed.). (1990). Introduction. *Making Face, Making Soul/Haciendo Caras. Creative and Critical Perspectives by Feminists of Color.* San Francisco: Aunt Lute Books.

Baca Zinn, M., L. Weber Cannon, E. Higginbotham, & B. Thornton Dill. (1986). The costs of exclusionary practices in women's studies. *Signs: Journal of Women in Culture and Society,* 11 (21), 290–303.

Barrera, M. (1991). Café con leche. In C. Trujillo (ed.), *Chicana Lesbians: The Girls Our Mothers Warned Us About* (pp. 80–83). Berkeley, CA: Third Woman Press.

Castillo, A. (1994). *Massacre of the Dreamers: Essays on Xicanisma.* Albuquerque: University of New Mexico Press.

Enríquez, E. & A. Mirandé. (1977). Liberation, Chicana style: Colonial roots of feministas chicanas. *De Colores: Journal of Chicano Expression and Thought* 4 (3), 7–21.

García, A. M. (1989). The development of Chicana feminist discourse, 1970–1980. *Gender & Society* 3, 217–238.

Gonzales, S. (1977). The white feminist movement: The Chicana perspective. *Social Science Journal* 14 (2), 67–76.

González, D. J. (1993). La Tules of image and reality: Euro-American attitudes and legend formation on a Spanish-Mexican frontier. In A. de la Torre & B. M. Pesquera (eds.), *Building with Our Hands: New Directions in Chicana Studies* (pp. 75–90). Berkeley: University of California Press.

Lanigan, R. L. (1988). *Phenomenology of Communication: Merleau-Ponty's Thematics in Communicology and Semiology.* Pittsburgh: Duquesne University Press.

Lorde, A. (1984). The uses of anger: Women responding to racism. In Lorde's *Sister Outsider* (pp. 124–133). Trumansburg, NY: Crossing Press.

Lugones, M. (1987). Playfulness, "world"-traveling, and loving perception. *Hypatia* 2 (2), 3–19.

Martínez, J. M. (1996). *Phenomenological communication and political identity: Ethnic assimilation and cultural recovery at the end of the millennium.* Unpublished manuscript. Presented as a visiting scholar, Millersville University, Millersville, PA.

——. (1997). Radical ambiguities and the Chicana lesbian: Body topographies on contested lands. In T. D. Sharply-Whiting & R. White (eds.), *Spoils of War: Women of Color, Cultures and Revolutions.* New York: Rowman & Littlefield.

Merleau-Ponty, M. (1962; 1984). *Phenomenology of Perception.* New York: Humanities Press.

——. (1964). On the phenomenology of language. In Merleau-Ponty's *Signs* (pp. 84–98). Evanston, IL: Northwestern University Press.

Moraga, C. (1983). La güera. In C. Moraga & G. Anzaldúa (eds.), *This Bridge Called My Back: Writings by Radical Women of Color* (pp. 27–34). New York: Kitchen Table/Women of Color Press.

——. (1986). From a long line of vendidas: Chicanas and feminism. In T. de Lauretis (ed.), *Feminist Studies/Critical Studies* (pp. 173–190). Bloomington: Indiana University Press.

Moraga, C., & G. Anzaldúa (eds.). (1983). *This Bridge Called My Back: Writings by Radical Women of Color.* New York: Kitchen Table/Women of Color Press.

Pérez, E. (1991). Gulf dreams. In C. Trujillo (ed.), *Chicana Lesbians: The Girls Our Mothers Warned Us About* (pp. 96–108). Berkeley, CA: Third Woman Press.

——. (1993). Speaking from the margin: Uninvited discourse on sexuality and power. In A. de la Torre & B. M. Pesquera (eds.), *Building with Our Hands: New Directions in Chicana Studies* (pp. 57–71). Berkeley: University of California Press.

Ramos, J. (ed.). (1987). *Compañeras: Latina Lesbians.* New York: Latina Lesbian History Project.

Rich, A. (1980). Compulsory heterosexuality and lesbian existence. *Signs: Journal of Women in Culture and Society* 5 (4), 631–660.

Ruiz, V. L. (1993). Star struck: Acculturation, adolescence, and the Mexican American woman, 1920–1950. In A. de la Torre & B. M. Pesquera (eds.), *Building with Our Hands: New Directions in Chicana Studies* (pp. 109–129). Berkeley: University of California Press.

Sandoval, C. (1991). U.S. third world feminism: The theory and method of oppositional consciousness in the postmodern world. *Genders* 10, 1–24.

Sedgwick, E. K. (1990). *Epistemology of the Closet.* Berkeley: University of California Press.

Trujillo, C. (ed.). (1991). *Chicana Lesbians: The Girls Our Mothers Warned Us
About.* Berkeley, CA: Third Woman Press.

Zavella, P. (1989). The problematic relationship of feminism and Chicana Studies.
Women's Studies 17, 25–36.

4

♦ ♦ ♦

THE POWER OF LANGUAGE

From the Back of the Bus to the Ivory Tower

Christine Marín

This essay depicts my story, the story of a Chicana from the mining town of Globe, Arizona. It describes who and what I am in the context of *familia,* growing up in a mining town, and attending schools there. It also describes my coming to terms with the formation and the power of language. Many voices will appear throughout this journey. I set out to describe the various incidents that helped shape my identity as a Chicana through the power of language.

MY FAMILY BACKGROUND

Thousands of workers from northern Mexico, including my grandfathers, came to Arizona in 1919 to mine ore for mining companies in the Globe-Miami area. Mexicans were given the hardest, most dangerous jobs and paid the lowest wages. They worked in tunnels four thousand feet underground without respirators and safety equipment. Anglo miners worked under similar conditions, but Mexicans made only half as much as Anglos did, even though they did the same work and worked the same number of hours. The mining companies controlled the towns of Globe and Miami and opposed the idea of Mexican miners and their families socializing with Anglo miners and managers.

My father, Lupe Trujillo Marín, was born in Torreón, Coahuila, Mexico, in 1921, and was an infant when he and his mother and his siblings returned to Miami after a brief stay in Mexico. There were seven children in the family, three of whom are now deceased, as is my grandmother, Natalia Trujillo Marín. She was born in Aguascalientes, Mexico, in 1892 and died in Globe in 1965. My grandfather, Alejandro Trujillo Marín, worked at the Iron Cap Mine in Miami. He died of silicosis, also known as "miners' lung disease" or *tísico,* as the Mexicanos called it. It's an irritation that gradually eats away at the lungs; the miners suffered horrible deaths as a result. The Mexicanos who worked underground at the mines wrapped handkerchiefs or cloth around their mouths to protect themselves, thinking that thereby silica dust would not affect them if they inhaled it. But they were wrong. It wasn't until the 1940s that Arizona laws made it possible for miners to be protected from this lung disease by requiring that they wear respirators while they worked below the surface.

My mother, Eulalia Rentería Marín, was born in Miami, Arizona, in 1921. She had seven brothers and sisters, five of whom are now deceased, as are her parents. Her mother, Natalia Chacon Rentería, emigrated with her mother from Chihuahua, Mexico, through Juárez and then through El Paso. Her father, Francisco Rentería, was from Spain. As a young man, he came to the United States and eventually made his way to Brice and Tyrone, New Mexico, to work in the copper mines. He settled there and raised a family. The Rentería family then moved on to Miami, where Francisco worked as a miner for the Miami Copper Company. Miami was a company town with many immigrants from different backgrounds and nationalities who worked at the various mines, but it was the Miami Copper Company and the Inspiration Consolidated Copper Company that prospered and built the town.

My parents did not learn how to speak English until they entered elementary school. All Mexican children attended segregated schools where they were forced to speak English and were sometimes punished if they spoke Spanish. One of my mother's earliest and most vivid memories is the shame and humiliation she experienced when she and a group of Mexican and Mexican-American children were singled out by their Anglo teachers and forced to undergo examinations for *piojos* [head lice]. As she tells her story, the Anglo teachers would wear gloves and prod the children's heads with rulers, long sticks, or combs to see if head lice were evident. The examinations revealed that neither the Mexican nor the Mexican-American children in her group had them. Anglo children were never examined for piojos.

My mother did not graduate from Miami High School, but she completed the tenth grade. The weight and burden of the Depression years in the 1930s affected our family as well as other Mexican families. She and her brothers and sisters had to work to help support the family. My mother was a "cleaning girl" in the homes of Anglo families who lived on Inspiration Hill. Important Anglo mine workers and administrators lived in this neighborhood that had its own elementary school and company store. Only Anglos were allowed to shop there, but that changed. Later on, other miners and their families were allowed to purchase goods there.

My mother remembers that some Anglo women didn't always want to pay her the wages she had earned for cleaning their homes. The phrase she frequently heard was "Catch you next time, hon." Needless to say, she didn't always make up her lost wages. On some occasions, the Anglo women allowed the Mexican and Mexican-American women to take home leftovers from uneaten meals. And because they did, the Anglo women felt they didn't have to pay them their wages. My mother and her sisters worked and helped save money in order for their brothers to attend high school.

After the death of his father around 1935, my father's family moved from Miami to Globe to be closer to family. In 1939 my father graduated from Globe High School. He enrolled in the Civilian Conservation Corps in 1939 and worked in Arizona, at Camp Verde for six months and at Camp Pine for another six months. He recalls that the Mexican-American enrollees in the CCC camps were segregated and worked together in groups and that his commanders and officers were all Anglos.

MY STORY

I was a war baby, born in 1943, two months premature, at the Gila County Hospital in Globe. My brothers and sisters were born in Miami at the Inspiration Consolidated Copper Company hospital. I grew up on Euclid Avenue, that up-and-down unpaved canyon street that turned into a rushing arroyo after a hard rain. That's where we working-class Mexican, African-American, Apache Indian, and Anglo (mainly Italian) families lived. Kids from South Slav and Serbian backgrounds lived on Euclid, too. There were kids with Chicano nicknames, such as "Titi," "Suki," "Papooney," "Tingo," and "Teco," as well as "Poogie," "Bebeeo," and "Toonie." I was a real tomboy growing up on Euclid because I hung around with my older brothers. Sometimes it was a rough-and-tough neighborhood, and I had my share of fistfights with other kids. On Euclid, we didn't speak Spanish or Italian or Slovak, or any of the languages our parents and other grown-ups spoke. Our common language was English. Here on Euclid Avenue were Mexican-American children and children of interracial marriages between African Americans and Mexican Americans and between Mexican Americans and Anglos.

When I entered first grade in 1949, I attended Hill Street School, which was in the southeastern part of Globe. There were no school buses in our neighborhood. My parents preferred that I attend Hill Street School because it was closer to my grandmother's house, where I stayed after school until my parents picked me up.

From kindergarten through the sixth grade, children attended the same school. My classmates were a mixture of nationalities: Chinese, Italian, Mexican, Serbian, Irish, Cornish, Slovak, Apache Indian, and Mexican-American. Our fathers worked for the railroad, at grocery stores, gasoline stations, restaurants, hotels, movie theaters, liquor stores, or for Inspiration Copper. In school, we all spoke English with each other, both in and out of the classroom. We didn't know how to speak our native languages, but we picked up some slang words—usually the curse words—from each other.

Regarding my own language background, I was English-dominant. My parents didn't encourage me to speak Spanish at home, so I didn't learn to speak Spanish very well; however, I was always exposed to the language. As a result, I understood Spanish at a very young age. My grandmother, Natalia, didn't speak English, so my aunts translated my conversations when I was with her. Whenever I was spoken to in Spanish, I responded in English.

My parents and their friends spoke both English and Spanish with each other, and they could read and write in both languages. But throughout their lives, as children in school and as adults in the workplace, my parents were victims of the wrath of Anglo racism and prejudice against Mexicans and Mexican Americans. They certainly didn't want their children to experience this kind of negative and discriminatory treatment from Anglos, so they insisted that I learn English well. They were afraid that if I spoke Spanish, I would experience their shame of being poor Mexicans. Mexican Americans and Mexicans were terribly mistreated in Miami, Arizona, and that's a fact. Even now, the anger of my parents and some of their friends lies close to the surface whenever they recollect some of these experiences. As a result, my parents did not want me to experience what they had encountered, endured, and suffered. However, they believed that I should retain our Mexican culture; I was also taught to be proud of being of Mexican descent. My parents believed that I should speak better English than the gringo, so that he could not ridicule me the way they had been ridiculed in school and at work. "Learn to beat the gringo at his own game because you're better than him," was their motto and lesson to me and my brothers and sisters. I learned it well, and I understand the reasoning behind that idea.

I do not recall seeing or hearing anyone being ridiculed, embarrassed, or punished by our teachers for speaking Spanish. There were some Mexican children in my classroom who spoke Spanish at home but spoke English with us. There were no Mexican-American teachers or administrators when I attended Hill Street School in 1949–1955. My Mexican-American friends all spoke English. While we knew we were Mexican-American and were proud of our heritage and ethnicity—a pride we learned from our parents—we also knew we were Americans and never felt inferior to Anglos. How could we? We were as competitive as they were in school and in sports, and we knew we excelled at things they did not. We did not develop an inferiority complex about being Mexican-American. We weren't afraid of Anglos or intimidated by them—I certainly wasn't!

COMING TO CONSCIOUSNESS ABOUT THE POWER OF LANGUAGE

The reality of being a Mexican American whose mother tongue was English and who did not speak Spanish came in the form of a 1958 high school band trip and the song "La Bamba" by Ritchie Valens (I didn't even know he was Mexican-American!), which was quite popular. I wasn't any different from the other high school kids who learned the words of popular songs we heard on the radio. Anglo and Mexican-American kids would sit together in the back of the bus and sing loudly and attempt to drown out the singing of those kids who sat toward the front of the bus. The game was to see who could sing the best and the loudest, and consequently drown out the singing of those in front.

On one band trip we sang "La Bamba." I didn't realize we were singing so loudly and in Spanish! My "voice" came out in the form of Spanish lyrics, although I was unaware of it. My Mexican-American identity shone through. I remember how proud I was for singing in Spanish, even though I didn't understand all the words of the song. I didn't know what a *bamba* was or what a *marinero* was. I hadn't heard those words before, and I wondered if my Mexican-American girlfriends knew the meaning of the song. I stumbled over the words, mispronouncing many of them. Suddenly, one popular Anglo girl sitting toward the front of the bus stood up in the middle of the aisle and shouted out loud so that everyone could hear: "Hey, you Mexicans! This is America! Stop singing in Spanish!" She proceeded to loudly sing "God Bless America" and "My Country 'Tis of Thee." To my surprise, her Anglo friends joined her in singing those patriotic songs. Well, our group of Mexican-American girls was not to be outdone. We sang the words to "La Bamba" even louder, and this infuriated her even more! Eventually, our band director jumped up from his seat and demanded that we all shut up. That stopped the singing. I could see that our band director was agitated, but I wasn't sure if it was because of that stupid, racist remark from that little twerp or because of all the noise throughout the bus.

It didn't take me long to figure out what had happened. I realized that the girl and her friends did not resent being outsung but resented the fact that we were singing in Spanish, using words that weren't even a part of my everyday vocabulary! All I was doing was singing a song. I felt like getting up out of my seat and beating up that insensitive, stupid girl—and good! But I didn't. I learned the power of both the English and Spanish languages on that band trip. And what a lesson it was! The Spanish language posed a threat to that girl, and it made me feel proud of being a Mexican American despite the fact that I didn't speak Spanish. I felt superior to her because I knew two languages and I could understand both English and Spanish, while she could only understand English.

In high school, I was an above-average student but certainly not one who made straight A's. I excelled in English and writing assignments, and my work was noticed by my English teachers, especially Mrs. Ethel Jaenicke. She hoped I would attend college after high school, something I hadn't thought was possible. She spent extra time with me and encouraged me to continue my writing. Unfortunately, my father's pay didn't stretch far enough to pay for a college education. My parents, however, knew the value and importance of a good education and wanted their children to continue on to college. They made great sacrifices to help all of us begin our college education and were encouraging, nurturing, and understanding about our struggles to stay in school. It was ultimately up to us to somehow find the money to stay in school and continue our education.

After graduation from Globe High School in 1961, I moved to Phoenix, where I lived with my older brother and his wife. A friend of his helped me get a job as a salesgirl at Jay's Credit Clothing, a Jewish-owned clothing store in downtown Phoenix. Customers bought their goods on credit. The clothing lines were fashionable, stylish, and overpriced. Most of the customers were African Americans, Mexicans, Mexican Americans, and some Anglos. Mexican-American saleswomen were paid a small weekly salary but earned most of their money through sales commissions. Making those sales was very competitive, and I didn't do so well. I couldn't speak Spanish well enough to assist Spanish-speaking customers who came into the store, which left me frustrated and embarrassed. One of the senior Mexican-American saleswomen felt sorry for me; she noticed how desperately I struggled with the language. She often gave me her own sales after she had assisted Spanish-speaking customers by putting my name on her sales tickets. She knew I would be attending Arizona State University in August and needed to save money for school. She took me under her wing and spoke to me of her childhood wishes of going to college, though her family couldn't afford to send her. This woman worked in that clothing store for many years. She taught me another lesson about the power of language: bilingualism paid well—monetarily well! I decided to recapture my lost native tongue and consciously worked on speaking more Spanish so that I could earn more money.

At ASU, I enrolled in liberal arts courses and had many interests. I took classes in psychology, sociology, history, and English, to name but a few. One college adviser even suggested that I major in Spanish because "Mexicans make good Spanish teachers and you could always find a job teaching it." If he only knew how badly I spoke the language! I didn't want to major in Spanish. Chalk up two more lessons learned about the power of language. First, someone assumed I spoke Spanish simply because of my surname and brown-colored skin. Second, by knowing the Spanish language, I would always be guaranteed a teaching job. However, I didn't want to be a teacher.

Throughout some of my college years, I lived in a women's dormitory where I easily made friends with women from different social classes and backgrounds. I also met Mexican Americans who were truly bilingual and spoke Spanish constantly. Some of them were from mining towns such as Clifton, Morenci, Superior, San Manuel, and Sonora, Arizona; from agricultural areas such as Glendale, Chandler, and Tolleson; and from urban areas such as Phoenix and Los Angeles. I took the required liberal arts courses in elementary and intermediate Spanish, which were not designed for native speakers (they are now). I didn't do well. Since I had no formal training in Spanish and had not taken Spanish classes in high school, my reading and comprehension skills were below average. My writing and verbal skills were also poor. I wanted to speak Spanish as well as my friends, but I couldn't. They laughed at me and playfully teased me about my attempts to speak Spanish, but they also helped me. I took their teasing in stride. In return, I used my English skills to help them with their English and writing assignments.

During my freshman year, an English professor insulted my character and intelligence when she accused me of taking credit for a writing assignment she believed was written by someone else. According to her, the essay was extremely well written, but I couldn't have written it because "Mexicans don't write that well." "You people don't even speak the language correctly." Another hard lesson to learn about the power of language! This time the lesson was that my skin color and Spanish surname—not my language proficiency and ability in English—served as criteria to discriminate against me. My English ability was questioned and discredited. The academy had silenced my English voice. No matter how hard I tried, I couldn't convince her I had written that essay and that I had not paid someone to write it for me, as she presumed. This incident angered me. I had done what my parents said—be better than the gringo through language. But since this gringa professor had power and status, she felt she could accuse me of cheating. Needless to say, I dropped the class and never spoke to her again. I didn't care whether she believed me or not.

I was a part-time and full-time student at ASU in the early to mid-1960s, and I struggled financially in order to obtain an education. I couldn't always afford to pay college tuition and school expenses and desperately tried to balance school and work by taking odd jobs on and off campus. I was determined to get my degree. In 1967 I applied for and accepted a full-time position as a clerk in the acquisitions department at Hayden Library, where I had been a part-time student employee. I worked in a typing pool with other women and took advantage of the tuition waiver available to full-time employees of the university that enabled me to enroll in classes. I was a student again. A year later, I was promoted to clerk typist in the reclassification unit, where I learned a lot about the Library of Congress classification system and the importance of record-keeping and cataloging materials. I liked working with books and periodicals and reference sources.

In 1970 I applied for and was hired for a bibliographer position, where I learned all aspects of verifying English-language bibliographic entries and citations for monographs, serials, periodicals, and government documents, among others. I learned the intricacies of checking and verifying library holdings and how to use bibliographic tools and sources. I grew intellectually in my work. Because of my knowledge of library-related information, I became the "expert" and "voice" for my classmates and their friends who either were unfamiliar with the library system or found learning how to use book or serial catalogs confusing. I taught them how to use the library's catalogs and reference tools and encouraged them to enjoy the library setting. My job empowered me. I had learned a new code—the library code.

The year 1970 was an important one for Mexican-American students at ASU in other ways. My friends were beginning to call themselves "Chicanos" as a term of self-identification and tossed aside the term "Mexican Americans." For them, the term "Chicano" meant empowerment, and they found a new identity as Chicanos. But it was not a new word to me. I had heard it used by my parents and their friends when I was growing up in Globe. My father called himself a Chicano, and so did his friends from his military service days in World War II. For them the word "Chicano" was used in friendship—as a term of endearment, as a term of identity.

Now my college friends were using the word "Chicano" differently and in a defiant manner, with the word "power" after it: "Chicano Power!" For them and for me, it became a term of self-identity. The word was an assertion of ethnic and cultural pride, a term heard in a new form of social protests and associated with student activism and civil rights militancy. Chicanos throughout the Southwest were caught up in the Chicano Movement, a civil rights movement. They made new demands—that they become visible rather than invisible on their college and university campuses—and wanted a voice. They demanded courses that described the history, culture, and experiences of Chicanos in the Southwest. They wanted Chicano counselors and professors to teach bilingual-bicultural education courses and courses in social work on their campuses. Arizona State University was going to be at the forefront in making these changes. Two scholars, Dr. Manuel Patricio Servín and Dr. H. William Axford, played an integral role in this demand for change. Hayden Library was to be the setting that allowed students to legitimize history, culture, art, language, and literature by acknowledging the presence of Mexican Americans, Chicanos, and Mexicans.

In 1970 Dr. Servín coordinated the College of Liberal Arts' American Studies program and taught Mexican-American and Southwestern history courses. As a faculty member in the history department at the University of Southern California, he had experienced Chicano student demonstrations on his campus. He supported César Chávez and the United Farmworkers in southern California. Dr. Axford was hired as the university librarian for Hayden Library. At the University of Colorado-Denver, he had encountered Chicano student protesters who demanded that university officials establish a Chicano Studies program on their campus. He knew Rodolfo "Corky" Gonzales and the demands the Crusade for Justice was making on the UC campus, including changes in the library system. Now Hayden Library would be the setting for similar changes, and my work experiences in the library—combined with my contact with Chicano students and organizations and my knowledge of community activism— would enable me to help make those changes. Little did I know then how much of an influence Drs. Servín and Axford were going to have on my academic and professional career.

Servín and Axford quickly became my friends; the scholar and the librarian took me under their wings. They anticipated what Chicano students were going to do: demand that their library have books *by* and *about* them. They were right, and they gave students their voice. This is where I came in. Not long after his arrival, Dr. Axford came to the bibliography department and asked if anyone was familiar with Chicano materials. Being the only Chicana in the department, I was the one who spoke up.

In 1969 my friends had organized the Mexican American Students Organization (MASO) on the ASU campus, and I attended the meetings. MASO students came from various Arizona places, including mining towns, cities, and rural towns. The majority spoke English, so meetings were conducted in English; the MASO newsletter was written in English, with a few slogans in Spanish thrown in for effect, such as *¡Basta Ya!, ¡Viva La Raza!, Con Safos,* and *¡Viva La Huelga!* By 1970, I had attended

Chicano Movement–related meetings, had participated in United Farm-worker rallies in Phoenix, and had leafleted pro-union literature urging the boycott of lettuce sold at Safeway stores. I became well acquainted with Chicano Movement ideologies and with the events of the times.

I met with Drs. Axford and Servín and listened to a new idea that they proposed to me. Dr. Axford suggested that I become the bibliographer for the Chicano Studies Collection, with my first task being to conduct an inventory of the library's holdings of Chicano-related materials. Dr. Servín provided me with various bibliographies listing the Chicano Studies' holdings of university libraries in California. I kept a record of the library's strengths and weaknesses in Chicano Studies by searching publishers' catalogs, listing the titles we didn't have, and marking them as available for purchasing. In that meeting with Drs. Axford and Servín, I learned that it was their intent to build a Chicano Studies Collection that would support Servín's teaching and research needs in Chicano Studies and the needs of those students who would enroll in the American Studies program. Dr. Axford wanted to strengthen the library's holdings in Chicano Studies so that he would be prepared to justify those holdings to Chicano students when they demanded that the library have them. I agreed to become the bibliographer for the Chicano Studies Collection. I was the staff of one. In essence, Axford and Servín empowered me to take over the Chicano Studies Collection. I became the expert, the liaison for scholars, students, and researchers. The Chicano Studies Collection became another means by which my voice was heard. I now had the opportunity to tell others of my culture, of which I was proud.

In the meantime, MASO students were concentrating on staging demonstrations on campus when the fall semester began in 1970 and demanding the establishment of Chicano-content courses and programs. I suggested to the MASO leadership that they meet with Dr. Axford so he could explain the nature of my new assignment and they could have some input into the development of the Chicano Studies Collection.

Dr. Axford was open to the idea of meeting with MASO. I agreed to work with MASO representatives in selecting books for the Chicano Studies Collection. It was a positive relationship, reflective of Dr. Axford's philosophy of open access to library materials and sources. Chicano students began to utilize the library, and brown faces were now appearing in greater numbers in the study areas in and around the collection. Soon I was collecting and saving MASO newsletters, leaflets, minutes from meetings, membership lists, and other Chicano movement materials for my own interest. Dr. Servín encouraged me to collect these materials for the library and planted the seed in my mind to someday build a Chicano Studies archives. What a great idea! He also encouraged me to return to school and enroll in his courses to familiarize myself with the historical literature of the Southwest. It was my fate and destiny to encounter Drs. Servín and Axford and to find a new direction that would satisfy my intellectual growth and development. I learned more about Chicano history from Dr. Servín's classes, where I was exposed to the writings, research, and thought of Chicano scholars and writers. He also gave me the opportunity to do research and helped me publish my first article about the Chicano Movement in a scholarly journal that he edited. In 1974 my scholarly voice came through.

Outside the classroom, I continued to be exposed to Chicano Movement ideas and activities, and I easily made friends and contacts who would lead me to those elusive materials that are archival prizes in academic libraries today. I was challenged to improve my Spanish language skills by those individuals who were community activists. They spoke in both English and Spanish, and I learned what the term "codeswitching" meant. As a reflection of the times, MASO students changed their name in 1971 to MECHA, which stands for Movimiento Estudiantil Chicano de Aztlán.

I've continued working at Hayden Library, where I am now the curator/archivist for the Chicano Research Collection. I have built the Chicano Studies Collection into an important archival repository. During the last ten years, I've been an adjunct faculty associate in the Women's Studies program, where I have taught the courses "La Chicana" and "Women in the Southwest." I have assigned my students to write about the history of Chicanas in their families, to become curious about their family histories, and to incorporate oral history into their research. Through this assignment, they give voice to their own family histories, and they acquire their own voices in the discovery of their identities. Their manuscripts, as well as those of others, are in the Chicano Research Collection. These materials provide information about the past. Students, researchers, and scholars from all over the world have access to records, documents, oral histories, photographs, diaries, correspondence, videos, pamphlets, leaflets, and posters about the history, culture, and heritage of Chicanos, Chicanas, and Mexican Americans in the United States. I am proud and honored to preserve these records for future Chicana and Chicano scholars. It is these materials that transmit the voices of *nuestra raza* vis-à-vis the printed page.

As I conclude my journey and the sharing of my story of growing up in an Arizona mining town, I have come to discover the many voices and modes of communication I had available to me and how they have contributed to the formation of self and identity. These voices have empowered me, educated me, sensitized me. Empowerment came through my work as an archivist and MASO/MECHA student, my scholarship, and my work in academe. My English voices as a young child, in school, and throughout ring clear: the discrimination in academe that I encountered in my English class and also my knowledge of the intricacies of library language. My Spanish voices are also evident: in the back of the band bus in high school; when, for economic survival, I was a salesclerk; and when, through activism, I worked for change in the Chicano community. My empowerment coming full circle is evident through the sharing of my voice in my scholarship and my roles as teacher, lecturer, and historian. From the back of the bus to the ivory tower, I have learned the power of language.

5

...

CHALLENGING TRADITION

Opening the Headgate

Ida M. Luján

My body dreads the arrival of spring. Long before my senses of sight and smell detect the faint climatic warming, the budding of awakening plant life and the lengthening of each day by a few more seconds, then minutes, of daylight, my body has fully integrated this realization. I awake grudgingly, earlier than usual, with a vague sense of anxiety in my stomach that makes itself more clearly felt as the minutes tick by. It feels huge and white, like a rising ball of yeast dough. I try to push it back down by going back to sleep, but it's stronger than I am. It's a yearly event whose source I ritualistically try to deny. Then I realize my body has responded to the beginnings of spring runoff. The *acequias* [irrigation ditches or channels] in northern New Mexico will soon be flowing with ice-cold irrigation water. Part of my brain tries vainly to distract me by pointing out vegetable seed packets and potted daffodils all around town. It's no use. My body is locked into fight-or-flight mode, gearing up for battle. The annual ditch cleaning and distribution of water for irrigation is the battle scenario. The battlefield is in my psyche and in the memories and associations I have forever linked, as a corporeal experience, between the arrival of spring and the irrigation season.

Historically, water has played a vital role in the development of arid northern New Mexico. It has always been a scarce natural resource. Its availability over the centuries has authorized the establishment and continued survival of agricultural communities and subsistence farming, and continues to play a determinative role in attracting or limiting commercial development in this region. Water use and management have, therefore, preoccupied diverse generations of northern New Mexican settlers and have been dominant factors in our socioeconomic well-being. Numerous types of organizations whose aim is to develop and administer water resources for irrigation are recognized by state law. One of the oldest and, certainly, most important of these organizations has been the community acequia association. The institutionalization of water diversion and crop irrigation has evolved over centuries of indigenous systems onto which seventeenth- and eighteenth-century Spanish colonists overlaid the experience and technology of irrigation acquired largely during Spain's Moorish period in the Middle Ages. "Acequia" comes from the Arabic word *as-saquiya,* and can refer to either the irrigation ditch or channel itself or to the association of members organized around the acequia.

Acequias were built for the benefit of all villagers dependent on water for irrigation, livestock, and domestic use. Labor for the construction, annual cleaning, and general upkeep of the ditch was, and continues to be, contributed by the *parciantes* [landowner-water users] according to the amount of water use and acreage irrigated. Water is intended to be distributed impartially and in proportion to the land farmed. The acequias' method of operation and organizational structure have remained relatively unchanged over the centuries of their existence. Typically, the parciantes meet annually or biannually to elect a *comisión* [commission] consisting of three landowner-parciantes that serves as the governing body and to elect a *mayordomo* [ditch manager]. The mayordomo is paid a nominal annual salary for his labor over the irrigation season. Parciantes are assessed annual ditch dues, which are paid in either labor or money, for ditch cleaning and general repairs. The elected governing body, mayordomo, and parciantes meet annually during the early springtime to designate the ditch-cleaning schedule and to establish the irrigation cycle for the spring and summer seasons or for as long as the mountain snow runoff permits.

In addition to fulfilling their primary purpose of water delivery and equitable distribution of available water, acequia organizations have played a fundamental role in the promotion of cooperative efforts, community participation, and problem-solving. Often, this may be the only organization within the community that has the status of a local quasi-governmental body, and the elected officials may play leadership roles with respect to community issues other than water administration. On the other hand, the paucity of water in this region has resulted in a long history of conflicts, disputes, and misunderstandings leading to various means of resolution of such conflicts: self-help measures, judicial adjudication, legislation, or decades of unrelenting argument and conflict.

Communities in northern New Mexico are steeped in traditionalism. As in many agrarian communities, a division of labor strictly along gender lines assures continuity and observation of traditional customs. With the introduction of modern farming equipment and practices, the need for communal efforts by men and women to bring in crops or otherwise to work in cooperative groups has virtually been eliminated. The business of water administration and distribution has long been men's domain. The acequia in my community, until recently, has been no exception to this rule.

Coyote is the village that I claim as my hometown. It is a community of approximately three hundred people located in Río Arriba County in the red-soiled Jemez Mountains, about eighty-five miles northwest of Santa Fe. Farther south, outside of Santa Fe, these red-soiled mountains were named the Sangre de Cristo [Blood of Christ] mountain range by the Spanish settlers. The Santa Fe National Forest surrounds Coyote and its neighboring communities. A well-known tourist guidebook states that Coyote was established in 1862. I wonder how that can be when my grandmother was born outside of Coyote in Río Puerco in 1899, and she was preceded by several generations of the Serrano and Martínez families who had settled in that area long before. In this rural farming and ranching community, the only real employers are the Forest Service and the Jemez Mountain School District.

In truth, however, I did not spend much of my childhood in Coyote. My maternal grandmother and my mother's stepfather lived in Mesa de Poleo [Mint Mesa], and this is truly where I lived as a child. Mesa de Poleo is located about three miles west of Coyote on a beautiful mesa overlooking Coyote and the Abiquiu Reservoir. This area is lushly forested and mountainous at an elevation of about eight thousand feet. My paternal grandparents homesteaded over one hundred acres on this mesa in the late 1800s.

My father died in 1961, just prior to the judicial adjudication of water rights in the acequia that serves the property he inherited from his parents. For a number of years after his death, my mother rented the property to tenants who assumed responsibility for its general upkeep in exchange for farming and grazing privileges. They also assumed the responsibility for irrigation and attendance at annual acequia meetings. Just before I completed high school in 1975, my mother built a home of our own on the property. At about that time our small family undertook the farming and irrigation responsibilities that had previously been carried out by others. At the age of eighteen, just before I went off to college, I, the elder of two children, began to attend acequia meetings with my mother.

The memories I now associate with spring were literally incorporated into my physical being in my late adolescence. This is what I now associate with spring's arrival—old, middle-aged, and young men standing or squatting in the shade or *resolana* [sunshine] of the *sacristía* [sacristy], the traditional meeting place outside the locked church, depending on the state of the spring weather. My mother and I are the only women. The men's disgust at our presence is only thinly veiled. The other women dutifully wait in their husbands' vehicles, ladylike and uninvolved in the fray and the dust and the harsh words swirling mere yards from them. They will not acknowledge us at these acequia meetings; however, the next day at Mass we will greet one another warmly, embrace, and inquire about more genteel activities.

Battling to control internal torrents of emotion so strong, I can't easily find my voice. I cringe inside at her daring, her power, as my mother takes on those men. She challenges their disrespectful treatment of her, their failure to notify her of acequia meetings or ditch cleaning, and their participation in other parciantes' unlawful trespass and appropriation of her water. I want to protect her, to spare her from this yearly drama, yet I'm so intimidated by them, by her. I'm proud of my mother for standing her ground and her determination to protect her children's property. "What do you, a woman, need water for?" they ask. "You need to concern yourself with your house." Women's domain. I choke on my anger at the unequal treatment merely because of our gender and the casual disregard of our property rights. I fear the harshness and the anger in the words they hurl at us. Fear, anger, and outrage battle for supremacy and combine to strangle my voice.

An ancient and arbitrary mayordomo invokes my deceased father's name and their friendship as he seeks to bind us to a suspect and undisclosed agreement granting access to a portion of our water in perpetuity to the mayordomo. I am outraged at the attempted manipulation and reliance on a man incapable now of speaking out against the lie. Do they think my mother stupid and my father so cavalier or neglectful of his children's rights?

Obstinate, they refuse to recognize the relevance of water rights adjudicated by the court more than fifteen years before. They turn a blind eye to legal documents and instead demand allegiance to water distribution based on anachronistic calculations determined by ancestral homestead patent holders in the last quarter of the nineteenth century. We urge their adherence to acequia regulations drafted decades ago in a formalized Spanish that falsely suggests a more egalitarian era. They smile patronizingly or shout their opposition, tyrannically and irrationally scoffing at the need for regulations and disdaining any hint of governmental relevance suggested by written regulations. They insist on following unwritten rules practiced over decades or they instantaneously construct new rules to oppose our requests for notification, voting procedures, equitable treatment. Over the years, my mother and I make numerous and frustrating visits to lawyers and the State Engineer's Office to speak out against the injustices and the arbitrariness, and to seek a remedy. We search for and review statutory materials, other acequias' regulations or bylaws; we translate existing bylaws into English; we propose new bylaws—so much effort to introduce procedural equality. These are the memories my body remembers.

In the early years, I tape-recorded these spring meetings with twin goals of self-protection and putting them on notice that I was there to stay. The yearly reenactment of rageful responses, the ridiculous assertion that recording these proceedings was illegal, and finally, the threat of physical harm unless I turned off the tape recorder, further imprinted the physical memory. I have not yet tried to bring myself to listen to the briefcase full of that history, those memories, those voices that, twenty-two years later, are the cause of my anxiety on awakening. The powerful sound of high water rushing turbulently into a *compuerta* [headgate] triggers other memories—my late-night vigils on muddy ditch banks at our compuerta, shovel in hand, ready to confront the cowardly theft of that precious water. The smell of irrigated fields and dew-covered ground is powerfully associated with memories of my heart pounding in my chest, fear constricting my throat, and the sound of rushing water filling my hearing. Above all, I recall in a physical way that my need to stand strong had to be greater than my fear.

I stood alongside my mother and, years later, stood alone and con-

fronted men who, while they were my antagonists in that particular setting, also played different roles in which I stood on equal footing. I was
welcomed by them or I deferred to them as circumstances required. In
their other roles they were Penitentes [members of a Catholic brother-
hood], my relatives, my neighbors, and my elders. I also played different
roles—young girl, my mother's daughter, student. Each of our many roles
had profound significance for me as I journeyed from sheltered adolescence into uncharted young adulthood, and began to sculpt my female
and racial identities. Interactions with these people in their different
roles profoundly influenced the person I would become. Certainly one
challenge has been to reconcile those seemingly conflicting multiple
identities. No other role, however, had as significant an influence on me
as that of a young woman challenging tradition and asserting my voice
and place in an institution that was not yet ready to hear from me or to
make room for me.

In many ways, this early adversarial relationship planted powerful
seeds of empowerment. I learned some incredible lessons about standing
up to intimidation. My mind seems not to remember the lessons. In the
face of contemporary obstacles it wonders whether I can rise to the occasion, handle it. My body remembers, though. . . .

In 1979 I began my law school career, the only Chicana in an all-
white class in Texas, probably the only Catholic in a Baptist institution. I
graduated in 1981 in a class of fifty-one, and for the first time in Baylor
Law School's history, the women graduates outnumbered the men. During my twenty-seven months there, I encountered physical violence from
my male classmates, racial putdowns from law professors, and verbalized
expressions that I did not belong in that institution. To most of my classmates, I was invisible, and accordingly disregarded. For a handful of male
classmates, however, my presence required them to take some action
against me, including forcibly pushing and elbowing me in the hallways.
It strikes me as peculiar now that I did not seriously consider leaving or
backing off. My classmates' and professors' behavior—their intimidation
and attempts to silence me—occurred in a temporary, artificial setting and
did not have the effect they probably intended. I believe that the early
experiences embedded in my physical being enabled me, reminded me
that I knew how to stand my ground in a hostile and threatening environment that was not ready to make room for me.

The last few years have brought transition to my acequia and its membership. I am the first woman to hold the position of chair of the acequia commission. I nominated myself in 1995 when the member of the commission who served as chair died before the end of his term. My young cousin who threatened to assault me for tape-recording the meetings is now soliciting my investment in his entrepreneurial Amway marketing efforts, and is proposing cooperative efforts to secure state and federal funding for acequia improvements. Ironically, these efforts require the acequia commission's adoption of bylaws. I recently completed the drafting and filing of those bylaws. The older men are dying. In the last three years, three men have died of respiratory and circulatory illnesses. As I extend my condolences to the families and revisit memories of my various positive and negative interactions with these men, I am saddened by their absence. I also find it ironic that the organic causes of their deaths have mirrored my spring anxieties, my racing heart and labored breathing.

I have revised the parciante list to reflect their widows' assumption of their water rights, acequia responsibilities, and entitlement to notices of acequia meetings. One widow has begun to exercise unaccustomed rights to vote, pay ditch dues, and participate in decision-making and problem-solving.

I preside over meetings in a new, modern conference room—part of the new Forest Service complex—where we sit at laminated tables in comfortable office chairs, and have access to indoor bathrooms and a photocopier. Now, some of the wives come in and sit away from the conference table. I look forward to a time when meetings will include more women, although what I anticipate realistically is a new and unknown interchange with *varones* [young men] replacing their fathers. I send out written notices of meetings and outstanding fines and prepare written agendas, minutes, and a detailed report of the unspent funds. I stick to the agenda. I conduct the meetings primarily in Spanish, and I prepare all written documents in English. I do it purposely because it introduces an element of intimidation that serves as my *baque* [backup] when my anxiety level rises. I can draw on the official trappings of an office, formal surroundings, and written documents to equalize the balance of power. I am cognizant of the exploitation of their illiteracy or their discomfort with English. English feels like a weapon in my hand. My use of it feels cold and calculated. I mediate for myself between what feels like self-protection and what feels like *sinvergüenzada* [shamelessness].

So I compensate and work twice as hard to explain everything in Spanish as well as in English for the benefit of the one Anglo parciante. I account for every cent and I keep detailed and thorough records of every action I take because I know I am under scrutiny. I am exhausted after these meetings.

With the coming of fall I am genuinely saddened by the diminution of the runoff and the knowledge that the season won't permit another cutting of alfalfa, a good cash crop. In this season I once again read with pride the literature and history books that depict the acequia system as a remnant of the introduction of Moorish irrigation systems into medieval Spain that was eventually exported to this outpost of Spanish territory. I am also relieved. I long for blankets of snow quietly covering and nurturing the fields without inducing any anxiety on my part. When the spring and summer battle ends for another year, I can once again feel the stirring of my blood and *norteño* [northern] pride, and appreciate the "Agua Es Vida" [Water Is Life] bumper stickers when I hear the water's more mature and less turbulent journey down the acequias.

6
◆ ◆ ◆

MEXICAN BLOOD RUNS THROUGH MY VEINS

Aurora E. Orozco

The reason I am writing this *testimonio* is because I want my children to know who I am and the way I was raised—the reality of life of a Mexican and African woman. I want to show them that although there were very hard times, the unity, respect, and love of *familia* helped me grow into a woman who loves education. Although I didn't have the opportunity like there is today, I had the desire—*las ganas*—and vision to help my children educate themselves and help others, if possible, to do the same.

I was born in Cerralvo, Nuevo León, on May 8, 1918, daughter of Lorenzo Estrada Phillips and Gertrudis Gonzales Toscano. My father was born in Jamaica, son of a black man and an English woman. When he was a very young man, his father and mother died, so he became a sailor. After many years at sea, he lived in Veracruz, Mexico. He traveled to many places in Mexico and finally settled down in Cerralvo, Nuevo León. In those days, Cerralvo was a booming mining town. Because he spoke English fluently, he was hired as a foreman and bookkeeper for one of the American companies.

After a few years, he married my mother, Srita. Gertrudis Gonzales Toscano, daughter of Juan Toscano, an Italian, and Gabriela Montemayor Gonzales, a Mexican. While living in Cerralvo they had eight children. I had five sisters and two brothers. I was the fifth in the family. Things were going well, my father was making money, and one of my sisters was taking music lessons—there was money to pay for her classes. We lived in a big *jacal* [hut] made of adobe and painted white. This was our living room and bedroom. We had four beds, chairs, and a center table, and in the middle of the yard there was another jacal that was the kitchen. It was very big. Part of it was for the cooking. It had a big chimney. On one side of the chimney it had a place where you could put chopped wood. The other side had cupboards for pots and pans. In the middle we had a big dining table. The other part of the jacal was big, and in the winter, beds were moved in there. The heat from the chimney kept us warm. Outside of the kitchen jacal, there was a well where we got our water. We used to draw water from the well, pulling the rope with a pail on the end.

My mother had rose bushes and other plants, and a garden where she grew corn, squash, and beans. The place was surrounded by a tall *tapia* [wall]. It had a door to the front of the jacal and one in the back of the property. We were happy, but then came the Revolution. The Carrancistas would come and steal everything from the American mining company, so it decided to leave. The town was devastated and people were left without work. That's when my father left.

He came to the United States and worked in San Antonio for a while, and then went to work at a ranch in Bishop, Texas. One day my mother received a letter from my father. He wanted the family to come to Texas. My mother made all the arrangements. I remember how all the family got into this black 1920 Ford. My mother closed her house and we went to Vallecillo, a small town where the train stopped. From there we went to Reynosa, Tamaulipas. How excited I was to be on the train. I had heard people talk about the train but to be riding it was a dream, stopping along the way in these small towns and looking at the people and children running to the train to sell tacos, empanadas, candy, and *agua limonada* [lemonade]. To me, everything was a new adventure.

It took all day to reach Reynosa. There were so many people, cars, carts, and soldiers everywhere. That night we slept in my mother's friend's house. Early in the morning we were awakened by the sound of the bugle from the army base. Later in the day, my aunt Ignacia Toscano came to take us to Texas. By the next day we were in Mercedes, Texas, at the house of my aunt María Gonzales. How different everything was! The houses were made of lumber, and the people would go to work in the fields—some man came to take them to work in a truck. I remember hearing this woman who used to scream every morning, "A nicle, a nicle!" They used to get a nickel for selling a bushel of spinach, carrots, or squash.

My father came to Mercedes, and we left for Bishop, Texas, to live on a ranch owned by a German man, Mr. C. Davis. My brother and older sisters would go to the field to help my father. My sister Tules (Gertrudis) and I stayed home with my mother. This was a very different life from the one we had in Mexico. I remember my sister Tules would cry and say, "I want to go to our adobe home." At the ranch we saw rattlesnakes, spiders, wild birds, and many wild flowers. We liked to see how they milked the cows. We didn't speak English, but we played with the Davis children and somehow we understood one another. They liked to trade their biscuits for our tacos of flour or corn tortillas.

We eventually returned to Mercedes to live. My family used to work in the fields. Some truckers would pick us up every morning and take us to the ranches to work and bring us back in the evening. In our home, we spoke Spanish. My father was the only one who spoke English. All our relatives spoke Spanish, and all our neighbors in the barrio did, too. The barrio was where most of the Mexicans lived; a few owned their houses, but most people rented their houses. Some had one room, others had three rooms; all had outhouses and no electricity. We had kerosene for the lamp and we had a wood stove. There was a water pump in the middle of the yard, and every family was given $1.50 allowance a month for water.

There were *tiendas de comida* [grocery stores]. Near the stores was a pretty white house. People said it belonged to a man who was a bootlegger. I remember seeing the Texas Rangers come to his house and dig in the backyard to see if they could find tequila bottles. All the neighborhood kids used to say, "Mira los Rinches [Look at the Rangers] looking for tequila."

A few blocks from the house was the Catholic church, Nuestra Señora de la Merced [Our Lady of Mercy]. We used to go to church and to catechism there. The teachers were nuns, and they were very mean. Maybe it was hard to teach children who could not understand English, I don't know. We did learn, and I made my First Communion. There were baptisms, weddings, and *pastorelas* [Christmas religious comedies]. I remember this lady who used to have a pastorela at her house. She had people play different parts in the pastorela, which lasted all night. These people wore different costumes. Everybody enjoyed this religious comedy, and at midnight she served tamales and coffee and gave candy to the children. People looked forward to this pastorela.

During Lent, there were *misiones* [missions] at the church, and because so many people attended, some had to stand outside. On Palm Sunday, everyone was eager to take the blessed palms home, and on Easter Saturday there were big tubs of *agua bendita* [holy water]. People came with bottles and jars to take the blessed water home. On the next day, Easter Sunday, the church was full. In those days there were no picnics, no barbecues, and no trying to show off new clothes at church.

Less than two months later came the Mexican holiday, Cinco de Mayo. People got together to hear the Mexican consul, who would come to town to speak. There were lawyers and some societies that took part in these events. The people, with so much respect, would stand in the sun for hours, listening to these men. The same thing happened during *las fiestas patrias,* which were celebrated the fifteenth and sixteenth of September. They still felt the love and respect for Mexico.

In those years there were no *quinceañeras* ["sweet fifteen" parties] held for girls. People were very poor—they were trying to survive. Weddings were small, and big fiestas were held at the bride's home. Food consisted of *cabrito* [young goat], rice, beans, and, of course, tequila. The dance was held in the patio.

Funerals were something that every family got involved in. Neighbors would go to the house and help the family dress *el difunto* [the deceased] while a man fixed the table with a white sheet where they laid the deceased. Women brought flowers from their gardens and put them in pails filled with water by the table where el difunto lay. Some brought candles, others came with food, and some took turns making coffee for the men who would stay up all night at the wake, known as *el velorio.* The next day people walked in the funeral procession to the church and then to the cemetery, where someone would speak and give thanks on behalf of the family.

The Anglo community didn't have anything to do with Mexicans except in things related to business, at drugstores, in doctors' offices, in lawyers' offices. The other contact with Mexicans was hiring them to work as maids, cooks, drivers, and other kinds of jobs. Their barrios were nice. Some of their houses were made of brick and wood, and their lawns were kept clean. They had paved streets, electric lights, and running water. Some had cars. The town was divided by the railroad tracks. Most of the Mexicans lived on the north side; the Anglos lived on the south side, away from the *bodegas* [warehouses] of fruits and vegetables.

In Mercedes, I was enrolled in North Ward School, a brick building containing first through fourth grades. The teachers were Anglo and the students were Mexican. Many of them had recently come from Mexico. I felt lonely and scared. I didn't know any English, and I did not understand what the teacher was saying. After a while, my parents enrolled me in a private Mexican school. I stayed in that school until I learned how to read and write, and then I returned to North Ward School. This time I began to understand what the teacher was saying. Slowly I practiced my English and began to do better in class. In those days, the grades were assigned according to the ability of the student; slow learners were put in low first and the others in high first. We were prohibited from speaking Spanish in class and on the playground, but everyone spoke Spanish behind the teacher's back. I was one of the students who spoke Spanish in class, so my teacher, Mrs. White, would make me stay after class. With a red rubber band, she would hit my poor hands until they nearly bled. But she never broke my spirit and determination to speak my native language. It is *my* language—that is what my parents taught me—and it is going to stay with me all my life. How I hated Mrs. White!

The Anglo teachers wanted to change our customs, but it was impossible. After school we ran to our homes in the barrio—to our Spanish, our songs, our food, our friends, and our relatives who were our life. How could they think that a few hours in school could change our culture that we loved? The teacher taught us all about the Anglo customs, but when we got home, it was a very different world. When I was in the fourth grade, every Monday morning the principal, Mrs. Day, would come and speak to the class: "You Mexicans come from very ignorant people without ambition, dirty, and full of lice. You will never amount to anything in your lives." Many times some of the students cried because what she said hurt us. We didn't have anyone to defend us. Our parents didn't speak English, and they were not about to take off from work to come and fight for us. They were Anglos, and therefore we should not say anything.

Our teacher said that we should pay tribute to the Pilgrims because they were the ones who had come to establish a home for us. We would sing a song that went like this:

> The Pilgrims come from overseas
> To make a home for you and me
> Thanksgiving Day, Thanksgiving Day
> We clap our hands, we are so glad.

Some afternoons the teacher would let us sing our school songs. Some students asked if we could sing in Spanish, and she said yes. "Sing the one I like—Valencia," she said. The boys answered "yes," and this is what they sang:

Valencia son tus noches perfumadas
Con olor de naranjo en flor.

[Valencia, your nights are perfumed
with the smell of orange blossoms.]

The boys would also sing other verses:

Valencia no te quites los zapatos
Porque da la pestilencia.

[Valencia, don't take off your shoes
because of the stench.]

We laughed and clapped, and the teacher would say, "I love that song!"

In the late 1920s, I remember how we would hear that things were getting hard. No money. No work. At school during Christmas time, we each received a little brown sack with one apple and one orange. We were at the beginning of the Great Depression. We were very poor. Many students came to school barefoot. Some didn't have jackets. Many times we didn't have any tacos to take to school. In the cafeteria we had a corner where a bunch of us sat to eat our tacos made of refried beans, potatoes with *chorizo* [Mexican sausage], or eggs. At school many white students were given tickets for their lunch, but none were given to the Mexicans. So we ate what we had, and the white students used to make fun of our tacos. How times have changed! Now the gringos eat plenty of tacos, and some companies have become rich selling tacos.

We used to hear that schools were going to be closed. Teachers were not being paid. Everyone was worried. Things were very bad. Some of the students talked about going back to Mexico with their families. President Herbert Hoover was asking the illegal immigrants to return voluntarily to Mexico. Many families, seeing their terrible situation, decided to leave. There were no jobs, and if any job surfaced, American citizens were hired first.

It was during the Depression that many white men came to the Rio Grande Valley looking for work. They came on the freight trains, and the Mexicans gave them the name *trampas* [tramps]. They would come to the barrios asking for food, and everyone gave them tacos and coffee, and some befriended them.

We moved to a better barrio and house. My father was working as a foreman for a German company that opened a factory making buttons from oyster shells. He would take a group of men to the lakes and get the oysters. Others took out the oysters, and the shells were put in big tanks of clean water in the factory. Women worked there, cutting buttons from the shells. The pay was a dollar for a full pail. One of my sisters worked there and used to make seven dollars a week—that was a very big salary during the Depression.

When I was in high school, Franklin Roosevelt was elected president. He promised that he was going to see that everyone got a job. He ordered the federal government to give jobs to all young men ages sixteen to twenty who would work for the government in the forest, and their families would receive the money. Many young men left home to go to work.

In those days there were rumors that a group who called themselves the League of United Latin American Citizens (LULAC) was organizing to work on behalf of Mexican Americans. They would encourage younger generations to finish school, get scholarships, go to college, and become professionals in order to fight for our people—*nuestra gente*—in discrimination cases. This, of course, was for U.S. citizens only. Some Mexicans resented that LULAC was excluding them because they were not citizens. Some of our own people began to call themselves Latin (Latin American) instead of Mexican and decided they didn't want to speak Spanish. They hoped that by doing this they would be accepted by the Anglos. This was a mistake. There were some people who would tell us, be proud of being of Mexican-American, Azteca, Indian, Spanish, or African descent. We were always made to feel ashamed of our heritage in school, at work, and even at church. That's wrong. We didn't know where we came from. Some families did not let their children speak Spanish because they thought it degraded them. To me, that's wrong; you are more educated and superior (instead of inferior) if you are bilingual and can speak two languages instead of only one.

It was 1938 when I finished school, and we still didn't have any Mexican-American teachers.

In the late 1930s, I worked in a store owned by a Jewish family. Most of the businesses were owned by Jews. I had worked very hard to learn to speak and pronounce English very well. I used to read every book I could get my hands on. Maybe it was because I used to see my father reading, so it helped me. That's what I was told when I was hired. Most of the customers were white. It was at this time that we started to hear about the war in Europe, and that maybe the United States could become involved. Everyone was worried and talked about it, especially if they had young men in their families.

For us, life remained the same. Mexicans were still looked down upon. I remember that it was only when elections were going to be held that whites who were running for office would find a Mexican American who was well-known in the community. They would befriend him and have him campaign in the barrios to get their votes. The whites would invite them to barbecues and dances, and make promises if they won.

In those years, the gringo—the white man, the boss—would recommend you through a letter to rent a house, get a loan at the bank, get out of jail, enter a hospital, and even help you get a passport or get credit at a grocery store, because we still had a lot of discrimination against Mexicans and Mexican Americans. For example, a Dr. Maldonado came to Mercedes in the late 1930s. He didn't stay long, because he couldn't find anyone who would rent him a house in the Anglo neighborhood, simply because he was a Mexican, even though he was educated and a medical doctor. That didn't matter.

In the 1940s, the news was about the war in Europe. The United States was preparing for war. Many young men enlisted in the military; some were drafted. Many Mexicans enlisted in various branches of the service—they were promised citizenship. Almost every family had someone in a military branch. Every family was alert to the news from the front. When Pearl Harbor was attacked, it was a very sad Sunday. I remember that we sat in front of the radio, listening to President Roosevelt speak to the nation about the terrible Japanese attack on Pearl Harbor. We knew some young men who were there at the time of the attack. Later, news started arriving of soldiers and sailors who had been hurt or killed. The war in Europe was getting worse. My oldest brother, Roberto, fought in the war. He was in Italy during the Battle of the Bulge, and his unit was forty-five miles from Berlin when World War II ended. When the bodies of soldiers came home, the whole town attended the funerals. I remember Miguel Gonzales, my neighbor, who was killed in Germany, so young and friendly. He sang beautifully. There were few men left in town—so few, it was very hard for single girls to get a date. People made a joke about this, saying that all the single girls used to go and see the male mannequins at the main store to remember what men looked like.

There was plenty of work in the vegetable and citrus warehouses but no men were available, so women began doing men's work there. Some women left home and went to work in factories making clothing, machines, and all kinds of armaments for the soldiers. Soon, men from Mexico started to come to this side and were hired everywhere to do all kinds of jobs. The immigration authorities—La Migra—didn't bother them. Once the war ended, everyone was glad. Some families were sad because some of their members didn't return alive. Factories closed, leaving many without work, and at the same time, the troops were coming home. There wasn't work for everyone. For this reason, the order was given to deport all Mexicans back to Mexico. La Migra raided factories, restaurants, laundries, bakeries, and stores. They would load them up in trucks and deport them to Brownsville and Reynosa.

During the 1940s, we continued to face discrimination from the gringos. Mexicans were still considered to be dirty, lazy, and without ambition. Some parents decided not to teach Spanish to their children; they wanted them to speak only English and to say that they were Spaniards instead of Mexicans. You heard comments like *"Se creen gringos"* [They think they're white] from other Mexicans who saw how these parents made their own children act *agringados* [anglicized] in order to fit in and be accepted by the Anglos.

It was the 1940s when young men created another language they called caló. They used words like *carnal* to mean "friend" and *vato* to mean "guy." These young men formed groups called *pachucos* in many barrios throughout the Southwest. They adopted this pachuco style from Mexican movie stars/comedians like Tin Tan and su carnal Marcelo. They dressed in colorful shirts, wide-legged pants that narrowed at the bottom, long chains that hung from the pockets, and colorful hats with brims.

We began to have Mexican-American lawyers, doctors, teachers, and engineers in our community around the decade of the 1940s. Many times discrimination toward them was due to the fact that they spoke English with a Spanish accent. The bilingual individuals started to get more jobs—they could communicate better with persons who spoke only Spanish. Some of the schools that Mexicans attended were in terrible condition. When Dr. Hector Pérez García formed an association called the American G.I. Forum, it was to pressure the state to provide better and equal educational opportunities for our children, including bilingual education for children who didn't speak English. Bilingual education has been successful, although the Anglos deny this. LULAC kept encouraging parents to educate their children because they would become the leaders of the future. They knew that being able to speak English *and* Spanish would be of great benefit and value. I had that same experience when I started school. It was so hard to listen to the teacher speaking English. I felt sad and lonely because I didn't understand a word she was saying.

At the end of the 1940s, there were more jobs; many of the ex-soldiers went to college and vocational schools, and started a better life. By this time, I was working in a dress shop called Lee Ann's, and in 1949, I met my future husband. We were married in 1950. My husband's name was Primitivo Orozco. He was born in Guadalajara, Jalisco, and was an expert bootmaker.

A few months after we were married, we came to Cuero, Texas, in Dewitt County, a town with six thousand residents. The reason we came to Cuero was because my husband would be able to make more money than he was making in Mercedes, Texas. The white residents are German and Polish. Their ancestors came from Europe in the nineteenth century and received land that Mexico was giving to newcomers just for saying they were Catholic. Some of them came later, after Texas won its independence, and acquired land illegally by burning the Mexicans' houses and running them off their land. That is why some of these ranchers in south Texas have big ranches and lots of cattle. Cuero also has lots of blacks; most of them are descendants of slaves who were brought to Dewitt County. There are also Mexican descendants of Indians who used to live in the region. When my husband and I moved to Cuero, we quickly noticed the racial differences of the people who lived in this town.

We noticed the Jim Crow laws. These laws were established in 1870 to prohibit marriage between blacks and whites. Tennessee was the first state to pass such a law. Blacks and whites could not sit together in trains, hotels, barbershops, restaurants, and theaters. In 1885, it was prohibited for black children to go to school with whites. When we came to Cuero during the 1950s, we noticed the Jim Crow laws were present everywhere. The Mexican neighborhood was about two blocks from downtown. Most of the houses where poor whites lived were run-down. My husband's boss had to recommend us so we could rent a run-down house.

There were signs that said "No Blacks, no Mexicans" in doctors' offices, restaurants, hospitals, and swimming pools. Like colored people, Mexicans had their place. In the hospital, the basement was for blacks and Mexicans. In restaurants, Mexicans were forced to eat in the kitchen. There were Catholic and Baptist churches for Mexicans on the west side of town.

We noticed that most Mexicans who lived in Cuero felt inferior to the Anglos because they didn't have any rights. They had to go to their boss and ask for a recommendation so they could rent or buy a house, furniture, or a car. The merchants perceived that all Mexicans were dirty, drunks, and thieves. There was an apartment house near where I lived. I decided to go and try to rent an apartment, but the owner told me they didn't rent to Mexicans. Years passed, and my husband and I eventually bought the house where our children were raised.

I remember that after a few weeks in Cuero, we decided to go to the movie theater. We went in and sat on the right side and enjoyed the movie. When we came home, a friend asked, "Where did you sit?" I told her, and she said, "It's a wonder that you were not asked to move." I asked why. "Because that side is for whites, the left side is for Mexicans, and the balcony is for blacks," she said. I told her, "I wouldn't move. My money is as good as any white person's."

People told me that many years ago they had a school for Mexicans in a run-down building on the west side of town. Mexicans referred to it as *"la escuela de piojos."* The Anglos called it "the school of lice" because they associated Mexicans with having lice. Students felt mistreated and not properly taught, and as a result, many dropped out of school. Many of them could not read or write, and had to find someone to help them with their paperwork. Many Mexican children never even had an opportunity to go to school. Those families who lived on farms or ranches were told by their gringo *patrones* not to send their children to school; it wasn't necessary for them to become educated. They felt hurt and left out and didn't have anyone to help them. Los Mexicanos lived at the mercy of the Anglos. I feel that if some of these children had had the opportunity to be educated, they could have become teachers, lawyers, or other professionals, and would not be looked down upon as being full of lice, dirty, and dumb.

My children did not attend this school because when my oldest daughter, María Teresa, started school, segregation had ended. After the era of segregation had passed, the school district closed Daule School, a school for blacks. Daule was the name of a black school principal. Today, all children—Anglos, Mexicans, and blacks—go to the same school.

You had to fight for your rights in Cuero, Texas. I decided to fight for the rights *de mi familia* when I went to the Buchel Bank to ask for a loan of $125.00. My husband's boss had already spoken to the banker, Mr. Henderson, so I went to his office and talked to him. He didn't seem very friendly. When I finished speaking, he waited a while, then said, "I don't want to lend you any money. You Mexicans and blacks never pay it back. If you ask a black or Mexican the whereabouts of these people, they never know. You all are deadbeats, drunks, and thieves." I felt insulted, so I stood up and said, "You cannot say that about my race, you don't know. We have all kinds of people, just like in your race. We are not all the same. It's a shame you advertise in the newspaper about your loans. Why don't you say it's not for Mexicans and blacks?" He stood up and said, "No one has spoken to me like that." I answered, "Maybe I am the one who had to tell you." I left and walked to the shop where my husband worked. At that moment, the phone was ringing. Mr. Bohne, my husband's boss, answered and said, "It's Mr. Henderson. He wants you to return to the bank." Mr. Bohne asked what happened. I told him the story, and he told me that everyone complained about Mr. Henderson. So I went back to the bank and Mr. Henderson let me have $125.00. I repaid the loan, and after that, he was very friendly. I still have an account with the bank.

My husband didn't get mad. I was the one who spoke better English and took care of business matters. After the incident at the bank, some people asked me if I wasn't scared. I said, "No, it's for the Mexicans in Cuero. We have to fight for our rights."

I had six children, and I promised myself to teach them to be good Mexican-American citizens and to be proud of their heritage. I was proud to be a Mexican, and I wanted to prove to the Anglos that we were not different from them. I also wanted to prove that it's not the color of the skin that makes the person. When my first daughter started school, I joined the Parent Teacher Association and would go to all the school board meetings. I wanted the teachers and principals to know that the education of my children was very important to me. I didn't work when my children were small. I raised them, read to them, sang to them, played games with them, and sent them to catechism.

In the late 1960s, I joined LULAC and was secretary for a year; I was chosen to be on the City Advisory Committee for about eight years. I also served on the grand jury three times. One of those times, I helped an illegal immigrant youth who was accused of something he didn't do. The young woman who was translating was not very fluent in Spanish and was unable to explain accurately what the young man was trying to say, so I told the district attorney that what the young woman was saying was wrong. He asked me to sit down and translate for this young man. He was found innocent.

Some Mexican-American professors and writers came from San Antonio and Kingsville to Cuero to speak to the Mexican-American community in the late 1960s. We formed a society called Texans for the Educational Advancement of Mexican Americans, which worked on behalf of the students. I was named president. We started to work with parents, students, and teachers and told them about their rights in school. We also alerted the parents about how in some schools, teachers were placing their children in classrooms for the mentally retarded because they could not speak English.

Another organization that I belonged to was called Familias Unidas, which was part of La Raza Unida, a political party founded by José Angel Gutiérrez during the 1960s. This was a time when many students and university professors decided to come together to protest and march against discrimination in the schools. The first Mexican-American teachers were hired in the late 1960s and early 1970s. This is what one Anglo school board member said in a meeting: "We don't hire Mexican-American teachers because they aren't qualified. We don't think they can do the job." During the 1970s, Familias Unidas reported the case to the State Department of Education. They came to Cuero and made them hire Mexican-American and black teachers.

When my youngest son started school, I decided to go to work. Things were costing more. We needed more money. My oldest daughter was in high school and needed more clothes and money for her school supplies, and we wanted her to go to college. On September 15, 1967, I started working at Lieberman's department store. They hired me because I was bilingual, had experience in sales, and was well-known. I worked hard and became one of the best salesladies in the store. I worked there for eighteen years. I also experienced discrimination and learned to work with people who were racist. One day the manager of the store told me she was going to fire me because I spoke Spanish to the customers. I responded, "Fire me if you like, but that is why the owner hired me, because I am bilingual and I can do my job in two languages. Remember, there are many people who don't speak English because people like you failed to give them an opportunity."

Mexican-American teachers and other community women were trying to help Mexican-American students. The teachers were having a problem with the superintendent, Dr. Sims, so my friend Mary Sánchez and I and many Anglos went to the school board meeting. Several members of Concerned Citizens for Education (of which I was a member) also attended. One of the school board members announced that Dr. Sims had resigned. The teachers were very happy. My involvement in school helped my children. They started to receive better treatment, and Mexican-American students began to take more of an interest in their studies.

I was interested in improving the educational system for our people. One way to voice our concerns was to serve on the school board. Father Jerry Mackin, a friend of the family, recommended me for a position that was vacant. I was interviewed, but they gave it to another person—a gringo. I remember a letter my daughter Cynthia, who has a Ph.D. in history, wrote to our Cuero newspaper: "The school wanted to keep its members 'lily white.' " There were no Mexicans or blacks on the board.

My first daughter was initiated into the National Honor Society and graduated with honors. Later she attended Victoria Junior College and again graduated with honors. All six children did very well in school; five of them were members of the National Honor Society and received many medals for excellence in academic subjects. My children are bilingual— they speak both languages. They went to the University of Texas at Austin and also attended Rice, Columbia University, and UCLA. They are professionals with degrees in public affairs, art, journalism, business administration, history, and electrical engineering. So to me, what I did on behalf of my children and other Mexican Americans was to fight a battle against discrimination in order for our children to have equal opportunities to succeed. Many people ask me, "How did you do it?" One doctor said, "You did better with your family than me. I have money and social standing." "Yes," I answered, "but my family had the will to study and work hard to get their education, with my encouragement and love."

I would like to offer some advice to parents of our younger and future generations. Teach them the importance of education. While they are at home, read to them in English *and* in Spanish. Teach them to be proud of their heritage, and tell them that going to school gives them the opportunity to be anything they want. I know many parents think that speaking Spanish makes them inferior, so they don't teach their children the language. That is wrong. You are making them feel ashamed of their Mexican heritage and Spanish language. Speaking both languages provides many more opportunities for them than for someone who speaks only one language. We need to teach our sons and daughters and grandchildren to be proud of being Mexican Americans whose ancestors include Indians, Spaniards, and Africans. We have deep roots that connect us to our ancestors, their customs, and their language. This is why I am proud to say that Mexican blood runs through my (our) veins.

THREE

INNOVATION

SPEAKING CREATIVELY/CREATIVELY SPEAKING

7

• • •

SEARCHING FOR A VOICE

Ambiguities and Possibilities

Erlinda Gonzales-Berry

When I first heard Sandra Cisneros talk about her work, I was struck by her frequent allusions to her "voice." *House on Mango Street,* she said, was very definitely her child voice; in her more recent poetry she had found a new voice. At that time, I had just completed my first novella, and it occurred to me that I had never consciously set out to find a voice; I had merely begun to write, and wrote until I felt I had reached the end of the line. I continued to reflect for some time on the question of voice, and finally concluded that during the time that elapsed between the conception of the story and the setting of it down on paper, some six months, I had indeed engaged in a search for a voice. Uncovering that voice, however, had required the peeling away of layer upon layer of voice-muffling circumstances. The problem had been one of not hearing the voice for the noise, the latter disguised as bilingualism, self-consciousness, time, and a deeply entrenched baritone register.

The fact that I was bilingual by historical accident and by academic training raised the first obstacle in my quest for voice. In which language would my voice speak? While I am certainly English-dominant in the social domain, my formal experiences in Spanish outnumber those in English. I lecture daily in Spanish, and I have read more literature in that language than I have in English. I have done some acting in Spanish, but never in English. On stage, Spanish offers me an immediate persona. My Spanish persona has a certain flair, is a risk taker, is a game player, is witty. The English me, on the other hand, is more conservative, insecure, highly self-conscious. In Spanish, I always felt loved and accepted. In English, I always felt like Alejandro Morales's Mateo in *Caras viejas y vino nuevo:* spied upon, on the verge of being judged: Did he or didn't he measure up? This same sense of self-consciousness assaults me when I try to act or write in English.

There were other issues regarding language choice that went beyond the purely psychological. There were the social and ideological implications of language choice. I was very conscious of the fact that a Spanish-reading audience is limited in the United States. I was more conscious of the fact that, given repressive native-language education policies in our country, most Chicanos are not literate in Spanish; thus the primary audience I wanted to reach would be excluded should I choose to write in Spanish. I had noted in my academic studies on other Chicano writers that those who in fact did write in Spanish were, in the main, college professors formally trained in that language, and that their use of Spanish as the primary vehicle for creative expression in a sense constituted an elitist phenomenon.

I also remembered Marise Condi's words regarding this matter. Her solution and that of fellow Caribbean women writers, she said at a public lecture, had been to turn to "orature." If indeed they were sincere in their efforts to reach their people, they must return to the familiar oral mode. I could see her point clearly, but at that moment, I had a need not only to inscribe the collective wisdom of my people but also to tackle the demons that inhabited private, interior spaces. I thought of Aristeo Brito, a Chicano from Arizona, whose words reached me via letter many years ago: *"Espero que se siga escribiendo en Español puesto que allí es donde radica nuestra autenticidad."* [I hope that individuals will continue writing in Spanish, for that is where our authenticity lies.] I wanted to believe those words, but to do so would mean denying the authenticity of the works of Rudolfo Anaya, Sandra Cisneros, Cherríe Moraga, Gary Soto, Arturo Islas, and the many other Chicanas/os who write in English.

And what of the conflict that surely must assault writers who choose the colonizer's language to reveal the cultural reality of the colonized? If it was authenticity I wanted, was codeswitching not the more appropriate vehicle? How many Chicanas/os did I know who could resist the urge to subvert the English language system, to violate its formal constraints with a sound dosage of Spanish syntax, phonology, and lexicon? If codeswitching was in fact the "authentic" Chicano language, then the early movement poets were on the right track. But I am not a poet. Imagery and symbols elude me, and if there is a lyrical bone in my body, I have yet to find it.

I could say that in the end I heeded Albert Memi's (1965) prediction that sooner or later it will dawn on colonized intellectuals and writers that to them belongs the task of rescuing the mother tongue from oblivion, of returning to the people the precious jewel that hegemonic practices sought to grind into the ground.

But in the real end, I can only say that when I finally finished peeling back this layer, the first words uttered by my voice were in Spanish. Perhaps I should say in "spanish." Bill Ashcroft, Gareth Griffiths, and Helen Tiffin (1989:4–5), in their illuminating study of language and post-colonial literatures, assert,

> We need to distinguish between what is proposed as a standard code, English (the language of the erstwhile imperial centre), and the linguistic code, english, which has been transformed and subverted into several distinctive varieties throughout the world. The language of these "peripheries" was shaped by an oppressive discourse of power. Yet they have been the site of some of the most exciting and innovative literatures of the modern period and this has, at least in part, been the result of the energies uncovered by the political tension between the idea of a normative code and a variety of regional uses.

In a similar fashion, it was clear to me that my choice of Spanish did not mean that I would limit myself exclusively to a formal code, or *el español culto,* which I had mastered in graduate school. Certainly this code would provide the foundation, but I had no intention of repressing "peripheral" codes that I knew would surface: popular forms, particularly those of my native dialect (forms like *izque,* which one editor attempted to replace with the more generally used *dizque*); caló (that presumed male code that females are not supposed to use); calques (those shameless obiter dicta that betray the obstinate presence of the "bi" code that underrides the "consciously selected" language of the moment, which itself is always "other" to my "other" *idioma*). And, of course, I knew that English (sometimes english) would not fail to impose itself, reminding Spanish monolingual readers of the "difference"—historical, cultural, linguistic, psychological *(y la lista podría volverse catálogo)*— that marked my text for Chicanidad rather than Mexicanidad.

Such code alternations would allow me to grope for meaning beyond that afforded by a single language. They would allow me to inscribe "difference" in the most trenchant way possible. And I knew also that my writer's gaming sense would tempt me to throw in yet other languages. I am speaking of languages that did not belong to me by birthright, but that I had collected in my baggage of "high culture" as I struggled to meet the requirements for advanced degrees: French, Portuguese, German, all languages of a dazzling Western tradition whose attempts to repress "difference" were being set back light-years by Chicana/o writers. Yes, it was indeed "spanish" that my brain transmitted as I struggled to construct an identity made of words that betrayed me at every turn, an identity made of texts that came before mine, made of a history and of memory—both personal and collective.

Having made the decision regarding language, I turned to the actual process of narrating. I began in the third person, and after several weeks of writing, I stopped. It all sounded so stilted, so unnatural. I found, as did Eco (1985:19), that I "was embarrassed at telling a story." This seemed odd to me, for I knew that on stage I had no problem telling my part of the story. By relating writing to acting, I finally grasped an important point: on stage I was not myself, but someone else, and it is in the becoming of someone else that immobilizing self-consciousness dissolves. How many times had I told my beginning students of language to leave their "English selves" outside the classroom, to allow themselves to acquire a new "Spanish self"? Only then would they lose their self-consciousness and begin to acquire the new language. I finally concluded that if, in fact, I felt insecure about putting my *own* voice on the blank paper, why not let someone else speak for me? I decided to turn the task of narrating over to Mari, the main character of the novella. Thus, hiding behind a mask, believing that it was no longer I who spoke but, rather, a young woman who probably had a great deal in common with myself, I felt free from self-consciousness and from fear of exposure.

I now found myself confronting a third layer of voice-muffling experiences. This layer was perhaps less dramatic than the others, but nonetheless problematic. I go back to Sandra Cisneros's references to her child voice. My own point of departure in *Paletitas de guayaba* was childhood, but at the ripe age of forty-plus, I could no longer hear my child voice. Too many years and too many experiences had intervened. My adolescent voice seemed more accessible, but I soon realized that adolescence had been a silent time, a time for dreaming, but not a time for speaking. No, those were the silent and painful years, the years of interrogation. Why, I queried my maker, was I not born a male? Did not every family deserve at least one male? Why not this family? Why five females? What great sin had my father, a rancher to boot, committed to deserve such punishment? And was I not the best fit to be that male? My maker was even more silent than I.

I didn't realize then that what I was really asking was not why I had been born without that organ that would have made me heir to the culturally determined position of privilege but, rather, how the exclusive discourse and practices that privileged *that* organ over others originated in the first place. I soon overcame the disappointment and frustration that accompanied my discovery of the marginal status of women by wrapping myself in Athena's veil, or in what Luce Irigaray (1983:239) has called "the mask of femininity that one sees in mythology beginning with Athena." The acceptance of this veil, of course, meant acceptance of my condition of female-in-waiting. Alas, adolescence was a time neither for action nor for speaking.

When I finally began to hear a voice from my past, it was the voice of a young woman. It was an angry voice with a deep resonance and an imposing urgency. It wanted to run free like the waters of a ruptured dam careening through a narrow canyon in search of unknown open spaces. I was indeed relieved when I discovered in this impetuous voice a marvelously humorous timbre that tempered the narrator's saucy tongue. The only problem with this voice was that it sometimes tired and became vulnerable. When this happened, a mature voice stepped in to counsel, to comment, to judge. This intrusion persisted throughout the narration. Finally, a reconciliation of these two voices was reached in the following passage:

> Cuando hice los apuntes en un cuadernito, la verdad es que no tenía ninguna intención de que todo aquello llegara a formar un texto. . . . No sabría decir exactamente cuándo me dio por juntarlo todo, digo los apuntes del viaje y las memorias de postviaje. Una vez decidida a construir el texto, me pareció lógico empezar en el principio y proceder en forma cronológica hasta el fin. . . . A medida que iba escribiendo a máquina (y editando) los apuntes, los cuales me parecían de alguna manera auténticos y objetivos precisamente por ser apuntes, se me aferraban los recuerdos no-apuntados y, por lo tanto,

menos empíricos pero no menos insistentes. (*Paletitas de guayaba*:32)

[When I took notes in a little notebook, the truth is that I never had the intention that all of that would become a text. . . . I don't know exactly when I decided to bring it all together, I mean the notes about the trip and the memories of the trip. Once I had decided to compose the text, it seemed logical to begin at the beginning and to proceed chronologically until the end. . . . As I was typing and editing the notes, which seemed to me in some way to be authentic and objective, precisely because they were notes, the memories, not written down and consequently less empirical but no less insistent, kept latching themselves on.]

Thus the inconsistencies in voice recorded in young Mari's journal could be attributed to the hand of the mature Mari, the reader and preserver of the original text, who could not resist the temptation of editing and perhaps even embellishing. The result of this narrative strategy is that, in addition to justifying the dialogical tension created in the monologues, it added a self-reflecting or narcissistic (to use Linda Hutcheon's [1980] metaphor) dimension to the work.

The fourth layer alluded to in the beginning of this commentary was the result of my formal academic training. The department in which I did my graduate work was composed almost entirely of male professors who assigned works written by males, and who interpreted female characters from a male perspective. In fact, my first exposure to Sor Juana was through the baritone voice of my male professor of Latin American literature. During those years of formal training, I learned to revere the canonical literary figures and to look with patronizing disdain at women writers. My own dissertation focused on male Chicano writers. Once freed from the straitjacket I donned in graduate school, I was free to explore the world of women's culture. But even as I wrote, I worried a great deal about the weight of my academic baggage.

In moments of doubt, I feared that perhaps Mari's worldview was too masculinist. At other times I conceded to myself that because she was trapped in the contradictions of living in a phallocentric society, her character bore witness to those contradictions. The nagging fear that perhaps my writing was too masculine was not assuaged when, after my first public reading, a female colleague said to me, "You write like José Agustín!" Ten years earlier I would have considered her comment a compliment of the highest order, for in those years, I had had a dashing literary affair (in my imagination, to be sure) with this young Mexican writer. Upset by her comment, I approached a friend, a feminist critic, and asked her what she thought. "Don't worry about it," she said. "When women narrate well, their style is always compared to male writers or attributed to male influence." What I yearned to hear was that I wrote like Sandra, like Denise, like Ana, like Cherríe, like Helena María, Gloria, Margarita *y otras, tantas otras,* who had given me the nerve to write.

As I read more women writers, and consciously scrutinize their female voices, I find that vigorous narration is indeed not the exclusive domain of male writers. What is of consequence, however, is that we not get lost in the argument over the existence or the nonexistence of an exclusive language of women, but that we abrogate male language and that we seize that language to speak, with authority, of female experience(s) and, more important, the specificity of Chicana experiences. That we appropriate and revise myths, particularly those that have had as their primary goal the immobilization and the silencing of women. Thus, following in the footsteps of María Fernanda Alegriá, Rosario Castellanos, Margarita Cota-Cárdenas, and numerous other Mexican and Chicana writers, I created my own revised version of the Malinche Myth. In the following passage we hear not the traditional discourse of betrayal ascribed to the mythohistorical figure but, rather, what she might have said about herself as she evaluated history from a female perspective:

> *Quiero que comprendas mis acciones para que algún día cuando te hiera la violencia de las palabras, "hijo de la chingada," entiendas los motivos que me impulsan. Mira, las mujeres en esta sociedad, igual que lo serán en la tuya, son meros objetos, son muebles, son la propiedad de sus padres y después de sus esposos. El único honor que se les otorga en esta cultura, es ser sacrificadas, siempre que sean vírgenes. ¡Gran honor! Mira, los sacerdotes, los príncipes, los mercaderes, los artesanos, los guerreros, todos son varones. Las mujeres somos primero los espejos que reflejan la imagen del varón para que se percate de quién es; después somos sus jugetes en el petate y, en fin, receptáculos e incubadoras de sus granos de*

maíz. Se nos reliega al mundo de la sombra y del silencio; pero ese silencio engendra la palabra que se revuelca en nuestra misma hiel y se vuelve rencor, injuria y también canto; y a esta palabra se le agrega otra y otra y terminan en fin siendo una larga y fuerte cadena que nos envuelve y nos estrangula. Podemos rendirnos ante ella, expirar asfixiadas de palabras que nunca encontraron voz, o podemos conjurar, con todos los agüeros del cielo y del infierno esa voz y volcarla sobre el mundo de los grandes señores. Ante ella, ellos recularán en temor y demostrarán sus verdaderas tendencias—la soledad, la resistencia oculta tras máscaras y órganos sexuales que disparan cual arcos y flechas, arcabuces y escopetas. (pp. 75–76)

[I want you to understand my actions, so that one day when the violence of the words "son of the fucked one" slaps you in the face, you will understand the motives that pushed me. Listen, women in this society, just as in yours, are mere objects, they are furniture, they are the property of their fathers and later of their husbands. The only honor society bestows upon them is to sacrifice them, that is, if they are virgins. What an honor! Look, the priests, the princes, the merchants, the artisans, the warriors—all male. We women are first of all the mirrors that reflect the male image so they will know who they are; later we are their playthings on the mat; and finally [we are] receptacles and incubators for their kernels of corn. We are banished to the world of shadow and silence, but this silence engenders the word that churns around in our own bitterness and becomes resentment, outrage, and also song; and to this word another one fastens itself and yet another, to finally become a long, solid chain that envelops and strangles us. We can be over-powered by it, die asphyxiated by words that will never find their voice, or we can conjure up, with all the omens of heaven and hell, that voice and turn it against the world of the great masters. Before it they will recoil in fear and will show their true tendencies—solitude, resistance shrouded by masks and sexual organs that discharge like so many bows and arrows, harquebuses and muskets.]

As an appropriator of language, I have also dared to invade the "bawdy linguistic preserve" of male language (Ostriker 1982:88). My motivation stemmed not from a need to imitate males for the sake of imitation, but from a need to break the bonds of silence and to cease to support, as Cixous (1981:50) would have women writers do, the limiting "realm of the proper." Thus Mari's mouth finds its peer in the mouth described negatively by Luisa Valenzuela (1982:90): *"La Boca. De la cual no deben emerger las culebras de las malas palabras; las palabras malas, aquellas que podrían perturbar el preestablecido orden del discurso masculino."* [The Mouth: From which the serpents of filthy words should not appear, those that could perturb the preestablished order of masculine discourse.]

> *¿Le puedo llamar pochita? . . . Cabrón, llámame lo que te dé la gana porque ya me imagino lo que me llamas en tu mente. Tetona, culito lindo. Esas palabritas, mano, las llevas impresas en los ojos. ¿De veras crees que me gusta que me desvistas con los ojos, a la vez que te acaricias instintivamente los cuates? ¿Verdad que tenía razón mi amiga con su diálogo imaginario que inventó cuando viajó por México en camión? ¿Todo bien, señor? ¿Negativo el autoexamen de cáncer de los testículos? ¿Verdaderamente crees que me gusta? Hijo, que retrasado mental, que poco sabes de las mujeres.* (p. 47)

> [May I call you pochita? . . . You jerk, call me whatever you want, because I can imagine what you call me in your mind. Big tits, sweet ass. Those juicy words, bro, are imprinted onto your eyes. Do you really think I like it when you undress me with your eyes, while you instinctively caress your balls? My friend really hit the nail on the head with the dialogue she invented while she traveled through Mexico by bus. Is everything all right, señor? Negative on the self-exam for testicular cancer? Do you really think I like it? You cretin, how little you know about women.]

Despite its aggressive tone, this passage opens the door to laughter. In her study on humor in Chicana literature, Rebolledo (1985:91) points out that "women's humor as a social process has not been studied analytically." While it is not my intent here to do an analytical analysis of my own use of humor, I would like to call attention to the reactions to my humor, for I think they point out some interesting issues regarding male/female reader response.

The women who read portions of the text while I was working on it invariably commented on its humor. Only one male mentioned this aspect of the novella to me. Since males and male discourses are sometimes the subject of Mari's ironic vision, I cannot help but ask if male readers resent low-status (female) characters making disparaging remarks about males. Since men are accustomed to viewing themselves as subject, as creators of symbolic constructs, it must be difficult for them to accept a text that posits males as objects of the aggressivity underlying this female humor. What is perhaps more significant, however, is that I do this at all, for as McGhee (1976) and Levine (1976) point out, humorists tend to have more social power than others, and high-status persons use other-disparaging humor, whereas low-status persons use self-disparaging humor. Although I cannot state that the object of this text is to consciously raise the status of my female character by having her indulge in "other-disparaging humor," this may indeed be the case. And perhaps women readers have recognized and appreciated this inversion. The only thing that I can state with any degree of confidence regarding my use of humor is that I agree with Helene Cixous (1981:55) that it is time for women to turn to humor in order "to replace the tears that culture has caused women to shed," and that through humor I have been able to broach taboo topics, to poke fun at a variety of discourses and, not infrequently, at myself. That humor offers such rich possibilities and a sound antidote for the ambiguities inherent in writing from the margins has been the most important discovery in my search for a voice.

REFERENCES

Ashcroft, B., G. Griffiths, & H. Tiffin. (1989). *The Empire Writes Back: Theory and Practice in Post-Colonial Literatures.* London and New York: Routledge.

Brito, A. (1976). *El diablo en Texas: Literatura chicana.* Tucson: Editorial Peregrinos.

Cisneros, S. (1984). *The House on Mango Street.* Houston: Arte Público Press.

Cixous, H. (1981). Castration and decapitation. *Signs* 7 (1), 41–55.

Eco, U. (1985). *Postscript to the Name of the Rose.* Trans. William Weaver. New York: Harcourt Brace.

Gonzales-Berry. E. (1991). *Paletitas de guayaba.* Albuquerque: El Norte Publications.

Hutcheon, L. (1980). *Narcissistic Narrative: The Metafictional Paradox.* New York: Methuen.

Irigaray, L. (1983). Interview. In J. Todd (ed.), *Women Writers Talking* (pp. 231–245). New York: Holmes & Meier.

Levine, J. B. (1976). The feminine routine. *Journal of Communication* 26 (3), 173–175.

McGhee, P. (1976). Sex differences in children's humor. *Journal of Communication* 26 (3), 176–189.

Memi, A. (1965). *The Colonizer and the Colonized.* Trans. Howard Greenfield. New York: Orion Press.

Morales, A. (1975). *Caras viejas y vino viejo.* México, D.F.: J. Moritz.

Ostriker, A. (1982). The thieves of language: Women poets and revisionist myth-making. *Signs* 8 (1), 68–90.

Rebolledo, T. D. (1985). Walking the thin line: Humor in Chicana literature. In M. Herrera-Sobek (ed.), *Beyond Stereotypes: The Critical Analysis of Chicana Literature* (pp. 91–107). Binghamton, NY: Bilingual Press.

Valenzuela, L. (1982). Mis brujas favoritas. In G. Mora & K. Van Hooft (eds.), *Theory and Practice of Feminist Literary Criticism* (pp. 88–95). Ypsilanti, MI: Bilingual Press.

8

◆ ◆ ◆

SACRED CULTS, SUBVERSIVE ICONS

Chicanas and the Pictorial Language of Catholicism

Charlene Villaseñor Black

Even the most cursory review of contemporary Chicana art reveals that pictorial discourses of Catholicism pervade the genre. Images of the Virgin of Guadalupe, references to the Mexican home altar tradition, and depictions of grinning *calaveras* [skeletons] from Día de los Muertos are almost omnipresent. Scholars and critics, however, have long neglected the language of Catholic imagery in the work of Chicana artists. Consequently, the significance of Catholic icons in contemporary Chicana cultural production remains largely an enigma. This essay attempts to unravel this mystery through examination of this rich system of coded signs and the specific methods by which it is manipulated by Chicana artists. Case studies of four women artists currently residing in Albuquerque, New Mexico, demonstrate that Chicanas manipulate the visual language of Catholicism to a variety of ends: to articulate their identities as Chicanas, to question and re-create traditional gender constructions, to valorize and empower themselves as women, to record and validate their family histories, and to propose political change. In the hands of Chicana artists, Catholic imagery participates in contemporary discourses of gender, race, and social class.

Upon first glance, Chicanas' manipulation of the visual rhetoric of traditional religious imagery appears to subvert the Catholic Church's centuries-old control over artistic production. As Peterson's (1992) study of the imagery of the Virgin of Guadalupe clearly demonstrates, however, artists, patrons, and beholders have always manipulated Catholic imagery to a variety of political ends.[1] The set of coded signs that compose Catholic iconography, like any language, is not fixed but changes to respond to specific circumstances. Scholars are only now beginning to trace and unravel the refashioning of Catholic pictorial discourses throughout history. Therefore, contemporary cultural production is ripe for the following analysis.

Although Catholic imagery and discourses are predominant features of Chicana artistic production, one should not oversimplify the inquiry. Chicana visual language, like its verbal counterpart, Chicano Spanish, is composed of a variety of pictorial choices and strategies arising from the multicultural origins of Chicana identity. Chicana artists choose from among the many different representational strategies of the North American, European, Mexican, Chicano, Native American, and Mesoamerican visual traditions to articulate their identities. In other words, Chicana visual language, like Chicano Spanish, is multidialectical.[2] It crosses the borders of various pictorial traditions, paralleling Chicano Spanish, which, as theorized by Gloria Anzaldúa (1987), traverses the linguistic borders of English, Spanish, Tex-Mex, and Nahuatl. Thus, this essay analyzes the variety of representational languages open to Chicana artists and posits that language, in this case pictorial language, is a major site for the articulation of Chicana identity. In addition, this study asserts that Chicana visual language expresses cultural identity and solidarity as it consciously positions Chicana artists outside of mainstream postmodern movements.

Scholars have not previously attempted a sustained scholarly analysis of the pictorial languages of Chicana art or of the importance of Catholic discourses in Chicana cultural production. Instead, academicians have been engaged since the 1960s in (1) documenting the Mesoamerican legacy in Chicano art; (2) establishing Chicano muralism's ties to Mexican Social Realism; and (3) situating the muralist movement within Marxist lineages.[3] Although these directions have naturally arisen from studies of the Mexican Muralist Movement and *"los tres grandes"* (Rivera, Orozco, and Siqueiros), the time has come to consider other appropriate approaches, particularly to the art of Chicanas, whose voices have often been excluded from art historical discourse.

The reluctance of art historians and critics to analyze religious icons in Chicana art, however, is not surprising, given the Catholic Church's long legacy of colonization and oppression in Latin America. In addition, many scholars fail to understand the historical power, importance, and centrality of such images in Mexican Catholic culture. Images of saints are central to Catholic worship and serve to spur devotion. The devotion shown to an image by a worshiper transfers to the heavenly prototype depicted. The Church has repeatedly asserted the importance and necessity of its icons, symbols that have played key roles since the Church's inception.[4] Scholars who work on Chicana visual culture often fail to understand the nuances and importance of Catholic discourses in Chicana art.

Several trailblazing studies of Chicana art have laid important groundwork. The art historian Shifra Goldman, through two key works (1985, 1994), signaled the importance of the figural mode, describing Chicana art as "overwhelmingly representational" in character. She briefly pointed out the influence of the "vernacular art of the Southwest" and in particular of "home altars and the smaller *nichos* [religious niches] which are created and tended by women" (1985:194). The critic and artist Amalia Mesa-Bains (1990) penned the first comprehensive characterization of Chicana art, singling out the general traits of narrative, domesticity, social critique, and the ceremonial in the work of Chicana artists. Although her broad characterization has served as an important first step, additional research is necessary to address adequately the importance and specificity of the language of Catholicism in Chicana art.

A more recent study by Alicia Gaspar de Alba (1998), which focuses on the cultural politics of the seminal 1990–1993 exhibition *Chicano Art: Resistance and Affirmation, 1965–1985 (CARA),* initiates critical analysis not only of the content but also of the display and reception of Chicana art. She provides a historical overview of Chicana art from the 1960s and 1970s, positing the creation of a working-class Chicana aesthetic distinguished by the themes of "motherhood, regeneration, and female ancestry," as well as "iconography from Catholic ritual and pre-Columbian mythology" (1998:132–133). In addition, Gaspar de Alba's study contains one of the first significant analyses of Chicana lesbian imagery in the visual arts.

An exception to the general neglect of Chicana art is the scholarly attention given to the work of Yolanda López, the pioneering Chicana artist whose portraits and self-portraits of women as the Virgin of Guadalupe serve as the point of departure for many contemporary artists' elaborations of Catholic iconographies (see *CARA*:63, 136–137, cat. nos. 103–105; Chabram-Dernersesian 1992). Goldman (1990b:171) describes these images as "divested of any religious intent," a characterization consistent with López's self-identification as an atheist (1998a, 1998b). But we should not dismiss López's manipulation of the language of Catholicism as the object of scholarly inquiry. Although her imagery may not be Catholic in intent, her subversion and manipulation of traditional religious icons is both purposeful and traceable to a tradition of politicized and even playful subversion in Catholic art.

In fact, Catholic icons are almost omnipresent in the art of Chicanas. Why is this so? How and why are women artists claiming and reinventing this imagery? What kinds of meanings does this imagery produce—spiritual, cultural, subversive? What gender ideologies are being encoded in this imagery? I will consider these questions by examining the work of four contemporary New Mexican artists: Elena Baca, Lydia Madrid, Delilah Montoya, and María Baca.

ELENA BACA

Elena Baca, a native New Mexican printmaker, manipulates the language of Spanish Colonial religious icons in her artwork, which treats such themes as human suffering and redemption, her family's history and legacy, and her own identity as a Nuevo Mexicana. Through her reclamation and reiteration of the imagery of Catholic saints, Baca subverts and re-creates traditional gender ideologies. One may best observe Baca's re-use of the language of Spanish Catholicism in her self-portraits and her portraits of family members, especially in her series of works portraying her grandmother. *Portrait of My Grandmother,* a nonsilver photographic print from 1994, presents the family matriarch in the guise of the Christ of Sorrows (fig. 8.1). Depicting her grandmother as a bust-length figure with eyes raised to heaven, adorned with both a halo and a crown of thorns, Baca constructs her as the Man of Sorrows, the image of Christ at the moment of his greatest humiliation—after the scourging, mocking, and crowning with thorns. Her expression pensive and long-suffering, she is fashioned as the Christ of the "Ecce Homo" [Behold the Man!] sequence of John 19:4–6.[5]

Baca's moving homage to her grandmother, after whom she was named, is firmly rooted in her family's history. The mother of eight children, Elena Baca the Elder dedicated her life to caring for two invalids— her institutionalized son, Miguelito (or Michelo), and her husband, Juan. Her halo, which subsumes the crown of thorns, testifies to the Catholic conception of the redemptive quality of suffering. As Christ's physical

Figure 8.1. Elena Baca, *Portrait of My Grandmother,* 1994. Cyanotype. Artist's collection, Albuquerque, New Mexico. Photograph by Delilah Montoya.

suffering and sacrifice redeemed humanity, so her grandmother's suffering was the salvation of the family. Thus, Baca makes sense of her family's travails by using the language of Catholicism.

Baca's grandmother is portrayed again in *Atocha Dream* (1996), a five-color lithograph that is a hybrid portrait/self-portrait (fig. 8.2).[6] The composition consists of a large upside-down cross seen against a cream-

Figure 8.2. Elena Baca, *Atocha Dream,* 1996. Lithograph. Author's collection, Albuquerque, New Mexico. Photograph by Delilah Montoya.

colored background with gold constellations and clouds. Baca's own image appears in the bottom half of the cross. On axis with the self-portrait, the elderly grandmother Elena appears in the top of the cross. They are inextricably linked, positioned anagrammatically. The upside-down cross and the alignment of the two portraits encourage the beholder to read the image as an anagram and to contemplate the visual and verbal puns of Elena-Elena and Grandmother-Self.

In this image, Baca recasts the language of Spanish Colonial religious art to situate herself as heir to her grandmother's wisdom and suffering. Specifically, she fashions herself in the guise of the Santo Niño de Atocha [Holy Child of Atocha], an image of the seated Jesus dressed as a pilgrim that is renowned for curing illnesses and as the patron of prisoners (Nunn 1993; Lange 1978). This devotional cult is important throughout Mexico and New Mexico, with major centers in Zacatecas and Chimayó. Against the backdrop of Albuquerque's Sandía Mountains, Baca presents herself with the attributes of the Holy Child. Like the Christ Child, Baca is seated in a frontal position, a pose long associated with wisdom in the context of the Catholic Church.[7] In her left hand she holds a crutch, which substitutes for Jesus' staff, and her right hand supports a "crown of thorns" gourd.

Baca's grandmother floats above her in the dark, starry night. Stars issue from her upraised left hand and flow into the surrounding space, linking her to Baca as the source of identity and strength. The stars create constellations in the form of a crown and a rocking chair, "grandmotherly" attributes. In the bottom half of the composition, a heart, symbolic of love, and a butterfly, representing transformation, flank Baca's image.

The positions of the two figures in this family portrait point to another major theme in Baca's work, the passage of wisdom from the old to the young. The alignment of the images of the two Elenas locates Baca as heir to her grandmother's roles of caretaker and sufferer, as does the use of the Holy Child of Atocha iconography. Furthermore, the "crown of thorns" gourd held in her right hand refers to the redemptive nature of suffering.

Baca's self-fashioning as a saint, while clearly modeled on the life of her grandmother, also reflects personal tragedy in her own life. As a child, sickness seemed a normal part of family life to Baca: "Growing up, some children hear heroic war stories or tales of walking in twenty feet of snow to school. I heard stories of sickness," she has written (E. Baca 1996:4). As a child, she accompanied her grandmother every Friday to visit her disabled Uncle Michelo in the Training Hospital at Los Lunas, New Mexico. Baca's grandfather suffered for years from Parkinson's disease and eventually died in a hospital in Las Vegas, New Mexico.

In retrospect, Baca's *Atocha Dream* seems hauntingly appropriate, for the years 1995 and 1996 were spent caring for sick and dying relatives and friends. In December 1995, her Aunt Agnes was admitted to the hospital. Baca spent Christmas caring for her, a reversal of their traditional roles: "When I was a child she took care of me while my mom worked. She braided my hair, walked me to kindergarten, and made us fried baloney and mustard sandwiches for lunch. Now it was my turn to care for her" (E. Baca 1996:3). Shortly thereafter, two friends died of AIDS.

As a result of a serious car accident in 1995, Baca herself experienced intense physical suffering. *Atocha Dream* comments upon the accident and the long physical recuperation that followed it. The crutch she holds in *Atocha Dream* symbolizes her strength and triumph over physical suffering. Significantly, it replaces the staff of the Holy Child of Atocha, a sign of guardianship and pilgrimage. Thus, as a result of her physical suffering, Baca has earned the roles of caregiver and patroness of the sick, roles ultimately inherited from her grandmother. "Some things you just have to go through . . . really beautiful things can come from suffering" (E. Baca 1997).

By depicting herself as the Christ Child or her grandmother as the Christ of Sorrows, Baca claims for Chicana women the redemptive powers of suffering, thereby valorizing Chicanas' traditional roles in new ways. But while concerned with women's issues, Baca, like many Chicanas, regards mainstream feminism as insensitive to Chicanas. To her, feminism is "unrealistic" and "unnecessary." "I come from a family of strong women. My grandmother had eight kids, five girls. My family is very female-oriented. . . . My mom raised me as a single parent. . . . This was the norm when I grew up" (E. Baca 1997).

Family history and identity, saintliness and suffering, losses and memories, the passage of wisdom from one generation to the next—these are the themes of Baca's art. Taken as a whole, they articulate her identity as a native Nuevo Mexicana. Perhaps no work expresses Baca's regional New Mexican identity like her 1993 *Milagros* print series. Printed on white paper in blues, brown, and gold, collaged snapshots of her family and other nostalgic mementos appear amidst images of her grandmother's and her own hands. They proudly record and chronicle the history of Baca's rural working-class New Mexican family.

Illness and suffering are major themes in the series. The sixth print, which features an old snapshot of Baca's ailing grandfather, poignantly gives visual form to what the artist calls "the beauty of the grotesque" (fig. 8.3; E. Baca 1997). Her grandfather's gaunt figure, propped up in a wheelchair, is one of great pathos. A handwritten prayer, perhaps written on his

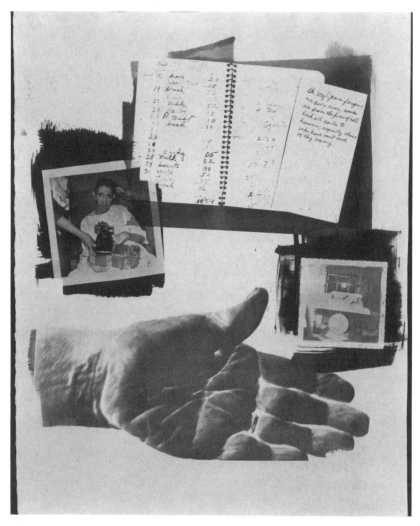

Figure 8.3. Elena Baca, *Milagros: #6,* 1993. Cyanotype. Artist's collection, Albuquerque, New Mexico. Photograph by Delilah Montoya.

behalf, also appears. It reads: "Oh my Jesus forgive us our sins, save us from the fires of hell, lead all souls to heaven, especially those who have most need of thy mercy." Next to the prayer is a mundane record of daily existence, a page from a small spiral notebook listing expenses for bread, milk, garlic, and other necessities. The large image of her grandmother's hand is placed at the bottom of the scene, a photographic signature.

The seventh print depicts Baca's Uncle Michelo looking out from

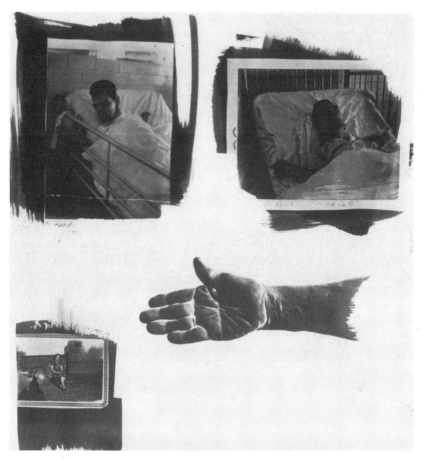

Figure 8.4. Elena Baca, *Milagros: #7,* 1993. Cyanotype. Artist's collection, Albuquerque, New Mexico. Photograph by Delilah Montoya.

behind the bars of his hospital bed in another moving image of illness (fig. 8.4). The snapshot unapologetically records his physical and mental disabilities. He appears in another photo, labeled "Miguel Baca 10–69," in an eerie, Christlike pose. Below is the hand of his mother, the artist's grandmother, testifying to her years of caring for him. The loving acceptance of the sick seen here speaks to a particularly Catholic notion of charity and the redemptive nature of caring for the less fortunate. Significantly, it is a concern with a long history in Spanish art, the most famous expression of which would be the "dwarf" portraits of the Golden Age court artist Diego Velázquez.[8]

Through the inclusion of family souvenirs such as snapshots, her grandmother's handwritten prayers to the Madonna, and her grandfather's farm accounts, Baca's family members became artists working in conjunction with her. Thus, Baca blurs here the distinction between fine art and vernacular forms of expression. Simultaneously, she elevates the most humble details of her family's existence, even the financial accounts that proudly and matter-of-factly record her family's rural origins. The chance drips of color framing the collaged objects lend an accidental quality to her work and remind the viewer of the chance accidents of life.

Baca's work validates and records her family's history as it examines the intersections of physical suffering and personal identity. In her images, her grandmother is omnipresent, the powerful yet saintly matriarch. By chronicling and constructing her family's past, Baca's images create her present reality and identity. "I like telling stories, but my way of doing it is a visual way." As the keeper of the family's history and Catholic devotions, Baca performs roles traditionally assigned to Chicana women in the family. These roles have become increasingly important as her grandmother ages and begins to lose her memory. In addition, Baca has begun recounting the family history verbally to her Aunt Agnes, who suffers from memory loss. One day her aunt lamented to Baca, "It's too bad someone couldn't just write it all down" (E. Baca 1997). Baca is doing just that in her prints. Her desire to chronicle her family's history and to do so in a representational manner places her within the tradition of Chicana art outlined by Mesa-Bains (1990).

The representational strategies and imagery employed by Baca clearly situate her within the continuing tradition of Spanish Colonial art. These strategies include the attempts to replicate the effects of reality, the elaboration of Catholic signs and symbols, and the elevation of vernacular forms of expression to the level of high art. Baca's artwork displays her identification with her Spanish past. Her self-identification is not unusual in the context of New Mexico, where many people of Spanish/Native American descent identify as Hispano, and where the artistic and linguistic legacies of Spanish colonialism persist to this day.

LYDIA MADRID

One finds a diametrically different pictorial language in the work of Lydia Madrid, a politically active multimedia artist who has exhibited all over the country and is currently a professor at the University of New Mexico.

In contrast to Baca's reworkings of Spanish Colonial pictorial languages, Madrid's enigmatic, deeply personal, and profoundly suggestive imagery focuses on the indigenous roots of Chicano Catholicism as it draws upon Native American discursive practices. This approach has been labeled "Chicano Neoindigenism" by Goldman and Ybarra-Frausto (1990). Madrid's art, however, is unusual in the context of Chicana cultural production because it transforms Native American visual languages into a state of almost pure abstraction. While the viewer is free to respond to her images as pure form, Chicano or Native American viewers are likely to find numerous recognizable points of reference. "A person with non-Western experience can understand my art, especially the space. You can't approach it with only a knowledge of Italian art. There are significant differences between Western and non-Western expressions and perceptions of space" (Madrid 1997a). Madrid's compositions are spacious and minimalist. The surfaces are articulated by large patches of stained color, carved indentations, pencil lines, and pictographic symbols. In imitation of indigenous pictorial modes, the viewer's eye is free to roam Madrid's images, to meditate upon the symbols.[9] According to Madrid, it takes time for the beholder to uncover and decode the various political references in her art.

Madrid's enigmatic approach is aptly demonstrated by her four wood panels executed in mixed-media drawing: *Wood: A según te lo digan* [Wood: As It Is Told to You]; *Ocean: A según lo hagan* [Ocean: As It Is Made/Done]; *Navigation: Reading the Water;* and *Trailblazing: Reading the Ground.* The first two panels function as a pair. Stylistically, they cross the visual borders of Native American, Mesoamerican, and Spanish Colonial pictorial languages. In conscious imitation of indigenous representational modes, pictographic objects are scattered across the pictorial fields of both panels. Similarly, the use of line and color emphasizes the two-dimensional. Even their titles demonstrate Madrid's crossing of linguistic borders through her use of both English and Spanish.

A pair of brown walking sticks and a white arrowhead dominate the first panel, *Wood: A según te lo digan* (fig. 8.5). The meaning or identification of these shapes, however, is not stable. The walking sticks (the "wood" of the title?) also read as pilgrims' staffs, a wishbone, or twigs to start a fire (stylized red flames appear below). The positioning of the white arrowhead is similarly precarious. Its shape is reminiscent of the Aztec obsidian knife and even reads as a heart, a particularly multilingual

Figure 8.5. Lydia Madrid, *Wood: A según te lo digan,* 1996. Mixed media drawing and carving on wood panel. Artist's collection, Albuquerque, New Mexico. Photograph by Delilah Montoya.

sign in Mexican culture, since, depending on your point of view, it can reference either indigenous heart sacrifice or the Spanish Colonial cult of the Sacred Heart. In fact, because Madrid's heart bears a small red gash on its right side, it seems more strongly associated with Catholic heart worship (Montoya 1994; Sussman 1991; Sebastián 1989). In the artist's words, "It doesn't stay put" (Madrid 1997a).

Below the white arrow/heart/blade, other enigmatic shapes challenge the beholder. Most important, a large black *nudo* [knot] appears here, a symbol that recurs frequently in Madrid's art. According to the artist, the knots represent labyrinths or paths. More metaphorically, they refer to relationships, self-perception, the process of becoming. The paths represented by the knots, the landscape, and the walking sticks point to the theme of travel in this work. Travelers and intercessors are major themes in Madrid's art. A playful word association in Spanish is inscribed on the bottom left: *"nudo desnudo"* [nude knot].

These objects appear within a very open, spacious composition. Madrid intentionally incorporates the open spaces as "conversational" or "transitional" spaces. She describes this process grammatically. For her, identifiable objects are like nouns; open spaces are like verbs: "Nouns stop time. . . . A lot of Western art is about nouns. . . . Identifying objects isn't what it's about" (Madrid 1997a). The spaces in her compositions, which allow the eye to roam freely, indicate activity, movement, transitions.

The other panel, *Ocean: A según lo hagan,* features as its main element a blue boat, seen from below, that glides into the panel from the top of the composition (fig. 8.6). Its form responds to the white heart/blade seen in the *Wood* panel. According to Madrid, the boat also represents the sacrificial obsidian blade of the Aztecs (as does the white heart). To the left is a black-and-white checker pattern, a reference to Native American landscape. On the right, a black curved shape depicts the celestial dome of the indigenous cosmos. At the bottom of the panel, the black remains of a charred boat appear to smolder. A stylized yellow zigzag that represents the plumed serpent Quetzalcoatl defines the right margin.

The numerous references to Quetzalcoatl, to boats, to Native American landscape, and to both Mesoamerican and Christian sacrifice demonstrate that one of the underlying themes of these panels is the Spanish conquest of the Americas. "The Conquest is a real interesting issue for me, because I have both sides in me. . . . I'm a real mutt. . . . I'm a mix in several ways—in language, in culture, and in my genealogy. But this allows me a foothold in a number of places. I understand both the indigenous and the European, but I have an indigenous attitude" (Madrid 1997a). The prominent knots also refer to the history of the Americas. "History is convoluted. . . . It's a real knot of things going on. It's a very hard thing to untie" (Madrid 1997a).

Two final works by Madrid further testify to the Neoindigenist orientation of her art. The three mixed-media drawings that compose her *Señor del Monte/mū Xandohu* triptych again cross the borders between Mesoamerican and Spanish Catholic pictorial languages, a strategy

Figure 8.6. Lydia Madrid, *Ocean: A según lo hagan,* 1996. Mixed media drawing and carving on wood panel. Artist's collection, Albuquerque, New Mexico. Photograph by Delilah Montoya.

indicated in the title itself, which juxtaposes the appellation of a specific Christ figure, Our Lord of the Mountain, with the Otomí name for the spirit of the same site. The first panel includes numerous Mesoamerican symbols, most prominently a large, stylized maguey plant in the bottom left. The second panel features a succulent red heart at the top, and below it, a handprint. These objects call to mind the Aztec goddess Coatlicue, who wears a necklace of hearts and hands.[10] The final panel of the triptych features a pair of Yaqui deer antlers emerging upside down from the top of the drawing and a stylized representation of Quetzalcoatl.

Madrid's art demonstrates the ways in which Chicana artists transform the pictorial language of indigenous art and, to a lesser degree, of
Spanish Colonial traditions. Her transformations are imaginative, especially when viewed in contrast to the heavy-handed quotations from
Mesoamerican art in early Chicano murals.[11] Although her compositions
may appear understated, even minimal, her representational strategies
are political in nature. The way in which the most important objects
literally cling to the margins of the images provides a commentary on
Madrid's feelings as a Chicana and on the current marginalized status of
Chicano and indigenous cultures in the United States. The empty spaces
left in the heart of her compositions also have personal meaning: "To have
this space at or near the center is also a reminder that a person's 'core' is
where strength lies—rather than around the edges. It also contradicts the
illusion that strength comes from the 'outside.' So the issue of 'margin' is
not just political, it is also personal. It isn't just general, it is specific and
focused. It's not just about how a Chicana lives in the world, but how I
live with myself" (Madrid 1997b).

Elena Baca and Lydia Madrid define the two poles of Chicana pictorial languages. Baca's imaginative reworkings of the language of Spanish
colonialism strongly contrast with Madrid's minimalist transformations
of indigenous symbols and pictorial strategies. The artists Delilah Montoya and María Baca stand somewhere in the middle of this continuum
of Chicana visual languages. Both insist on their mestiza heritage as
they search to create appropriate alternative visual languages for Chicana
artists.

DELILAH MONTOYA

Delilah Montoya is an artist, activist, and teacher currently residing in
Albuquerque, New Mexico, whose art explores issues of Chicana identity
and ideology from her viewpoint as a mestiza in "occupied America"
(Montoya 1996a). A photographic printmaker, she has lived and worked
as an artist in California, Colorado, and Nebraska, where she spent much
of her childhood. Her approach is deeply grounded in El Movimiento
Chicano, and she offers her work as a conscious alternative to mainstream
art. Yolanda López was a powerful mentor and example. "I formulated
and saw my identity as being a Chicana artist," Montoya (1996a) has

Figure 8.7. Delilah Montoya, *Saints and Sinners,* 1992. Multimedia installation exhibited in the New Mexico Museum of Fine Arts, Santa Fe. Photograph by Delilah Montoya.

written. Her art reflects her struggle to give definition to that identity. Consistent with her vision as a Chicana activist, Montoya's art always involves the community or the viewer in the creation of its message.

Saints and Sinners, exhibited in the New Mexico Museum of Fine Arts in 1992, explored the topic of Chicano spirituality, one of the major themes of Montoya's art (fig. 8.7). Inspired by her grandfather's life as a *penitente* in the *hermandad* [brotherhood] of the *morada* [chapel] of San Ysidro, near Las Vegas, New Mexico, it engaged themes of family, Chicano identity, and political activism.

Intrigued by her grandfather's spiritual life, Montoya made the acquaintance of a modern-day penitente, Juan Sandoval, the *hermano mayor* [head brother] and founder of San José, a morada in Albuquerque's South Valley. Under his tutelage, she gained an intimate understanding of the secretive penitente devotions. Her experience with him was vital, particularly since traditionally women have been denied access to the penitential brotherhoods of New Mexico.[12]

The installation featured a large mural-sized photograph of Montoya's New Mexican grandfather's morada that served as a backdrop for an altar arranged on the floor. The backdrop, which measured nine by seven and a half feet, was composed of composite prints of the morada's interior taken under different light conditions. Montoya reassembled the images, taken under either cold blue moonlight or the warm light of morning, into a grid. The grid, in turn, revealed within itself the image of a cross. The light of the right side, representative of Christ's "good" side, is mostly warm, in contrast with the cool left side, Christ's "bad" side. "The mural's theme is dualism: one side is night, sin, death, darkness, juxtaposed against day, grace, resurrection, light" (Montoya 1992:16).

The altar consisted of a shallow blue trapezoidal box filled with red Jemez sand and a black *banco* [bench or shelf] spray-painted with the word "SIN" to hold offerings. In the sacred space of the altar, Montoya arranged numerous glass jars, candles, and other devotional objects. Fourteen of the jars depicted the Stations of the Cross. On one level, Montoya's jars represented sinners' opportunity to be transmuted into saints through Christ's sacrifice on the cross.[13] Simultaneously, Montoya manipulated the contents of each jar to present a contemporary political commentary. The roots of her homemade altar lie in the long Mexican folk tradition of erecting personal and community altars, as well as in the Native American practice of appropriating the earth itself as a sacred space (Mesa-Bains 1990).

The objects in the jars metaphorically evoked the events of the Passion of Christ. For example, Jar 2, entitled *Christ Receives the Cross,* contained fishhooks that reminded the viewer of Christ's painfully torn flesh. The hooks can also be traced to a long-standing Christian tradition of figuring Christ as a fish.[14] Jar 2 also included weights to remind the viewer of Christ's great burden of the cross. Montoya made His sacrifice relevant to the Chicano community through the inclusion of a photograph of an hermano carrying a cross in a Holy Week procession.

Figure 8.8. Delilah Montoya, *Saints and Sinners: Jar #6, Veronica*, 1992. Detail of multimedia installation exhibited in the New Mexico Museum of Fine Arts, Santa Fe. Photograph by Delilah Montoya.

The jar representing Station 4, *"El Encuentro"* or the meeting between Christ and His mother, featured an image of the Christ Child, a photograph of a local grandmother and her grandson, a transparency of a dead fetus, and three red thorns. The transparency, taken during Montoya's ten-year career as a medical photographer, documented the accidental removal of a fetus from a heroin-addicted mother by doctors who thought the woman had a tumor (Montoya 1996b). The doctors' mistake not only caused the death of the fetus but also left the woman unable to bear children. Montoya's jar raised questions for the viewer: Was this heroin-addicted mother's loss any less painful than Mary's loss of her Son? Why did the doctors so eagerly cut into her womb? What did they feel at the loss of this woman's child?

The sixth jar, which represented the episode of Veronica wiping Christ's face, provided another pointed political commentary. It contained a *paño* [handkerchief] image of the "Veronica" created in ballpoint pen by a New Mexican prison inmate (fig. 8.8). The legendary Veronica, supposedly a woman on the road to Calvary, compassionately wiped the perspiration from Christ's face with her veil. As she did so, Christ's visage was miraculously imprinted upon the veil, or *sudarium*. The tale of Veronica, whose name derived from *vera icon,* or "true icon," is a story of the revelation of Christ (Hall 1974). Montoya's jar thus reminds the viewer that Christ revealed Himself to the lowest members of society, even to prisoners. In fact, one of the Seven Acts of Mercy, which are central to Catholic concepts of salvation, is visiting the incarcerated. Thus, this miraculous "true icon" rendered by a prisoner speaks on many levels. In addition, the viewer is thereby reminded of the disproportionate number of Chicanos in the penal system.

Montoya's arrangement of the installation invited the beholder to examine the jars closely and to posit connections between the arranged objects and the Stations of the Cross. Several of the jars included objects donated by Albuquerque's Chicano community, a strategy that literally implicated certain viewers, as well as one that elevated ordinary people to the level of participatory artists.[15] The arrangement of the installation encouraged the beholder not only to inspect the jars closely, but it also demanded that the spectator literally kneel before the cross of the backdrop to do so. Numerous viewers touched the objects, rearranged them, or even censored them. Montoya (1992:22) wrote,

> The jars drew people into a closer investigation of the piece. Some held the jars while examining the contents, others knelt on the floor to view the candles and objects placed on the altar. Several even repositioned the jars and lit candles while weaving their own stories of the scene. Someone even censored *The Third Fall of Christ* by removing the crucifix and syringe and pouring the ashes to the ground. Audience members continued interacting with the installation by removing a rosary

and emptying and taking the dog tags from the jar which discussed military life.

While the themes of *Saints and Sinners* clearly derived from traditional Catholic discourses and specifically referenced New Mexican penitential practices, Montoya's installation consciously offered an alternative Chicana artistic language. By emphasizing the indigenous and mestizo elements of Catholic practice, she elaborated the traditional New Mexican language of Spanish Colonial Catholicism. Her inclusion of everyday objects donated by the community and photographs of local Chicanos, and her pointed political commentaries demonstrated her activist orientation.

Another major theme in Montoya's work, one already seen in the art of Elena Baca, is the transmission of knowledge from one generation to the next. Indeed, the installation, which honored her grandfather, also commemorated the collaboration between Montoya and Juan Sandoval of the morada of San José. What was unusual about the generational relationships at the heart of this piece was that Montoya positioned herself as the recipient of knowledge traditionally denied women in New Mexico, that is, knowledge of the activities of the penitential brotherhoods. Like Baca, she has explained that she is uncomfortable with a feminist label. "I've always had a little difficulty with that. . . . I come from a very strong matriarchal family. I'm a strong matriarch. In my family, women have always been empowered" (Montoya 1996b).

Similar issues can be found in Montoya's collection of twenty-six collotypes entitled *El Corazón Sagrado/The Sacred Heart* (1994).[16] The series, which began for Montoya as a historical investigation into the syncretic cultural icon of the Sacred Heart, portrays Albuquerque's Chicano community in a series of portraits staged against spray-painted murals by local aerosol artists. She assembled the series of twenty-six photographs into four groups that reflect different aspects of the cult of the Sacred Heart: the duality of life and death; the passions of the heart; love; and syncretism.

For Montoya, the Sacred Heart is the perfect expression of Chicano identity because it was forged during the violent *encuentro* of Spanish and Mesoamerican cultures in the sixteenth century. Because the Sacred Heart produces meaning in both a European and an Indian religious context, it stands for the process of *mestizaje* that formed Chicano culture.

Because of its syncretic nature, the Sacred Heart legitimizes all mestizos (Montoya 1996b).

The nineteenth-century collotype technique she employs lends her photographs a nostalgic quality. "As a cultural icon, the Sacred Heart endured in the hearts and minds of Chicanos for at least four centuries, giving the image an ageless quality" (Montoya 1994:10). The use of collotype also gives her images an air of historical authority designed to authorize the Chicano histories she has constructed. She further legitimizes her images by exploiting the camera's ability to record detail and thereby suggest facticity. Montoya, however, turns upside down facile assumptions about the "objectivism" of the camera lens and the "truth" it supposedly reveals.

> As an artist who is committed to revealing the topography of Aztlán through synoptic judgment, my viewpoint as the photographer, subject, and observer is a combination of insight and blindness, reach and limitation. Impartiality and bias together do not achieve omniscience, nor a unified master narrative, but rather a complex understanding of ever-changing multifaceted social realities. Since culture shapes reality we must recognize that the reality being addressed is filtered through the photographer's viewpoint. A question of paramount importance, then, is: How is the community's reality being represented? (1994:10–11)

The community's collaboration was a vital ingredient in the *Corazón Sagrado* series because it validated the series as a "part of our collective conscious. . . . My approach in representing the *Corazón Sagrado* as a cultural icon was to invite the community to collaborate with me in the realization of the project," a process of "creative interdependence" (Montoya 1994:11). Three dancers executed stylized poses and gestures in front of mural backdrops painted by local aerosol artists.[17] Montoya's collaboration with the aerosol artists, many associated with Albuquerque gangs, was both personal and political.

> The city was after these kids . . . they felt they had no future. These were real artists with integrity. They had sketchbooks and theories and ideas. They had mentors. Their art was very postmodern. They were true collaborators, working with each

other. They constantly reworked their own images; their walls were continually changing. I gave them a safe space to work in. We needed to give them solidarity. (Montoya 1997)

Montoya's portraits combine the language of Spanish Colonial religious imagery, nineteenth-century photographic technique, and the stylized *placas* [tags] of Chicano youth street culture. The placas serve as geographical markers that claim the space depicted (Sánchez-Tranquilino 1995). For example, *La Muerte and Infinity* depicts two figures placed against a spray-painted backdrop in a scene based upon the long tradition of *vanitas* [emptiness] imagery (fig. 8.9). Vanitas images, which contrast the transitory nature of life with the certainty of death, often encode gender ideologies that associate women with sex, sin, and mortality. The figure on the left is dressed as Doña Sebastiana, the New Mexican figure of death *(la muerte)*. She faces the viewer, her right hip thrust out seductively in a grotesque *contrapposto,* her long hair covering her shoulders. Her face is the macabre mask of the grinning calavera. Allusions to Doña Sebastiana's former beauty suggest to the viewer the transitory quality of life and link women's beauty to mortality.[18] La muerte has come for the young man on the right, who is poised to exit the scene. On the back of his T-shirt is the image of the Sacred Heart of Christ, which reappears in the open doorway and on the face of the clock on the backdrop. A spray-painted text, "TIMEZ UP," flanks his image.

Several of Montoya's other portraits demonstrate her translation of traditional religious imagery into a contemporary Chicano idiom. *La Familia* represents a local Chicano family as the Holy Family. Similarly, Montoya's cousin and her baby are valorized as the Madonna and Child in the portrait of that name. In *Jesús' Carburetor Repair,* the figure of Jesús labors at a workbench in a scene reminiscent of baroque images of St. Joseph in the carpenter's workshop. In *God's Gift* the sacrifice of Christ is made relevant to the contemporary beholder. A long-haired male figure, back to the viewer, faces the wall, his arms out in the pose of the Crucifixion. The figure wears a white shroudlike drapery from the waist down, clearly modeled on the loincloth, or *sendal,* worn by Mexican images of Christ.

The paired images of La Malinche and El Matachín portray characters from the New Mexican fiesta of the Matachines (figs. 8.10 and 8.11). They comment upon syncretism as they question traditional gender and

Figure 8.9. Delilah Montoya, *La Muerte and Infinity,* 1994. Collotype. Artist's collection, Albuquerque, New Mexico. Photograph by Delilah Montoya.

racial ideologies. The first depicts the controversial figure of La Malinche, or Doña Marina, the "mistress" of the conquistador Hernán Cortés. Although she has long been condemned as the traitor who betrayed the Indians to the Spanish, Chicana feminists recently have been reevaluating her as a figure of strength, intelligence, and subversion.[19] Montoya's image of her comments on the gender constructs that confine Chicanas to the roles of virgin (the Virgin of Guadalupe) or whore (La Malinche). The portrait features an eleven-year-old girl wearing her white First Communion dress, rosary in her hands, against a sumptuous curtained setting. In contrast to the girl's virginal white dress, the ornate setting is reminiscent of a brothel. Montoya intentionally stressed this dichotomy. The girl is poised to enter womanhood, "at that liminal stage between kitten and cat," and thus her very physicality undermines the gender construct (Montoya 1996b).

La Malinche is paired with El Matachín, the *moro* [Moor] from the New Mexican fiesta. Montoya brings alive the myth of the Matachín by posing a Nigerian runner as the mythical "Moor." He stands before a

Figure 8.10. Delilah Montoya, *La Malinche,* 1994. Collotype. Artist's collection, Albu-querque, New Mexico. Photograph by Delilah Montoya.

tapestry of the brown-skinned Virgin of Guadalupe, displacing her figure, a juxtaposition that calls attention to the issue of race in the Americas. In front of the Matachín, a candle honoring the *Mano Poderosa* [Powerful Hand] flickers. This is a devotion to the hand of Christ popular in north-ern Mexico. Upon each of His five fingers is a member of the Holy Family. The choice of this particular candle is especially apropos because the

Figure 8.11. Delilah Montoya, *El Matachín,* 1994. Collotype. Artist's collection, Albuquerque, New Mexico. Photograph by Delilah Montoya.

hand is a syncretic sacred symbol with a long history in Muslim, Jewish, and Christian cultures.

Clearly, the language of Spanish Colonial religious art is central in Montoya's works. Her early works, however, rarely referenced religious iconographies, and it was only upon her return to New Mexico in 1980 that these issues began to surface in her art. This is not surprising, since the legacy of Spanish Colonial Catholicism is surprisingly strong in New Mexico, the only state to preserve a living tradition of *santero* art (Gavin 1994; Steele 1994; Varjabedian & Wallis 1994). Montoya, however, is philosophical about the role of religious iconographies in the pictorial languages of Chicana artists. She has remarked that Chicana artists are expected to produce religious art. While these images express and affirm Chicana cultural identity, saints' images are also "seemingly very safe . . . they aren't highly politically charged in the outside culture" (Montoya 1996b). Nonetheless, as evidenced in Montoya's art, the language of saints' imagery can encode covert power systems designed to prevent assimilation into the mainstream. As proposed in the opening of this essay, the system of coded signs that compose the language of Catholic religious art is easily manipulated to encode subversive commentaries on contemporary political issues.

MARÍA BACA

Like Delilah Montoya, María Baca is an artist and dedicated community activist whose work insists upon the mestizo and the indigenous sides of Catholic culture. She has thought deeply about the process of mestizaje and is eloquent on the subject of racism: "My paintings have been a deep healing process for my own psyche, a healing process from the legacies of racism. As mestizos we've all experienced the pain of conquest. I have learned the healing power of symbols through my work. Native American sandpainting ceremonies which heal the whole person have been a source of inspiration."[20] She added: "The most painful thing in my life is that I'm tricultural. I'm indigenous. I'm the Spanish conqueror. And then I live in a predominantly Anglo society." Baca feels that in many ways she was destined to be a healer. Artists, who live "between the cracks" as outsiders looking in, have a special ability to reflect the culture, to be the conduits of culture. Furthermore, Baca has spent her life as an observer: "Because of my visible Native American features, I was virtually invisible. I became an observer instead of a participant" (M. Baca 1997b). Baca has exhibited internationally. Currently, however, she refuses to sell her paintings in galleries. "Earlier I sold in galleries, but galleries took power away from my work. My paintings were going into a black hole and were robbed of their power [because they were being sold to private collectors].

I want people to see these paintings. These paintings are for the community, to help the healing process in the community" (M. Baca 1997b).

Interestingly, Baca's paintings employ the language of European fine art. She is heir to the post-Impressionist legacies of Paul Cézanne, whom she cites as a strong influence, and Pablo Picasso's Cubism. She works primarily in acrylics on canvas (or sometimes paper) but also in tempera and oils and has executed prints. In the tradition of the great "painterly" artists of Spain, such as El Greco and Diego Velázquez, or Venice's Titian, Baca works directly on the canvas, a technique that encourages bravura brushwork, spontaneity, and vitality. She often collages fabrics onto the canvas or builds up the pigment by adding plasters to produce highly textured impastos, effects heightened by her use of loosely woven canvas. Because acrylics dry quickly, they allow Baca to build up many luminous layers on the canvas. Baca's layers record the history of the piece. "Many of my paintings contain several other earlier paintings beneath the visible top layer" (M. Baca 1997b).

Baca uses religious icons in her paintings to offer solutions to problems in the community. Two canvases from 1996, *God Grant Me the Serenity* and *Puentes/Bridges,* were inspired by the struggles of parents raising children in Albuquerque's crime-ridden neighborhoods, amid the violence of drugs and gangs (figs. 8.12 and 8.13). In *God Grant Me the Serenity* the viewer looks down upon three women around a kitchen table, in the domestic heart of the home, drinking tea and drying the dishes. Bars on the window indicate that they are trapped, prisoners in their own home due to neighborhood violence. But they themselves have invited the violence into their home. On the left a television eerily glows with a scene of a gunman. The images of the Virgin of Guadalupe and the cross, visible in the background, are static, powerless icons in the face of the television. The dreamy quality of the scene, created through the painterly application of soft, rich colors, emphasizes the passivity and powerlessness of the women. They exist in slow motion. The young woman seated at the table crosses her arms in resignation while the standing figure looks up dreamily as she dries the dishes. The Cubist perspective contributes to a sense of looming chaos. The crazy tilt of the back wall, where the viewer finds the Virgin of Guadalupe and the cross, emphasizes the instability of these icons. The title of the piece, *God Grant Me the Serenity,* ironically refers to the "Serenity Prayer" made popular by Alcoholics Anonymous:

Figure 8.12. María Baca, *God Grant Me the Serenity,* 1996. Acrylic on canvas. Artist's collection, Albuquerque, New Mexico. Photograph by Delilah Montoya.

"God grant me the serenity to accept the things I cannot change, the courage to change the things I can, and the wisdom to know the difference." In the past, women in violence-wracked neighborhoods were often encouraged to pray. "Prayer should be the first step, but we have to take action" (M. Baca 1997b). The painting is thus meant as a warning, a Chicana call to arms. The grandmother figure at the table cranes her neck to turn and look up, imploring the viewer to take action.

Puentes/Bridges advocates acceptance of our indigenous roots as the solution to violence. It depicts a monumental, classical figure of a Spanish Catholic woman holding aloft a candle of hope. On the right is her indigenous son, who looks up to the figure of a Native American seed planter. Above his head a window reveals a building, representative of

Figure 8.13. María Baca, *Puentes/Bridges,* 1996. Acrylic on canvas. Artist's collection, Albuquerque, New Mexico. Photograph by Delilah Montoya.

the technology of the modern world. Two icons exist between mother and son: a Native American seed planter, rendered in blue and red, then re-imaged in negative on the floor, and a very indigenous-looking Virgin of Guadalupe. They are all bridges from one culture to the other: the woman, the boy, the Virgin, the seed planter. The separation and sadness of the mother and son indicate the need for these bridges.

In her work, María Baca consistently images the Virgin of Guada-lupe as strongly indigenous. "I deliberately paint her very indigenous. I was always criticized for looking 'india'—'negra e india.' . . . The Virgin of Guadalupe has become terribly significant to me because I truly under-stand what she represents" (M. Baca 1997b). The indigenous Guadalupe represents for Baca the pain she felt growing up looking Native American and her eventual acceptance of, and pride in, her indigenous beauty. La Guadalupana is "the tip of the iceberg of the indigenous world. Her roots are indigenous. She represents the unconscious" (M. Baca 1997b).

Baca's commentaries on the Virgin of Guadalupe have been profoundly influenced by the theories of the Swiss psychiatrist Carl Gustav Jung. She further explains the importance of the Guadalupana as a symbol of hope:

> The Virgin of Guadalupe has become significant to me because she represents the painful psyche of the whole territory. She is the visible metaphor for the feminine unconscious that is lacking on a continent beaten down by our animus. We have to go deeper than the theories of whether the Spanish introduced her to control the indigenous peoples or whether she was created to replace Tonantzin, an indigenous goddess. We must begin to understand through the collective unconscious the goddess vision surfacing in people's psyches. We cannot separate ourselves from our natural desire for balance of both the feminine and masculine. It has taken centuries to see the growth and resurfacing of the feminine nature. When a belief system is destroying Mother Earth, our feminine instinct must surface and save us from extinction. So we enter the new millennium with a new sense of spiritual consciousness that is directed by the anima of familiar balance many tribes understand intuitively. (M. Baca 1997a)

Thus, *Puentes* expresses the theme of the dangerous imbalances of the modern world. According to Baca, the imbalance of ego and instinct, conscious and unconscious, intellect and intuition, masculine and feminine, threaten our very existence. This explains the increasing alienation and violence of our society. The antidote is to reembrace our sacred, feminine, indigenous natures: "I see us in the future reembracing our indigenous religions. The future lies in our past" (M. Baca 1997b). In *Puentes,* Baca draws attention to the sacredness of indigenous religions by highlighting the seed planter with gold leaf.

Baca's realization that we as a society are destroying ourselves by privileging science, technology, and the intellect over the earth and nature is intimately linked to her acceptance of herself as an indigenous person. These processes of self-realization were accompanied by a pow-

Figure 8.14. María Baca, *Responding to Life's Forces,* 1996. Acrylic on canvas. Artist's collection, Albuquerque, New Mexico. Photograph by Delilah Montoya.

erful series of dreams. These dreams resulted in a series of "panther paintings" that chronicled Baca's ongoing voyage to self-knowledge. The first of this series was finished in 1994, shortly after Baca returned from her first trip to Mexico. Entitled *Initiation: Panther Ceremony,* it recorded Baca's initiation into her indigenous perspective. The painting depicts her in the foreground, lying on her back amid tall grasses. She wears a cat headdress and holds a cat in her arms; she has been possessed by the spirit of the panther. In the background are the masked corn mothers who have come to rescue and initiate her. For Baca the painting represented a seminal moment in her life and her art—her acceptance of her indigenous self.

The panther theme continued in two self-referential canvases from 1996. *Responding to Life's Forces* depicts a nude contorted female who literally bends over backward as a woman and as a Mexicana (fig. 8.14). For Baca, the nude figure is a sacred symbol, a metaphor for the powerful feminine consciousness. In the painting, the nude comes face to face with

Figure 8.15. María Baca, *Sweet Dreams of You,* 1996. Acrylic on canvas. Artist's collection, Albuquerque, New Mexico. Photograph by Delilah Montoya.

a panther mask surmounted by an image of the Virgin of Guadalupe. "Beneath the Virgin of Guadalupe lies the panther" (M. Baca 1997b). Similarly, *Sweet Dreams of You* depicts a woman supine on the back of a black panther, which she embraces (fig. 8.15). This painting, too, is self-referential. "At this moment I am the instinct, the unconscious" (M. Baca 1997b). Baca has written, "In the Catholic faith we believe in The Father, The Son, and The Holy Spirit. I have come to believe that Instinct is the Father (Father-Mother), the Son is the Intellect born out of Instinct. The Holy Spirit (the Intuitive) is our Awareness that we are interconnected to everything and everyone, which is the belief of the Native American."[21]

In addition to her paintings, Baca chronicles the process of self-realization in poetry. Her "Dream #1" encapsulates in text the process of accepting her indigenous heritage. This process is described in rich, sensuous language:

The rio puerco flowed
right thru my kitchen today

under my table and around my chairs
it just kept flowing
bringing with it
my past
treasures
in shapes of masks
wooden figures
clay creatures I could never imagine
It brought me messages
stories I couldn't recall
only in my dreams
when all was still and the night was so black and too deep
spirits came out caressing my blood
whispering in my ears
telling me secrets I couldn't remember in the light
wild spirits filling my breath with their presence
pumping visions freely thru my veins
images hanging heavy near the ground
like overripe plums waiting to be plucked.

(M. Baca 1996a)

According to Baca, only when we accept our past, our treasures, our spirits, and our masks will we be healed as a society. Her manipulation of the coded symbols of religious art reflects these beliefs. She transforms them into Nativist, feminist emblems and couches them in Jungian terms. They express hope for humanity, but our salvation does not result from the sacrifice of Christ. Rather, the redemption of humanity will come from devotion to His mother, Nuestra Señora de Guadalupe, who is both earth goddess and the will of the feminine unconscious.

CONCLUSION

This essay analyzes the pictorial languages of Chicana artists. Specifically, I have endeavored to demonstrate the centrality of the coded language of religious icons and the specific ways in which Chicanas manipulate Catholic discourses. The work of Elena Baca, which self-consciously references Spanish Colonial pictorial practices, subverts the traditionally gendered messages of saints' images to valorize Chicanas' traditional caretaker roles in new ways. Elena Baca also manipulates the coded signs of Catholic art to validate her family's history, and thus her own identity as a Chicana. Lydia Madrid's art is unusual in its rejection of the figural mode of representation. Her nearly abstract art crosses the borders of various visual languages: Spanish/Spanish Colonial, Mesoamerican, and Native American. Madrid's visual language demonstrates the flexibility and mutability of these various systems of signs. Like Chicano Spanish, Madrid's Chicana visual language is constantly in a state of re-creating itself. Delilah Montoya reworks traditional Catholic imagery to encode subversive political commentaries informed by the Chicano Movement. Her work questions anachronistic racial and gender ideologies. By exploiting the camera's ability to suggest facticity, Montoya seeks to document and legitimize Chicano histories. María Baca's art challenges New Mexican conceptions of Hispano identity by insisting on acceptance of the indigenous and mestizo legacies of Catholic culture. She manipulates religious imagery to emphasize the indigenous aspects of cults such as that of the Virgin of Guadalupe. María Baca attempts to empower Chicanas to challenge racism and injustice in the community.

The prominence of Catholic discourse in these four case studies may evidence a regional phenomenon rooted in the context of New Mexico. The vitality of such colonial institutions as religious brotherhoods and the Spanish Colonial Arts Society, which sponsors exhibitions of religious images in the santero tradition, testify to the territory's strong connection to its Spanish Colonial past, as described by Varjabedian and Wallis (1994) and Kalb (1994). Cursory examination of the art of Chicanas from areas other than New Mexico, however, suggests that Catholic icons are more central universally in the visual language of Chicana art. The importance of Catholic discourse is not surprising, given Chicanas' traditional roles in fostering religious devotion in the family. What is surprising, though, is the almost complete lack of attention directed to this issue in the scholarly literature.

Much additional research remains to be done. Further investigation and documentation of the significance of Catholic icons in Chicana culture are necessary, as is consideration of the gender, social, and political ideologies encoded in religious art. As the number of Chicanas in the United States continues to increase, studies of regional cultural production become increasingly important.

ACKNOWLEDGMENTS

I owe a special debt of gratitude to the editors of this volume, María Dolores Gonzales and D. Letticia Galindo. This essay could not have been written without the friendship and generosity of the four artists—Elena Baca, María Baca, Lydia Madrid, and Delilah Montoya—who unselfishly gave of their time to participate in numerous interviews and provide me with extensive access to their work and inspiration. In addition, Delilah Montoya photographed all of the works of art. My colleague Geoffrey Batchen graciously took the time to comment on drafts and helped me refine my thinking on the language of Catholic imagery. My husband, Jamie Green, a lawyer by trade and editor by default, patiently and astutely edited this essay numerous times. ¡Mil gracias!

NOTES

1. The participation of religious imagery in political discourses has been examined most successfully for art produced in the sixteenth through eighteenth centuries. See Steinberg (1983), Peterson (1993), and Black (1995).

2. My thinking on Chicana pictorial and verbal languages has been strongly influenced by discussions with María Dolores Gonzales and by her essay "Sometimes Spanish, Sometimes English: Language Use among Rural New Mexican Chicanas" (1995). The essay by D. Letticia Galindo in this volume also helped me refine my thinking on the subject of Chicanas and language, as did Gloria Anzaldúa's *Borderlands/La Frontera: The New Mestiza* (1987).

3. This can be seen in the major studies in the field: *Chicano Art: Resistance and Affirmation, 1965–1985* (1990); Goldman and Ybarra-Frausto (1990); Goldman (1990a); and Barnett (1984). An important exception to the general trend in the scholarship is the essay by Tomás Ybarra-Frausto (1990), which briefly discusses the importance of religious imagery in Chicano art.

4. On the function of imagery within the Catholic Church and the various councils convened to establish official policies on art, see Freedberg (1989). On the history of censorship by the Inquisition throughout the Spanish Empire, see Kamen (1985), ch. 11, "Popular Culture and the Counter Reformation," esp. pp. 201 and 204. Further information on Inquisition censorship is in Crespo (1978). The specific Inquisition guidelines regulating religious imagery have been preserved in the seventeenth-century treatise by Pacheco (1990 [1648]).

5. In 1978 Yolanda López portrayed her grandmother in *Victoria F. Franco: Our Lady of Guadalupe*. See Chabram-Dernersesian (1992) and Mesa-Bains (1990). As Mesa-Bains points out, it is not uncommon for Chicana artists to valorize their mothers or grandmothers in their art.

6. The lithograph was printed in the Tamarind Collaborative, with the help of Raul Rabaça, in Albuquerque, New Mexico.

7. My thanks to Felipe Mirabal for kindly pointing this out to me.

8. For these portraits, see Brown (1986:148–154). The valorization of the lowly has its roots in the life and devotions of the mystic St. Francis of Assisi. For a succinct discussion of his elevation of lowliness, poverty, and humility, see Warner (1983), ch. 12, "Let It Be."

9. Madrid's representational strategies closely mimic those of both Native American and Mesoamerican art. See Turner (1996), vol. 22, s.v. "Native North American Art," esp. pp. 559–562, 581–584, 587, and 590–591. A cogent discussion of Mesoamerican style can be found in Robertson (1959).

10. The famous goddess, found on the top of the main double temple in the ceremonial center of the Aztec capital, Tenochtitlán, is now housed in the Museo Nacional de Antropología, Mexico City. The sculpture dates from between 1487 and 1520. For a reproduction and brief discussion, see Pasztory (1983). Chicana feminists have appropriated her as a symbol of the goddess of power.

11. Numerous murals employ direct quotations from Mesoamerican art. A quote from Mayan relief panel #24 at Yaxchilán inspired the mural by José Gamaliel González and the youth of Westtown, *La raza de oro,* 1975 (*CARA,* p. 44, cat. no. M29). Aztec warriors can be seen in Zarco Guerrero, *Culture, Brotherhood, and Pride,* 1976 (*CARA,* p. 46, cat. no. M36). Two Toltec warriors from Tula frame the mural by Antonio Burciaga, *Mitología del maiz,* in Gorodezky (1993).

12. On the penitentes in New Mexico, consult Varjabedian & Wallis (1994). The penitentes are officially called Los Hermanos Penitentes, the Penitent Brothers. They are a lay Catholic organization whose flagellant practices have been the object of much curiosity.

13. For the definitive study of representations of the Passion of Christ, consult Schiller (1972), vol. 2.

14. Christ is represented in such a way in the Golden Age Spanish painting *Christ in the House of Mary and Martha* by Diego Velázquez (London, National Gallery, 1618). See Brown (1986:16).

15. These objects included rosaries from Amalia García, the paño donated by hermano Juan Sandoval, and jar-sculptures given by Cecilio García-Camarillo.

16. This project was funded by the Center for Regional Studies of the University of New Mexico. Additional funding came from the College Art Association's Professional Development Fellowship Program.

17. The dancers were José García, Alicia Perea, and Eva Encinias. Mike Ippiotis led the team of local aerosol artists: Lloyd Hernández, Frank Carrillo, George Ramírez, Rel Maestas, Robbie Herrera, and Miguel Baca.

18. These ideas were codified by fourth- and fifth-century Church writers such as

St. Augustine and St. John Chrysostom. They linked Eve's beauty to death because mortality was a by-product of the fall in the Garden of Eden. See Warner's discussion of this in *Alone of All Her Sex*, ch. 4, "The Second Eve."

19. See Rendón (1976:96–97):

> We Chicanos have our share of Malinches, which is what we call traitors to la raza who are of la raza, after the example of an Aztec woman of that name who became Cortez' concubine under the name of Doña Marina, and served him also as an interpreter and informer against her own people. The malinches are worse characters and more dangerous than the Tio Tacos, the Chicanismo euphemism for an Uncle Tom. The Tio Taco may stand in the way of progress only out of fear or misplaced self-importance. In the service of the gringo, malinches attack their own brothers, betray our dignity and manhood, cause jealousies and misunderstandings among us, and actually seek to retard the advance of the Chicanos, if it benefits themselves—while the gringo watches.

This view of La Malinche, as well as machismo in the Movimiento Chicano, is analyzed in Chabram-Dernersesian (1992). For the newer view valorizing Malinche, see Rodríguez (1994:xiii) and Gaspar de Alba (1998:143–144).

20. Interview with María Baca, January 1997, conducted at her home in Albuquerque, New Mexico. She has been influenced by the discussion of sandpainting in Waters (1975:258–259).

21. Baca, gallery label, *Cinco Pintoras* exhibition, Downtown Gallery 516, University of New Mexico, Albuquerque, fall of 1996.

REFERENCES

Anzaldúa, G. (1987). *Borderlands/La Frontera: The New Mestiza.* San Francisco: Aunt Lute Books.

Baca, E. (1996). Qualifying review paper. M.F.A. paper. University of New Mexico.

——. (1997). Interview. Albuquerque, New Mexico, January.

Baca, M. (1996a). Dream #1. Unpublished poem.

——. 1996b. Gallery labels. *Cinco Pintoras* exhibition. Downtown Gallery 516, University of New Mexico, Albuquerque.

——. (1997a). *The Virgin of Guadalupe.* Unpublished paper.

——. (1997b). Interview. Albuquerque, New Mexico, January.

Barnett, A. W. (1984). *Community Murals.* Cranbury, NJ: Associated University Presses.

Black, C. V. (1995). *Saints and social welfare in Golden Age Spain: The imagery of the cult of Saint Joseph.* Ph.D. dissertation, University of Michigan.

Brown, J. (1986). *Diego Velázquez: Painter and Courtier.* New Haven: Yale University Press.

Chabram-Dernersesian, A. (1992). I throw punches for my race, but I don't want to be a man: Writing as—Chica-*nos* (*girl, us*)/Chicanas—into the movement script. In L. Grossberg, C. Nelson, & P. Treichler (eds.), *Cultural Studies* (pp. 81–95). New York: Routledge.

Chicano Art: Resistance and Affirmation, 1965–1985 (CARA). (1990). Los Angeles: Wight Art Gallery, University of California.

Cockcroft, E. S., & H. Barnet-Sánchez (eds.) (1990). *Signs from the Heart: California Chicano Murals.* Albuquerque: University of New Mexico Press.

Crespo, V. P. (1978). La actitud de la Inquisición ante la iconografía religiosa. *Hispania Sacra* 31, 285–322.

Freedberg, D. (1989). *The Power of Images: Studies in the History and Theory of Response.* Chicago: University of Chicago Press.

Galindo, D. L. (this volume). Caló and taboo language use among Chicanas: A description of linguistic appropriation and innovation.

Gaspar de Alba, A. (1998). *Chicano Art Inside/Outside the Master's House: Cultural Politics and the CARA Exhibition.* Austin: University of Texas Press.

Gavin, R. F. (1994). *Traditional Arts of Spanish New Mexico: The Hispanic Heritage Wing at the Museum of International Folk Art.* Santa Fe: Museum of New Mexico.

Goldman, S. (1985). Portraying ourselves: Contemporary Chicana artists. In A. Raven et al.(eds.), *Feminist Art Criticism: An Anthology* (pp. 187–205). Ann Arbor: University of Michigan Research Press.

——. (1990a). How, why, and when it all happened: Chicano murals of California. In E. S. Cockcroft and H. Barnet-Sánchez (eds.), *Signs from the Heart: California Chicano Murals* (pp. 22–53). Albuqueruque: University of New Mexico Press.

——. (1990b). The iconography of Chicano self-determination: Race, ethnicity, and class. *Art Journal* 49 (2):167–173.

——. (1994). *Dimensions of the Americas: Art and Social Change in Latin America and the United States.* Chicago: University of Chicago Press.

Goldman, S., & T. Ybarra-Frausto. (1990). The political and social contexts of Chicano art. In *Chicano Art: Resistance and Affirmation, 1965–1985* (pp. 83–95).

Gonzales Velásquez, M. D. (1995). Sometimes Spanish, sometimes English: Language use among rural New Mexican Chicanas. In K. Hall & M. Bucholtz (eds.), *Gender Articulated: Language and the Socially Constructed Self* (pp. 421–446). New York: Routledge.

Gorodezky, S. (1993). *Arte chicano como cultura de protesta.* México, D.F.: Universidad Nacional Autónoma de México.

Hall, J. (1974). *Dictionary of Subjects and Symbols in Art*. New York: Harper & Row.

Kalb, L. B. (1994). *Crafting Devotions: Tradition in Contemporary New Mexico Santos*. Albuquerque: University of New Mexico Press.

Kamen, H. (1985). *Inquisition and Society in Spain in the Sixteenth and Seventeenth Centuries*. Bloomington: Indiana University Press.

Lange, Y. (1978). Santo Niño de Atocha: A Mexican cult is transplanted to Spain. *El Palacio* 84 (4), 2–7.

López, Y. M. (1998a). Personal communication. May.

———. (1998b). *An artist's proposal to the Chicano Movement: Rethinking the image of women*. Paper presented at Image of Devotion, Icon of Identity: The Virgin Mary in the Americas, conference sponsored by Centro Alameda in association with the Smithsonian Institution, University of Texas at San Antonio (downtown campus), May 14–16.

Madrid, L. (1997a). Interview. Albuquerque, New Mexico, January.

———. (1997b). Written communication. Albuquerque, New Mexico, February.

Mesa-Bains, A. (1990). El mundo feminino: Chicana artists of the Movement: A commentary on development and production. In *Chicano Art: Resistance and Affirmation, 1965–1985* (pp. 131-140).

Montoya, D. (1992). *Saints and sinners*. M.A. thesis, University of New Mexico.

———. (1994). *El Corazón Sagrado: The Sacred Heart*. M.F.A. paper, University of New Mexico.

———. (1996a). *Artist statement*. Unpublished manuscript.

———. (1996b). Interview. Albuquerque, New Mexico, December.

———. (1997). Personal communication. January.

Nunn, T. M. (1993). *Santo Niño de Atocha: Development, dispersal, and devotion of a new world image*. M.A. thesis, University of New Mexico.

Pacheco, F. (1990 [1648]). *El arte de la pintura*. Ed. Bonaventura Bassegoda i Hugas. Madrid: Cátedra.

Pasztory, E. (1983). *Aztec Art*. New York: Harry N. Abrams.

Peterson, J. F. (1992). The Virgin of Guadalupe: Symbol of conquest or liberation? *Art Journal* 51 (4), 39–47.

———. (1993). *The Paradise Garden Murals of Malinalco: Utopia and Empire in Sixteenth-Century Mexico*. Austin: University of Texas Press.

Rendón, A. (1976). *Chicano Manifesto*. New York: Macmillan.

Robertson, D. (1959). *Mexican Manuscript Painting of the Early Colonial Period: The Metropolitan Schools*. New Haven: Yale University Press.

Rodríguez, J. (1994). *Our Lady of Guadalupe: Faith and Empowerment among Mexican-American Women*. Austin: University of Texas Press.

Sánchez-Tranquilino, M. (1995). Space, power, and youth culture: Mexican American graffiti and Chicano murals in East Los Angeles, 1972–1978. In B. J. Bright & L. Bakewell (eds.), *Looking High and Low: Art and Cultural Identity* (pp. 55–88). Tucson: University of Arizona Press.

Schiller, G. (1972). *Iconography of Christian Art.* Trans. Janet Seligman. Greenwich, CT: New York Graphic Society.

Sebastián, S. (1989). *Contrarreforma y barroco: Lecturas iconográficas e iconológicas.* Madrid: Alianza.

Steele, T. J., S.J. (1994). *Santos and Saints: The Religious Folk Art of Hispanic New Mexico.* Santa Fe, NM: Ancient City.

Steinberg, L. (1983). *The Sexuality of Christ in Renaissance Art and Modern Oblivion.* New York: Pantheon.

Sussman, E. (ed.). (1991). *El Corazón Sangrante: The Bleeding Heart.* Seattle: University of Washington Press.

Turner, J. (ed.). (1996). *The Dictionary of Art.* New York: Macmillan.

Varjabedian, C., & M. Wallis. (1994). *En Divina Luz: The Penitente Moradas of New Mexico.* Albuquerque: University of New Mexico Press.

Warner, M. (1983). *Alone of All Her Sex: The Myth and the Cult of the Virgin Mary.* New York: Vintage.

Waters, F. (1975). *Masked Gods.* New York: Random House.

Ybarra-Frausto, T. (1990). Arte Chicano: Images of a community. In E. S. Cockcroft and H. Barnet-Sánchez (eds.), *Signs from the Heart: California Chicano Murals* (pp. 54–67). Albuquerque: University of New Mexico Press.

9

***

CALÓ AND TABOO LANGUAGE USE AMONG CHICANAS

A Description of Linguistic Appropriation and Innovation

D. Letticia Galindo

As a collective entity, Chicana voices have historically been ignored, silenced, deprecated, and marginalized by both in-group *(nuestra Raza)* and out-group (Euro-Americans—both male and female) members across ethnic, class, and sexual orientation lines (Anzaldúa 1987, 1990; Galindo 1994; Pérez 1991, 1996). For the aforementioned Chicanas-Tejanas, along with countless other Chicanas who grew up in the Southwest, there are vivid memories of being punished, ridiculed, and ultimately silenced by Anglo teachers for speaking Spanish. Educational institutions coerced us to make lifelong linguistic choices: either retain Spanish and acquire English or lose Spanish and acquire English.

Anzaldúa (1987) speaks of another strategy to stifle the female voice: assign her a derogatory label. This strategy originates within the infrastructure of *la familia* and extends to *la vecindad* and *la comunidad.* It includes labels like *habladora* [someone who speaks too much or lies]; *malcriada* [someone who talks back to parents/elders; not being well-bred or respectful]; *chismosa* [someone who gossips or likes *chismes*]; *repelona* [someone who complains and whines]; and *hocicona* [someone who talks excessively, a loudmouth]. Growing up in west Texas, I, too, heard these labels in addition to *maldicienta* [someone who curses/uses expletives a lot] and *malhablada* [someone who curses, insults others, confronts others]. These labels seem to imply that women have deliberately stepped outside the boundaries of what constitutes "female" language use and behavior and have appropriated what is considered to be male discourse: the use of expletives or *maldiciónes* in order to *hablar pesado*—which literally means to speak heavily—when confronting, challenging, insulting, or taunting others. To reiterate Anzaldúa's point about assigning stigmatizing labels to women who either consciously or unconsciously overstep their linguistic bounds, she makes the rightful observation that "in my culture they are all words that are derogatory if applied to women—I've never heard them applied to men" (1987:54).

Based on these descriptors, the profile of a traditionally raised Chicana shows her to be prudent in her use of language (don't use it to whine, complain, question, gossip, lie, etc.); it shows her to be cognizant of the social and cultural norms of language use based on age, gender, and social class and to speak accordingly; and it shows her tending to avoid expletives and other taboo-related language.

Although we acknowledge, but do not necessarily accept, the patriarchal structure and socialization practices steeped in Mexicano culture, including the demarcation of language codes and their uses/nonuses based on gender, the voices of women who break with tradition need to be reckoned with and heard. This essay, then, describes this multifaceted voice that is uninhibited, assertive, and innovative.

Conversational discourse that took place between two Chicanas who were former members of the *pachuca* subculture in Houston and Austin, Texas, served as the basis of linguistic analysis in order to capture and describe their uses of caló and taboo language. One of the women was also familiar with the subculture of female prisoners (hereafter referred to as *pinta*) because she had served time in Texas penal institutions. I intend to show how these women transcend cultural and gender boundaries traditionally assigned to many Chicanas.

Females are socialized at an early age to perform household duties, cater to/defer to males, be chaste/virtuous, and avoid vices like drinking and smoking. Rules pertaining to language appropriateness and use, in conjunction with these time-honored customs, are overtly stated or acquired through socialization and observation: speak like a lady, use proper language, don't speak out of turn, don't speak *como los hombres*—like men—whose linguistic repertoire often consists of taboo language in the form of expletives (e.g., *cabrón, pinche, chingar*) and caló (Anzaldúa 1990; Galindo 1993). A contradictory example is cited by Herrera-Sobek (1995) when she describes Evangelina Vigil's (1982) appropriation of expletives and caló in her poetry: "She [Vigil] most astutely initiates her onslaught on male sexism with the incorporation in her discourse of those specific taboo words traditionally off limits to 'nice, sweet, angelic, passive girls.' The Chicana is no longer limited in her verbal repertoire to 'pretty' or 'sweet-little girl' imagery. She is now free to utilize the full spectrum of poetic discourse previously available only to males" (1995: 160).

Like Vigil, who asserts her voice by using male-dominated street language which previously had been relegated to males, these Tejanas break with prevailing cultural and linguistic norms by appropriating caló and taboo language as their lingua franca (Galindo 1992). The adaptation of these linguistic codes symbolized personal empowerment and assertiveness, affirmation of in-group membership, and the antithesis of silence and repression as they recounted experiences of pachuca activity, buying/selling/using drugs, and prison life.

This essay intends to discuss the following: (1) the language varieties used and the terminology associated with these lifestyles; (2) the functions of these language varieties; (3) the use of taboo language, including expletives; and (4) how the appropriation of caló and taboo language facilitates the performance of particular speech acts, including boasting, challenging, insulting, and complimenting. By means of this analysis, we can see how these Chicanas shatter cultural barriers by going outside the confines of strict gender-specific roles and further transcend the language boundaries set forth for females by utilizing linguistic codes and adopting verbal strategies traditionally associated with males.

Conversational data were gathered in the barrio known as East Austin as part of a larger sociolinguistic study that sampled thirty-five Chicanas representing a cross section of ages, educational levels, occupations, and various regions in Texas as to their perceptions and attitudes toward *pachuquismo* and caló (see Galindo 1992). Three participants were part of this conversation: (1) the investigator; (2) Juanita (pseudonym), a thirty-six-year-old former pachuca and ex-pinta originally from Houston; and (3) Carolina (pseudonym), a twenty-three-year-old native Austinite and former pachuca and gang leader. The last two women were intimate friends who provided graphic accounts of their experiences as pachucas, inmates, and drug users within their respective barrios.

Pachucas are the counterpart of the *pachuco,* a dominant figure during the 1940s–1970s in cities and towns throughout the Southwest, including El Paso (the birthplace of the pachuco and pachuquismo) and Los Angeles. These subcultures are composed mainly of adolescents; however, there are pachucas/pachucos who are older than teens/young adults. They are characterized by their specialized jargon (referred to by the layperson as "pachuco" and by the linguist as "caló"), their attire (baggy pants, flannel shirts, white muscle shirts, head bandannas for males), and tattoos (usually on the hands, arms, neck, below the eyes, or between the eyebrows for females). The antiquated label of pachuco/pachuca has been replaced with *cholos/cholas* or "homeboys" and "homegirls" (Ornstein-Galicia 1987; Moore 1991; Galindo 1993; Harris 1994). These subcultures have been depicted in Hollywood films like *Zoot Suit, American Me, Mi Vida Loca,* and *Mi Familia.*

A brief discussion of these women's backgrounds revealed that Juanita had been a pachuca in Houston since she was fourteen years old. Gaining acceptance meant being able to fight and defend one's territory as well as participate in acts of theft. At seventeen, Juanita began doing time in Texas penitentiaries and served ten years for possession of half a pound of marijuana. Carolina had a reputation of being mean and tough; she and other family members were well-known in East Austin for dealing drugs and fighting. She was a high school dropout who dressed in Army fatigues and white T-shirt and always carried a knife and sometimes a gun. She considered herself a pachuca and a gang leader in junior high school. According to her, the pachuca from East Austin had to prove herself by participating in stealing and fighting. Carolina did drugs, including heroin, speed, and marijuana. Both women were willing to share their experiences with the investigator, who had taught Carolina's sister in junior high and knew other family members.

DISCUSSION

Language Varieties

The participants' linguistic repertoires were composed of three varieties: Spanish, English, and caló. "Linguistic repertoire" refers to the totality of linguistic forms available to a community of speakers or individuals (Blom & Gumperz 1989). Because both women were bilingual, a type of popular Spanish was selected by the interlocutors. Sánchez (1994) and Elías-Olivares (1976) describe this variety as one that shares characteristics with similar varieties from Mexico and Latin America, primarily rule simplification at the phonological and morphological level. This includes the omission of initial syllables (aphesis), as in the word *estaba* pronounced as *'taba;* the omission of fricatives in intervocalic position (sincope), as seen in the production of *mojao* instead of *mojado;* and the use of the suffix *-nos* for *-mos* in first-person-plural verb formation as in *vivíanos* vs. *vivíamos.*

English was used consistently throughout this discourse, perhaps to accommodate me when I asked questions in English; also, given the bilingual abilities of these women, they felt comfortable using either English or Spanish. The discourse contained elements of slang (john = bathroom, broads/chicks = women); specialized jargon reflective of drugs and prison life (pot = marijuana; get down = fight; the joint = penal institution); and expletives (fuck, bullshit), as indicated in the following examples from their discourse.

> There were these two broads *que* [that] would fight.

> . . . that was your survival in the joint.

> We had people that smoked a little pot, did some downers and stuff like that.

> You were expected to get down just like the dudes, you didn't just flash your weapons to be bullshitting around.

> I lifted her arm and cut that fuckin' tattoo off and handed it to her.

A linguistic product resulting from the meshing of cultures is Spanish-English codeswitching. Sánchez (1994) sees it as a type of verbal interaction characteristic of bilingual populations and as the most common communicative code used within the Chicano speech community. Elías-Olivares (1976) classified codeswitching—the alternation of codes (Spanish/English)—as being the rule rather than the exception among second/third-generation bilingual speakers in East Austin. I see codeswitching as a product of bilingualism that enables its speakers to be able to cross codes intrasententially and intersententially with great ease and facility, as seen in the following examples.

> The people *aquí en el Eastside me conocen.* [The people here on the East Side (of Austin) know me.]

> I pushed her hard, *y se metió la mano en la bolsa.* [I pushed her hard, and she put her hand in her pocket.]

> She already had two kids, *y ella todavía era pachuca.* [She already had two kids, and she still was a pachuca.]

Interestingly, this alternation also extends to caló, whereby many of these lexical items facilitated the switch from English:

I mean *fileros* [knives], chains, stuff like that.

I never got sent to *la pinta* [prison; penal institution], and I've been caught.

Most of the *chucos* [pachucos] that I know used to be *tecatos* [heroin users].

Since the 1940s, several scholars (Griffith 1947; Barker [1950] 1975; Coltharp 1965; Katz 1974; Ornstein-Galicia 1987) have described caló with the labels of *argot, patois,* and *pachuco.* Caló possesses linguistic roots dating back to fifteenth- and sixteenth-century Spain. It also has linguistic ties with Mexican indigenous language varieties such as Nahuatl, as well as English influence resulting from the language contact situation in the Southwest. It is known primarily for its unique and creative lexicon, such as *siról,* a lexical extension of *sí* [yes]; *chante* [Nahuatl origin *shantli,* which means "house"]; *ruca/ruco,* which means "woman/man"; and *bironga,* considered to be a lexical extension of the English gloss "beer" that has been assigned Spanish morphology *(-onga).*

In the Southwest, caló is culturally and linguistically linked with the pachuco/pachuca of the past and the present-day cholo/homeboy or chola/homegirl of urban barrios. Several Chicano scholars, including Ortega (1977), Reyes (1988), Galindo (1992), and Sánchez (1994), radically depart from the myopic view of caló users as criminals, delinquents, and pachucos/as and of their language activities as clandestine (as described by the aforementioned scholars of an earlier era). Instead, they view caló as a language of wider communication that has become an integral part of the linguistic repertoires of a cross section of Chicanas and Chicanos from various age groups, educational levels, socioeconomic levels, and professions.

Taboo Language

Spanish-based discourse included expletives that Grimes (1978) classifies as taboo language. Taboo language is that language or lexicon related to sex, sex organs, and bodily functions, as well as words considered to be expletives that intentionally convey negative or injurious effects to others when uttered (e.g., *hijo de la chingada* [son-of-a-bitch], *cabrón* [asshole or s-o-b], *pinche* [a noun that might translate to "asshole" or an adjective used with *cabrón* to imply "son-of-a-bitch"]).

An unresolved issue is whether some caló lexical items are expletives and whether some expletives are classified as being caló. George Alvarez (1967) classified caló as a "snarl" language and said that expletives like *chinga* and *pinchi [sic]*, which are analogous to the English word "damn," are included in their various forms in almost every caló utterance. Galindo (1992) discovered that Tejanas had varying opinions on whether *rallar la madre* [to curse at someone], *tirar chingazos* [throw blows/punches], and *'ta pinche* [it's a bitch] are part of caló. Some women saw these as essential components of the caló lexicon. I believe that certain lexical items cut across both classifications—expletives and caló—(e.g, chingar, pinche); however, a caló lexical item does not necessarily have to be an expletive (e.g., *chante, calcos*).

The use of expletives or the act of cursing as a verbal strategy was called *echando madres* by the women. Juanita described a woman inmate: "She was one of those loud people, man, *echando madres* and all that." Cursing (especially the use of the most common expletive in Mexican/Southwest Spanish, *chingar*) facilitated the description of actions including fighting (e.g., *tirar chingazos, meter chingazos* [hit, punch]); challenging (e.g.,*yo te chingo* [I'll hurt you], *tú no chingas conmigo* [You'd better not mess/fuck with me]); and boasting (*la más chingona* [the baddest]). Lexical items such as *cabrón* [male]/*cabrona* [female], *chingar* and its many variants, and *pinche* [damn] are considered expletives (in Southwest Spanish, these are referred to as *maldiciónes* [bad words]) within the Chicano speech community. Their level of intensity and meaning may be altered, depending on the power relationship and degree of intimacy between interlocutors.

Within the Chicano community, expletive use appears to be marked by gender; although Chicanas may possess receptive abilities regarding expletives, the latter are generally not produced by women. On the other hand, males are given what I refer to as "linguistic carte blanche" to use maldiciónes; for the most part, male and female members of the Chicano community are socialized to expect the utterance of "cabrón" or "chingado" from the mouths of males rather than females without serious repercussions.

In her poem *"Me caes sura, ese descuéntate"* (translated from caló as something like "I despise you, man; leave me alone" [Herrera-Sobek

1995]), Vigil (1982) lashes out at the Chicano male *through* her appropriation of English and Spanish expletives including "motherfucker," "chin-
gón," "tirar chingazos," and "cabrón." Herrera-Sobek observes how she
"demolishes her macho adversary with those linguistic weapons which
have traditionally belonged to the male domain" (1995:159). Vigil's unabashed display of linguistic creativity and innovativeness through her
use of expletives and caló characterize an in-your-face persona, someone
who conveys a "no chingues conmigo" attitude to both males and females
that may be attributed to growing up as a streetwise, barrio-grown Chicana from San Antonio.

Hughes (1992) perceives this view of distinct male-female swearing
practices as being deeply rooted across cultures. Coates (1993) attributes
gender differences as folk knowledge whereby in Britain people believe
that women talk more than men, that women gossip, and that men swear
more than women. Early language socialization based on gender demarcation reveals that females who curse are more likely to receive punitive
measures and harsher judgments from one or both parents than their male
counterparts. As a result, women who dare cross linguistic boundaries by
using expletives and/or caló become recipients of pejorative labels like
puta [prostitute], *cantinera* [a woman who frequents bars/cantinas], and
pachuca by out-group members (i.e., those males and females who do
not belong to these particular subcultures but are Chicanas/os). Elías-
Olivares (1976), whose ethnographic study on language variation and use
among a cross section of ninety-two Chicanas/os living in East Austin,
discovered from her subjects that the women who used caló often were
the ones who frequented the cantinas in the barrio, and thus they were
labeled as cantineras. Coltharp (1965) indiscriminately assigned such
labels to the women she saw (but did not talk to) with the males from her
study of caló use in El Paso, Texas. According to her, caló was and is a
male language, and the females who used it were either prostitutes or
mates of gang members. A more contemporary view of the consequences
women face as they dare cross male-dominated boundaries is offered by
Laura Cummings, who provides an ethnographic account of the evolution and description of the pachuco language in Tucson: "The positive
intentions of pachucas and cholas crossing boundaries . . . has often
resulted in forms of disenfranchisement as a consequence of the women's
divergence from prescribed 'female qualities and roles.' Disenfranchisement can be a social sanction in the form of 'talk' affecting the reputation

of the individual such as attributing 'aggressive' qualities of pachucas and cholas to imputed masculinity or at times, lesbianism" (1994:173).

These empirically based findings from East Austin, El Paso, and Tucson corroborate that the hurtful labeling from both in-group and out-group members continues: "pachuca," "cantinera," "puta," and "lesbian." This time these labels are for women who opt to use male-dominated verbal strategies rather than for women who speak too much.

Gal (1995) speaks of power and domination as being integral factors to consider in any theory that examines women's speech. She observes that speakers often redefine and play with language so that demeaning lexical items, when used in particular social contexts, can be perceived in terms of solidarity. Furthermore, forms considered to be stereotypically male that are appropriated by women might convey or symbolize nonconformity. In the case of Chicanas, expletive use could represent those forms that are perceived to be masculine in nature, including the use of caló. As a result of appearing to be nonconformists in regard to preconceived gender roles and expectations, including socially accepted language use, these women are often recipients of pejorative labels and, interestingly, are assigned qualities of aggressiveness, combativeness, and grossness (there is a word in Spanish that is used to describe someone who is vulgar in either words or actions—a *grosero* or a *grosera*) that are usually reserved for males, as seen in the aforementioned examples from both in-group and out-group members of the Chicana/o community. Yet extraneous variables—including generation, education, social class, social networks, group membership, feminist ideology, even urban versus rural upbringing—have contributed to and facilitated women's transition from traditional to innovative norms of language use in spite of societal repercussions and negative labels.

The Lexicon of Gangs, Drugs, and Prison Life

Within urban street culture in Chicano barrios across the Southwest, there exist specialized registers based on the lexicon of gangs, drugs, and prison life. Most of the lexicon produced is classified as caló and is found in dictionaries compiled by Fuentes and López (1974), Serrano (1976), and Polkinhorn et al. (1986).

The following caló terms described both males and females: *camarada(s)* [friend(s)]: *un camarada de mi apá* [a friend of my dad]; *chava* [young female]: *La chava había hecho tiempo conmigo dos veces.* [The girl/woman had done time with me twice.]; *chavalona* [young girl]: *'Taban unas chavalonas jambando.* [There were these young girls stealing.]; *chavalo* [young guy]: A lot of *chavalos cargan un filero.* [A lot of young guys carry a knife.]; *chuco/chuca* [abbreviated version of pachuco/pachuca]: *Más chuca que la fregada.* [I was really a hard-core pachuca.]; *pachucones* [lexical extension of pachuco]: *Muchos pachucones traían el cuete en un lado y el filero.* [Many pachucos had their gun on the side and a knife.]; *vato/bato* [guy/dude]: Never been anywhere except on the street *con vatos baratos.* [Never been anywhere except on the street with cheap, sleazy guys.].

Because the gang lifestyle involves defending turf and the barrio one is affiliated with, many terms pertain to fighting: *chingazos* [punches, blows]; *cuete* [gun]; *filero* [knife]; *pleito* [fight]; *brincar* [to hit or jump on someone]; *dar en la madre* [to beat up on someone]; *filerear* [to cut someone]; *hacer pedo* [to make trouble]. Part of the right to claim pachuca status was the ability to steal *[el jambo]* and to fight *[el pleito].* You also had to be able to fight *[tirar muchos chingazos]* in order to "hold down" a territory in your neighborhood. Juanita discussed the need to fight the "broad" who held the territory down as part of the gang lifestyle in Houston.

Drugs played a vital role in these women's lives because they used them, pushed them, or knew people who used them. Carolina stated, "I haven't seen a *chuco que esté limpio* [drug-free] or anything, most of the *chucos* that I know used to be *tecatos* [heroin users]." Juanita said that in Houston, people smoked a little pot and did some downers. Carolina's father was framed due to possession of *toques* [marijuana]. Carolina professed to have been an addict and stated that she was able to *conectar chiva* [score heroin]. Other drug-related terms include *carga* [heroin]; *grifa* [marijuana, joint]; *leño* [marijuana, joint]; *cargar* [to carry drugs]; *sonar un toque (toquear)* [to smoke a joint]; *fileraso de carga* [a fix of heroin]; and *fileraso de cranque* [a fix of speed].

Male prisoners from Washington corroborated the Tejana women's use of such prison-related terms as "the joint" [slang for "prison"] and "doing time" [serving a prison sentence], according to Cardozo-Freeman (1984). The most common terms include *pinta,* which denotes both the penal institution and a female convict. A snitch or informer is known as a *relaje.* In one instance, Carolina accused Juanita of being a relaje, of snitching to her father about her: "They also told me *que Juanita era relaje. Me relajates con mi apá.*" [They also told me that Juanita was a snitch. You told my dad about me.] Carolina used a similar expression *(puso el dedo),* which literally means "put the finger" on someone, when she described how some guy squealed on her dad, leading to his apprehension and eventual imprisonment: *"Entonces el vato fué y le puso el dedo a mi apá so a mi apá lo safanaron."* [Then the dude went and told/snitched on my dad, and they made him do time in the penitentiary.]

Juanita served ten years in the Texas prison system for possessing half a pound of marijuana. She made an interesting distinction between *el rancho* and *la pinta,* which both denote prison. According to her, *el rancho* was the term used by those who have actually been there and served time; *la pinta* was used by those who have not been there.

This collection of Spanish/caló lexical items that compose a major part of the women's linguistic repertoire reflects their knowledge of these terms used to describe aspects of their lifestyle within and across these subcultures.

Social Functions

Language is not used in vacuo, and as communicators who rely on social contextualization cues, we are cognizant and competent of the social rules of language—when to use what variety (codeswitching, caló), what style (formal/informal), and with whom (family, friends). Hymes (1989) refers to this ability as "communicative competence." Within this discourse, the women used a variety of codes in a mostly informal style with each other as friends and members of these subcultures. Reasons for their use are indicative of the social functions that language serves.

Both Chicanas were fluent in Spanish. Its use represents the language of a shared ethnic identity and conveys intimacy among its speakers. Quantitatively, English served as the dominant code or base language within this discourse. Functionally, it served to answer questions asked by the investigator and perhaps as an accommodation strategy to respond in the same code.

Codeswitching from English to Spanish and caló was a linguistic strategy utilized by both participants as they chose to traverse from one code to another, especially in the context of describing the nuances of urban life, gang membership, drugs, and prison life. Earlier examples of codeswitching indicate that use might be attributed to the participants' need to select the most appropriate term that meets their communicative needs during discourse (e.g., *limpio* to mean literally "'clean' of drugs, not using drugs"). The use of the Spanish phrase *se me va la onda* (literally "I lose my head" or "I go crazy") to describe Carolina's propensity for fighting and using her karate skills is comprehended by the other interlocotors.

Caló has been described as having many social functions, primarily from a male perspective, given that the bulk of empirical research conducted from the 1940s to the 1970s singled out men rather than women as the primary speakers of this linguistic variety. Hernández-Chávez et al. (1975) viewed caló as representing intimacy and brotherhood *[carnalismo]* among its users. Adolfo Ortega (1977) saw caló as a marker of group identity and as a group unifier. Galindo's (1992) study of caló use among Texas Chicanas revealed that it functioned to preserve ethnic/in-group membership, was a sign of assertiveness, and served as the linguistic medium for telling jokes/*chistes [bromeando]* among females and males in intimate settings. Cummings (1994) found that males and females from Tucson used caló selectively with peers to express solidarity and assertiveness.

In her examination of Chicano discourse, Sánchez (1994) mentions the use of caló within a type of verbal exchange called *cábula,* found in such speech acts as boasting, challenging, and insulting, and primarily documented among males. This study reveals how these women radically transcend cultural and gender boundaries through their systematic use of caló and adhere to social functions similar to those of their male counterparts: solidarity, in-group membership, and intimacy. Furthermore, we can see how these Chicanas are equally agile in the type of jive talk known as cábula that is depicted in the following examples:

(boasting) Juanita: *Yo era la Mexicana más chingona en los projects.* [I was the baddest Mexicana in the (housing) projects.]

(boasting) Carolina: *Yo controlaba a las negras de volada con chains y todo.* [I controlled the black females quite readily, with chains and everything.]

(boasting) Carolina: If I can stand up to my father and *tirar chingazos con mi apá* [and exchange blows with my father], I can do it with anyone!

(boasting) Juanita:	I lifted her arm and cut that fuckin' tattoo off and handed it to her. I say, *"¿Ay 'ta puta, quieres un tattoo?"* [I say, "There it is, whore/bitch, you want a tattoo?"]
(challenging) Juanita:	*Sabes que, puta, si no quieres que te patalee el culo, no chingues conmigo.* I pushed her hard *y se metió la mano en la bolsa.* [Listen here, whore/bitch, if you don't want me to kick your ass, don't fuck with me. I pushed her hard, and she put her hand in her pocket.]
(challenging) Carolina:	*Sabes que huerquia, tú no chingas conmigo porque yo te chingo.* [You know what, girl (young girl—this was meant to be an insult), you don't mess with me, because I'll beat you up.]
(challenging) Juanita:	*¿Qué quieres? ¿Que te corte uno de estos tattoos? ¡Yo te corto uno más de la volada!* [What do you want? Do you want me to cut off one of those tattoos? I'll cut one of 'em as quickly as possible!]
(insulting) Carolina:	They also told me *que Juanita era relaje. Me relajates con mi apá.* [They also told me that Juanita was a snitch. You snitched about me to my dad.]
(insulting) Juanita:	And the ones *más caidas de todas eran las de* Austin. Most of the chicks from Austin *eran puras tecatas,* uneducated, never been anywhere except on the street *con vatos baratos, bien pachucas.* [And the lowest (low-class) women were the ones from Austin. Most of the chicks from Austin were heroin addicts, uneducated, never been anywhere except on the street with cheap guys, they were very pachucas.]

In addition, compliments were part of their discourse as they talked about the prowess and ability of other pachucas: *"Como esa M——. Es más pachuca que la chingada.* She's still as good as she used to be *pa los chingazos."* [Like M——. She's a helluva pachuca. She's still as good as she used to be to throw punches/fight.] Juanita offered a hierarchical ranking of who reigned inside prison and got respect if others knew she could throw punches and wouldn't snitch. She complimented her *compañeras* from Houston: "The one thing when you go down there, if you're from the big city, you automatically have the respect. *Las meras chingonas eran de* Houston and then *si sabían que tirabas chingazos y que no te ibas a rajar,* you were automatically respected and left alone. The next biggest place people respected you was either Dallas or San Antonio."

Cursing as a linguistic strategy and stylistic device conveyed familiarity, bonding, and intimacy between the interlocutors. Juanita and Carolina exchanged words that sounded harsh and abusive if one did not know the context in which such words were used and the degree of intimacy between the interlocutors. In two instances, Juanita discussed Carolina's actions toward her: *"Esta cabrona me dijo que le iba a meter unos chingazos a mi vato una vez porque le había dado en la madre a un mojao."* [This woman/bitch (affectionate/intimate) told me that she was going to beat up my man because he had beat up a wetback (a pejorative label for an undocumented person).] When I asked Carolina if she was addicted to drugs and she responded "no," Juanita laughed and remarked, *"Pero si 'taba la cabrona."* [But she was, the bitch.] Risch (1987) indicates that women tend to use expletives, their own slang, as a means of bonding and being intimate with one another. This example among Chicanas supports her claim.

Other examples depict cursing as a powerful weapon used to convey to others that there would be grave consequences if the curser were harassed and provoked. Carolina described an incident during which another pachuca began taunting her. Carolina reacted to this by telling her: *"Sabes que huerquia, tú no chingas conmigo, porque yo te chingo."* [You know what, girlie, you don't fuck with me, because I'll beat you up.] Juanita described an incident where a young pachuca bumped into her and called her a *pinche puta* [damn whore]. She grabbed her and said, *"Sabes que, puta, si no quieres que te patalee el culo, no chingues conmigo."* [You know what, whore, if you don't want me to kick your ass, don't fuck with me.] These examples are reflective of what Grimes (1978) classifies as taboo language whose intent is malicious or injurious to the hearer, as indicated in the pejorative label *puta,* the use of *pinche,* and the expressions with *chingar.* These verbal insults and tauntings serve to instigate confrontation leading to fighting between parties. From my own personal experiences in elementary and junior high school, it was not uncommon for fights between females to occur when one's reputation was questioned (e.g., being called a *puta* or "bitch") or when one's mother was the target of the curse (e.g., *chinga tu madre,* "damn your mother").

Cursing crossed linguistic and stylistic boundaries and facilitated the *cábula* or "jive" among these females. Compliments were also spiced with expletives, and they were used to serve as praise of other women's fighting abilities and their loyalty to being a pachuca. For these women who shared similar street knowledge and experiences, it was a means of expressing their camaraderie and their solidarity as ex-pachucas who exemplified toughness, self-confidence, and defiance against cultural and gender-based norms.

CONCLUSION

This linguistic analysis of conversational discourse that centered around the topics of gangs, prison life, and drugs among these two Chicanas produced several important findings. First, the linguistic repertoires of these women were composed of a variety of codes: Spanish, English, and caló. The alternation of codes (codeswitching) was used extensively and represents a manifestation of the participants' bilingual ability and agility. Caló use facilitated the description of urban street culture as experienced by the women as they discussed gangs, prison life, and drugs. Closely linked to the language varieties used was the notion of style that influenced their use. For the most part, an informal, intimate style affected topic, speech act, context, and relationship between interlocutors. Second, the use of taboo language in the form of expletives to convey their life experiences reflected uninhibitedness and assertiveness on the part of the women to depart from traditional male-female role demarcations within the Chicano culture. Third, the social functions of these linguistic varieties during discourse conveyed intimacy, camaraderie, and bonding between women who shared similar life experiences and acquaintances. Fourth, women are equally capable of *cabulando,* and they do so within the speech acts of challenging, insulting, and boasting.

This research set out to depict a different persona of woman-as-communicator who is traditionally characterized as the spokesperson and promoter for the standard versus vernacular language. In stark contrast to Chicana/Mexicana women who tend to be the conservators of the standard linguistic norm (Spanish or English), these women were uninhibited and unconcerned about what out-group members (in this case, the investigator) thought if they cursed, used caló, or exchanged verbal insults. Furthermore, they displayed a strong sense of self that facilitated their crossing boundaries along linguistic, cultural, and social lines. Their unabashed use of what has been considered male-dominated language (caló) in the form of specialized verbal exchanges (cábula) exemplified the type of Chicana who felt comfortable revealing details about her life experiences as pachuca, gang member, drug user, and prison inmate to another Chicana, but an outsider.

I have been asked whether I believe these women would use this type of verbal discourse with males; I give a resounding "yes" because this is an integral part of their identity and their idiolect. They are not "performing" in caló or trying to intentionally shock anyone with their expletive use. Consequently, these Chicanas may be either atypical or the prototype of contemporary Chicana language users, at least in Austin, Texas. Lamentably, we do not have ample empirical scholarship to corroborate or refute such claims. The limitation of this research is that in obtaining data solely from two subjects, one cannot generalize about language use in the forms of caló and taboo language for the entire Chicana population nor for pinta/chola subcultures across cities/towns throughout the Southwest. Future studies should utilize larger samples of members of these subcultures in order to arrive at generalizations about specialized registers/jargons and their functions within these groups. Whereas early studies merely speculated that membership in these subcultures automatically meant the use of these linguistic forms, we do not have in-depth, ethnographic, sociolinguistic accounts of this occurring.

The profile of the contemporary Chicana is shaped by myriad variables, including residence, urban vs. rural setting, education, socioeconomic status, age, occupation, marital status, and sexual orientation. As she breaks the bonds of traditional gender roles, there is also a liberating of voice. It is a voice that is no longer silent, passive, or unidimensional. Her linguistic innovativeness and creativity are displayed through her selection of multiple codes—including caló and taboo language—that she manipulates to express her views and ideas and to empower herself and others.

ACKNOWLEDGMENTS

I would like to take this opportunity to thank Carolina and Juanita, who readily participated in this study and truly depict the voices of assertive, uninhibited, and creative Chicanas. Muchas gracias to the other mujeres who participated in the larger study and whose voices were heard and captured as they reflected on their uses of caló.

REFERENCES

Alvarez, G. (1967). Caló: The "other" Spanish. *International Society for General Semantics,* 24, 7–13.

Anzaldúa, G. (1987). *Borderlands/La Frontera: The New Mestiza.* San Francisco: Aunt Lute Books.

—— (ed.). (1990). *Making Face, Making Soul/Haciendo caras. Creative and Critical Perspectives by Feminists of Color.* San Francisco: Aunt Lute Books.

Barker, G. (1950). Pachuco: An American Spanish argot and its social function in Tucson, Arizona. Reprinted in E. Hernández-Chávez, A. Cohen, & A. Beltramo (eds.), *El lenguaje de los chicanos* (pp. 183–201). Washington, DC: Center for Applied Linguistics, 1975.

Blom, J., & J. Gumperz. (1989). Social meaning in linguistic structure: Codeswitching in Norway. In J. Gumperz & D. Hymes (eds.), *Directions in Sociolinguistics* (pp. 407–434). New York: Basil Blackwell.

Cardozo-Freeman, I. (1984). *The Joint: Language and Culture in a Maximum Security Prison* . Springfield, IL: Charles Thomas.

Coates, J. (1993). *Women, Men, and Language: A Sociolinguistic Account of Gender Differences in Language.* New York: Longman.

Coltharp, L. (1965). *The Tongue of the Tirilones: A Linguistic Study of a Criminal Argot.* University: University of Alabama Press.

Cummings, L. (1994). *Que siga el corrido: Tucson pachucos and their times.* Ph.D. dissertation, University of Arizona.

Elías-Olivares, L. (1976). *Ways of speaking in a Chicano community: A sociolinguistic approach.* Ph.D. dissertation, University of Texas, Austin.

Fuentes, D., & J. López. (1974). *Barrio Language Dictionary. First Dictionary of Caló.* La Puente, CA: Sunburst Enterprises.

Gal, S. (1995). Language, gender, and power: An anthropological review. In K. Hall & M. Bucholtz (eds.), *Gender Articulated: Language and the Socially Constructed Self* (pp. 169–182). New York: Routledge.

Galindo, D. L. (1992). Dispelling the male-only myth: Chicanas and caló. *The Bilingual Review/La Revista Bilingüe* 17 (1), 3–35.

——. (1993). The language of gangs, drugs, and prison life among Chicanas. *Latino Studies Journal* 4 (3), 23–43.

——. (1994). Capturing Chicana voices: An interdisciplinary approach. In M. Bucholtz et al. (eds.), *Cultural Performances: Proceedings of the Third Berkeley Women & Language Conference* (pp. 220–231). Berkeley, CA: Berkeley Women & Language Group, University of California.

Griffith, B. (1947). The pachuco patois. *Common Ground* 7, 77–84.

Grimes, L. (1978). *El tabú lingüístico en México: El lenguaje erótico de los mexicanos.* New York: Bilingual Press.

Harris, M. (1994). Cholas, Mexican-American girls, and gangs. *Sex Roles* 30 (3/4), 289–301.

Hernández-Chávez, E., A. Cohen, & A. Beltramo. (1975). *El lenguaje de los chicanos.* Washington, DC: Center for Applied Linguistics.

Herrera-Sobek, M. (1995). The street scene: Metaphoric strategies in two contemporary Chicana poets. In M. Herrera-Sobek & H. M. Viramontes (eds.), *Chicana (W)rites: On Word and Film* (pp. 147–169). Berkeley, CA: Third Woman Press.

Hughes, S. (1992). Expletives of lower working-class women. *Language in Society* 21, 291–303.

Hymes, D. (1989). Models of the interaction of language and social life. In J. Gumperz & D. Hymes (eds.), *Directions in Sociolinguistics* (pp. 35–71). New York: Basil Blackwell.

Katz, L. F. (1974). *The evolution of the pachuco language and culture.* Master's thesis, University of California, Los Angeles.

Moore, J. (1991). *Going Down to the Barrio: Homeboys and Homegirls in Change.* Philadelphia: Temple University Press.

Ornstein-Galicia, J. (1987). Chicano caló: Description and review of a border variety. *Hispanic Journal of Behavioral Sciences* 9 (4), 359–373.

Ortega, A. (1977). *Caló Tapestry.* Berkeley, CA: Editorial Justa Publications.

Pérez, E. (1991). Sexuality and discourse: Notes from a Chicana survivor. In C. Trujillo (ed.), *Chicana Lesbians: The Girls Our Mothers Warned Us About* (pp. 150–184). Berkeley, CA: Third Woman Press.

——. (1996). *Gulf Dreams.* Berkeley, CA: Third Woman Press.

Polkinhorn, H., A. Velasco, & M. Lambert. (1986). *El libro de caló: The Dictionary of Chicano Slang.* Oakland, CA: Floricanto Press.

Reyes, R. (1988). The social and linguistic foundations of Chicano caló: Trends for future research. In J. Ornstein-Galicia et al. (eds.), *Research Issues and Problems in United States Spanish* (pp. 75–97). Brownsville, TX: Pan American University.

Risch, B. (1987). Women's derogatory terms for men: That's right, "dirty" words. *Language in Society* 16, 353–358.

Sánchez, R. (1994). *Chicano Discourse: Socio-historic Perspectives.* Houston, TX: Arte Público Press.

Serrano, R. (1976). *Dictionary of Pachuco Terms.* Bakersfield, CA: California State College.

Vigil, E. (1982). *Thirty an' Seen a Lot.* Houston, TX: Arte Público Press.

10

•••

MÁSCARAS, TRENZAS, Y GREÑAS

Un/Masking the Self While Un/Braiding

Latina Stories and Legal Discourse

Margaret E. Montoya

Using personal narrative, this essay[1] examines the various masks *(máscaras)* used to control how people respond to us and the important role such masks play in the subordination of Outsiders.[2] It has as its characteristic motif the braiding together of the personal with the academic voice, legal scholarship with scholarship from other disciplines, narrative with expository prose and poetry, and English with Spanish. These linguistic and conceptual braids *(trenzas)* may be untidy *(greñas),* but they are distinctive, ethnically authentic, and challenging to conventional paradigms within the legal academy while subverting the dominant discourse.

> *Máscaras:* Un/Masking the Self
>
> . . . I put on my masks, my
> costumes and posed for each
> occasion. I conducted myself
> well, I think, but
> an emptiness
> grew
> that no thing
> could fill. I think
> I hungered for myself.[3]

OUTSIDER MASKS

Despite important historical, ethnic, and linguistic differences, stories of assimilation told from the various perspectives of subordinated groups have strains of similarities. In addition to the personal and collective pain that we experience because of societal pressures to assimilate, Latinas/os face the disquietude of being masked for some of the same reasons as other Outsiders. Being masked may be a universal condition in that all of us control how we present ourselves to others (Goffman 1959). There is, however, a fundamental difference in feeling masked because one is a member of one or more oppressed groups within the society. When members of the dominant culture mask themselves to control the impression they make, such behavior is not inherently self-loathing. But when we attempt to mask immutable characteristics of skin color, eye shape, or hair texture because they have historically been loathsome to the dominant culture, then the masks of acculturation can be experienced as self-hate. Moreover, for members of the dominant culture, unmasking does not involve the fear or depth of humiliation that it does for the subordinated, for whom the unmasking is often involuntary and unexpected.

For stigmatized groups such as people of color, the poor, women, gays, and lesbians, assuming a mask is comparable with being "on stage" (Harris 1990). Being "on stage" is frequently experienced as being acutely aware of one's words, affect, tone of voice, movements, and gestures because they seem out of sync with what one is feeling and thinking (Weigert et al. 1986). At unexpected moments, we fear that we will be discovered to be someone or something other than who or what we pretend to be. Lurking just behind our carefully constructed disguises and lodged within us is the child whom no one would have mistaken for anything other than what she was. Her masking was imperfect, still in rehearsal, and at times unnecessary.

For Outsiders, being masked in the legal profession has psychological as well as ideological consequences. Not only do we perceive ourselves as being "on stage," but the experience of class-jumping—being born poor but living on the privileged side of the economic divide as an adult—can induce schizoid feelings. As first-year law students don their three-piece suits, they make manifest the class ascendancy implicit in legal education. Most Latinas/os in the legal profession now occupy an economic niche considerably higher than that of our parents, our relatives, and frequently our students. Our speech, clothes, cars, homes, and lifestyle emphasize this difference. The masks we choose can impede our legal representation and advocacy by driving a wedge between self and our *familias* and communities. As our economic security increases, we escape the choicelessness and lack of control over vital decisions that oppress communities of color. To remain connected to the community requires one to be Janus-faced, able to present one face to the larger society and another among ourselves: Janus-faced not in the conventional meaning of being deceitful, but in the sense of having two faces simultaneously.

MASKING WITHIN THE LEGAL ENVIRONMENT

The legal profession provides ample opportunity for role-playing, drama, storytelling, and posturing. Researchers (Elkins 1978; Reich 1976) have studied the use of masks and other theatrical devices among practicing lawyers and in the law school environment. Mask imagery has been used repeatedly to describe different aspects of legal education, lawyering, and lawmaking. One distinctive example is Noonan's (1976) analysis exposing the purposeful ambiguity and the duplicity of legal discourse.

Some law students are undoubtedly attracted to the profession by the opportunity to disguise themselves and have no desire or need to look for their hidden selves.[4] Some law students, however, may resent the role-playing they know is necessary to succeed in their studies and in their relations with professors and peers. Understanding how and why we mask ourselves can help provide opportunities for students to explore their public and private personalities and to give expression to their feelings.

Desen/Mascarando Silencio / Un/Masking Silence

Esto es el exilio
este tenerme que inventar un nombre,
una figura,
una voz nueva.
Este tener que andar diciendo de dónde soy
que hago aquí.
Esto es el exilio
esta soledad clavándose en mi carne. . . .

[This is exile
this having to invent a name for myself,
a face,
a new voice.
This having to go around saying
where I'm from
what I'm doing here.
This is exile
this solitude biting into my flesh.][5]

MY STORY CONTINUES

My memories from law school begin with the first case I ever read in Criminal Law. I was assigned to seat number 1 in a room that held some 175 students. The case was entitled *The People of the State of California v. Josefina Chávez*.[6] It was the only case in which I remember encountering a Latina, and she was the defendant in a manslaughter prosecution. The facts, as I think back and before I have searched out the casebook, involved Josefina giving birth one night over the toilet in her mother's home without waking her brothers, sisters, or mother. The baby dropped into the toilet. Josefina cut the umbilical cord with a razor blade. She recovered the body of the baby, wrapped it in newspaper, and hid it under the bathtub. She ran away but later turned herself in to her probation officer. The legal issue was whether the baby had been born alive for purposes of the California manslaughter statute: whether the baby had been born alive and therefore was subject to being killed. The class wrestled with what it meant to be alive in legal terms. Had the lungs filled with air? Had the heart pumped blood? For two days I sat mute, transfixed while the professor and the students debated the issue. Finally, on the third day, I timidly raised my hand. I heard myself blurt out: What about the other facts? What about her youth, her poverty, her fear over the pregnancy, her delivery in silence? I spoke for perhaps two minutes, and when I finished, my voice was high-pitched and anxious. An African-American student in the back of the room punctuated my comments with "Hear! Hear!" Later, other students thanked me for speaking up and in other ways showed their support.[7]

I sat there after class had ended, in seat number 1 on day number 3, wondering why it had been so hard to speak. Only later would I begin to wonder whether I would ever develop the mental acuity, the logical clarity to be able to sort out the legally relevant facts from what others deemed sociological factoids. Why *did* the facts relating to the girl-woman's reality go unvoiced? Why were her life, her anguish, her fears rendered irrelevant? Engaging in analyses about The Law, her behavior, and her guilt demanded that I disembody Josefina, that I silence her reality that screamed in my head.

Perhaps my memory has played tricks with me. I decide to look for the casebook and reread the Chávez case. I'm surprised, after years of thinking about this case, to learn that her name was Josephine and not Josefina. My memory distorted her name, exaggerating for me her ethnicity, her differences.

The legal issue in the case is somewhat different from what I recall. The question presented is not only whether the baby was born alive for purposes of the California manslaughter statute (Cal. Penal Code § West 1947), but also whether the statute required that the baby be entirely separate from its mother, the umbilical cord cut, before being considered a person. The court concurred with the jury's finding that a baby in the process of being born but with the capability of living an independent life is a human being within the meaning of the homicide statutes. The appellate court affirmed the judgment of the lower court, concluding that a criminal act had been committed because of the mother's "complete failure . . . to use any of the care towards th[e] infant which was necessary for its welfare and which was naturally required of her" (*People v. Josephine Chávez* 1947:96).

The appellate opinion focused on the legal personhood of the dead baby, but questions of criminal intent, mens rea, and diminished capacity thread through the case. Contextualization of the facts through the use of gender-linked and cultural information would inform our understanding of the latter legal issues. Contextual information should have been relevant to determining the criminality of her behavior. Josephine Chavez's behavior seems to have been motivated as much by complex cultural norms and values as by criminal intent.

A discussion raising interpretive aspects of the gender-, class-, and ethnically based interpretations in the opinion, however, would have run counter to the traditional legal discourse (Elkins 1978). Interjecting information about the material realities and the cultural context of a poor

Latina woman's life introduces taboo information into the classroom. Such information would transgress the prevalent ideological discourse. The puritanical and elitist protocol governing the classroom, especially during the 1970s, supported the notion that one's right to a seat in the law school classroom could be brought into question if one were to admit knowing about the details of pregnancies and self-induced abortions or the hidden motivations of a *pachuca* or a *chola* (a "homegirl" in today's Latino gang parlance; Banks 1990; Scales 1990). Overtly linking oneself to the life experiences of poor women, especially pachucas, would emphasize one's differences from those who seemed to have been admitted to law school as if by right.

Information about the cultural context of Josephine Chávez's life would also transgress the linguistic discourse within the classroom. One would find it useful, and perhaps necessary, to use Spanish words and concepts to describe accurately and to contextualize Josephine Chávez's experience. In the 1970s, however, Spanish was still the language of Speedy Gonzales, José Jiménez, and other racist parodies. To this day, I have dozens of questions about this episode in Josephine Chávez's life. I yearn to read an appellate opinion that reflects a sensitivity to her story, told in her words. What did it take to conceal her pregnancy from her familia? With whom did she share her secret? How could she have given birth with "the doors open and no lights . . . turned on?" (*People v. Josephine Chávez* 1947:92). How did she do so without waking the others who were asleep? How did she brace herself as she delivered the baby into the toilet? Did she shake as she cut the umbilical cord?

I long to hear Josephine Chávez's story told in what I will call Mothertalk and Latina-Daughtertalk. Mothertalk is about the blood and mess of menstruation, about the every-monthness of periods, about the fear in the pit of the stomach and the ache in the heart when there is no period. Mothertalk is about the blood and mess of pregnancy, about placentas, umbilical cords, and stitches. Mothertalk is about sex and its effects. Mothertalk helps make sense of our questions: How does one give birth in darkness and in silence? How does one clean oneself after giving birth? How does one heal oneself? Where does one hide from oneself after seeing one's dead baby in a toilet?

Latina-Daughtertalk is about feelings reflecting the deeply ingrained cultural values of Latino families: in this context, feelings of *vergüenza de sexualidad* [sexual shame]. Sexual experience comes enshrouded in sexual shame; have sex, and you risk being known as *sinvergüenza* [shameless].[8] Another Latina-Daughtertalk value is *respeto a la mamá y respeto a la familia.* Familias are not nuclear or limited by blood ties; they are extended, often including foster siblings and *comadres y compadres, madrinas y padrinos* [godmothers, godfathers, and other religion-linked relatives]. Josephine Chávez's need to hide her pregnancy (with her head-to-toe mask) can be explained by a concern about the legal consequences as well as by the vergüenza within and of her familia that would accompany the discovery of the pregnancy, a pregnancy that was at once proof and reproval of her sexuality. Josephine's unwanted pregnancy would likely have been interpreted within her community and her familia, and by her mother, as a lack of respeto.

I sense that students still feel vulnerable when they reveal explicitly gendered or class-based knowledge, such as information about illicit sexuality and its effects or personal knowledge about the lives of the poor and the subordinated. Even today there is little opportunity to use Spanish words or concepts within the legal academy. Students respond to their feelings of vulnerability by remaining silent about these tabooed areas of knowledge (Finley 1989; Wildman 1989). The silence had profound consequences for me and presumably for others who identified with Josephine Chávez because she was Latina, or because she was female, or because she was poor. For me, the silence invalidated my experience. I reexperienced the longing I felt that day in Criminal Law many times. At the bottom of that longing was a desire to be recognized, a need to feel some reciprocity. As I engaged in his/their reality, I needed to feel him/them engage in mine.

Embedded in Josephine Chávez's unfortunate experience are various lessons about criminal law specifically and about the law and its effects more generally. The opinion's characteristic avoidance of context and its obfuscation of important class- and gender-based assumptions are equally important to the ideological socialization and doctrinal development of law students. Maintaining a silence about Chávez's ethnic and socioeconomic context lends credence to the prevailing perception that there is only one relevant reality (Minow 1987).

As a child I had painstakingly learned my bicultural act: how to be a public American while retaining what I valued as Mexican in the most private parts of my soul. My childhood mask involved my outward self: how I looked, how I sounded. By college, my mask included more subtle aspects of my personality and intellect: a polysyllabic vocabulary, years of tested academic achievement, and a nascent political philosophy wrapped up in the idea of being Chicana. Law school, however, challenged the effectiveness of my mask, jeopardized its coherence. My mask seemed brittle and permeable. At other times, it seemed solid and opaque. My cache of cultural, linguistic, and gender-linked disguises seemed inadequate; the private me was threatened with unwanted exposure. The private me was suffocating. The private me was leaking out.

I recall that my Criminal Law professor was supportive of my comments, even though his own Socratic dialogue had neither invited such remarks nor presented Josephine Chávez as a complex person worthy of our attention. I remember him as supportive partly because he later invited me and a small number of students to a social gathering at his home. I sensed that the invitation was a significant gesture of inclusion, that he viewed me as belonging in the way the other students belonged and in a way that I never felt. Over time, I figured out that my interpretations of the facts in legal opinions were at odds with the prevailing discourse in the classroom, regardless of the subject matter. Much of the discussion assumed that we all shared common life experiences. I remember sitting in the last row and being called on in Tax, questioned about a case, *Helvering v. Horst* (1940), involving the tax liability of a father for a gift of detached and negotiable bond coupons to his son. It was clear I was befuddled by the facts of the case. Looking at his notes on the table, the professor asked with annoyance whether I had ever seen a bond. My voice quivering, I answered that I had not. His head shot up in surprise. He focused on who I was; I waited, unmasked. He became visibly flustered as he carefully described the bond with its tear-off coupons to me. Finally, he tossed me an easy question, and I choked out the answer.

This was one instance of feeling publicly unmasked. In this case, it was class-based ignorance that caused my mask(s) to slip. Other students may also have lacked knowledge about bonds. Maybe other students, especially those from families with little money and certainly no trust funds, stocks, and bonds, also felt unmasked by the questioning. But I felt isolated and different because I could be exposed in so many ways—through class, ethnicity, race, gender, and the subtleties of language, dress, makeup, voice, and accent.

For multiple and overlapping reasons I felt excluded from the experiences of others, experiences that provided them with knowledge that better equipped them, indeed privileged them, in the study of The Law, especially within the upper-class domain that is Harvard.[9] Not knowing about bonds linked the complexities of class-jumping with the fearful certainty that, in the eyes of some, and most painfully in my own/my mother's eyes, I would be seen as *greñuda:* dirty, ugly, dumb, uncombed.

It was not possible for me to guard against the unexpected visibility—caused by class, gender, or ethnic differences—that lurked subtextually in the materials being studied. Such issues were, after all, pervasive, and I was very sensitive to them. Sitting in the cavernous classrooms at Harvard under the stern gaze of patrician jurists, mostly famous white male judges, was an emotionally wrenching experience. I remember the day one of the students was called on to explain *Erie v. Tompkins* (1938). His identification of the salient facts, his articulation of the major and minor issues, and his synopsis of the Court's reasoning were so precise and concise that they left a hush in the room. He had already achieved and was able to model for the rest of us the objectivity, the mental acuity that we/I aspired to. The respect shown for this type of analysis was qualitatively different from that shown for contextual or cultural analysis. Such occurrences in the classroom were memorable because they were defining: rational objectivity trumped emotional subjectivity. What they had to say trumped what I wanted to say but didn't.

I have no memory of ever speaking out again to sort out facts from my perspective, as I had done that one day in Criminal Law. There was to be only one Latina in any of my cases, only one Josephine. While I was at Harvard, my voice was not heard again in the classroom examining, exploring, or explaining the life situations of either defendants or victims. Silence accommodated the ideological uniformity but also revealed the inauthenticity implicit in discursive assimilation. As time went on, I felt diminished and irrelevant. It wasn't any one discussion, any one class, or any one professor. The pervasiveness of the ideology marginalized me and others; its efficacy depended upon its subtextual nature, and this masked quality made it difficult to pinpoint.

I had arrived at Harvard feeling different. I understood difference to be ineluctably linked with and limited to race, class, and gender. Learning about the varied experiences of students who had initially seemed to fit neatly into Us and Them categories was one of the profound lessons of law school. My life was eventually transformed by students of color from economically privileged backgrounds, self-described "poor farm boys" from Minnesota, the Irish daughters of Dorchester, the courage of a student with cerebral palsy. These and other students challenged the categories into which I forced my world. The kernel of that feeling I first associated with Josephine Chávez, that scrim of silence, remains within me. It is still my experience that issues of race, ethnicity, gender, or class are invisible to most of my white and/or male colleagues. Issues of sexual orientation, able-bodiedness, and sometimes class privilege can be invisible to me. I still make conscious choices about when to connect such issues to the topic at hand and when to remain silent. I'm still unclear about strategies and tactics, about being frontal or oblique.

Issues of race or gender are never trivial or banal from my perspective. Knowing how or when to assert them effectively as others react with hostility, boredom, or weariness can be a "crazy-making" endeavor. Sometimes it seems that every interaction requires that I overlook the terms of the discourse or that I affirmatively redefine them. My truths require that I say unconventional things in unconventional ways (Culp 1992).

Speaking out assumes prerogative. Speaking out is an exercise of privilege (Scales-Trent 1992). Speaking out takes practice. Silence ensures invisibility afforded by the "closet" in experiences of gay men and lesbians (Fajer 1992). Silence provides protection. Silence masks.

Trenzas: Braiding Latina Narratives

Let me show you my wounds: my stumbling mind, my
"excuse me" tongue, and this
nagging preoccupation
with the feeling of not being good enough.[10]

That I am writing autobiographically as a Latina is unusual; that I choose to do so in the context of legal scholarship is more unusual yet.[11] My purposes resemble some of the goals ascribed to African-American autobiography documented in the writings of Bell (1987, 1993), Williams (1991), Culp (1991), and Delgado and Stefancic (1993), among others. Autobiographical writing by African Americans has been described as serving descriptive and persuasive functions that are distinct from white autobiography. African-American autobiography "looks not backward over a completed career, but forward to what the black writer is doing and intends to do in the future" (Culp 1991:542).

Autobiographical writing and other forms of bi/multilingual expression in the legal academy and in legal scholarship legitimize multiple perspectives and validate personal experience. The writing of *mestizas* continues to expand the meaning of scholarship by including voices that "speak without the accents of ancestral power" (González & Treece 1992:xv).

Through shared language, goals, and visions, mestiza scholarship also connects us to those poets of Latinoamérica who "speak from the margins of the world system and from a position of exclusion" (González & Treece 1992:xv). Like them, we are engaged in a struggle to find ourselves as we reconstruct the world. Latino discourse "is not simply a locus of regret and imaginative explorations of other fictions; it is increasingly the site of a rehearsal of new relationships, new possibilities, new forms of struggle and often, at its best, a moving exhortation to find the self in the reconstruction of the world" (González & Treece 1992:xv). The exploration of personal agency through autobiography and the seizure of discursive space formerly denied to Latinas are regenerative acts that can transform self-understanding and reclaim for all Latinas the right to define ourselves and to reject unidimensional interpretations of our personal and collective experience.

STORYTELLING AS A CHALLENGE TO TRADITIONAL LEGAL DISCOURSE

The law and the practice of law are grounded in the telling of stories. Pleadings and judicial orders can be characterized as stylized stories (Delgado 1989). Legal persuasion in the form of opening statements and closing arguments is routinely taught as an exercise in storytelling. Client interviews are storytelling and story-listening events. Traditionally, legal culture within law firms, law schools, and courthouses has been transmitted through the "war stories" told by seasoned attorneys. Narrative laces through all aspects of legal education, legal practice, and legal culture. In these various ways, the use of narrative is not new to the legal academy.

Only recently, however, has storytelling begun to play a significant role in academic legal writing (Bell 1987; Cover 1983; Williams 1991). In the hands of Outsiders, storytelling seeks to subvert the dominant ideology. Stories told by those on the bottom, told from the "subversive-subaltern" perspective, challenge and expose the hierarchical and patriarchal order that exists within the legal academy and pervades the larger society (Matsuda 1987; Rajan 1992; Rosaldo 1989). Narrative that focuses on the experiences of Outsiders thus empowers both the storyteller and the story listener by virtue of its opposition to the traditional forms of discourse (González & Treece 1992).

Understanding stories told from different cultural perspectives requires that we suspend our notions of temporal and spatial continuity, plot, climax, and the interplay of narrator and protagonists (Rosaldo 1989). The telling of and listening to stories in a multicultural environment require a fundamental reexamination of the text, the subject, and the context of stories. The emphasis on critical scholarship (critical race theory, feminist jurisprudence, critical legal studies) and on narrative affirms those of us who are Outsiders working within the objectivist orientation of the legal academy and validates our experimentation with innovative formats and themes in our teaching and in our scholarship (Lawrence 1992).

Greñas: Un/Braiding Latina Narratives

Because I, a *mestiza,*
continually walk out of one culture
and into another,
because I am in all cultures at the same time,
alma entre dos mundos, tres, cuatro,
me zumba la cabeza con lo contradictorio,
Estoy norteada por todas las voces que me hablan
simultáneamente.[12]
[a soul between two worlds, three, four,
my head buzzes with the contradictory,
I am disoriented by all the voices that talk to me
simultaneously.]

PURSUING *MESTIZAJE* (OR TRANSCULTURATION)
IN THE LEGAL ACADEMY

The Euro-American conquest of the Southwest and Puerto Rico resulted in informal (Hernández-Chávez 1995; Espinoza 1990; Rosaldo 1989; Gómez 1973) and formal (Piatt 1990) prohibitions against the use of Spanish for public purposes. So, by inscribing myself in legal scholarship as mestiza, I seek to occupy common ground with Latinas/os in this hemisphere and with others, wherever situated, who are challenging "Western bourgeois ideology and hegemonic racialism with the metaphor of transculturation" (Morejón 1989:15–16).

As Latinas/os we, like many colonized peoples around the globe, are the biological descendants of both indigenous and European ancestors, as well as the intellectual progeny of Western and indigenous thinkers and writers. As evidenced by my names, I am the result of Mexican-Indian-Irish-French relations. I am also the product of English-speaking schools and a Spanish-speaking community. Claiming our mixed intellectual and linguistic heritage can attenuate the subordinating forces implicit in the monolinguality and homogeneity of the dominant culture. Anzaldúa (1987) has developed the idea of the "language of the borderlands. . . . There, at the juncture of cultures, languages cross-pollinate and are revitalized; they die and are born" (Preface). While I reject the idea that personal narratives can or should be generalized into grand or universalistic theories, our stories can help us search for unifying identifiers and mutual objectives. For example, the deracination of language purges words of their embedded racism, sexism, and other biases.[13]

Using Spanish (or other outlaw languages, dialects, or patois) in legal scholarship could be seen as an attempt to erect linguistic barriers or create exclusionary discursive spaces, particularly among Outsiders with whom Latinas share ideological, political, and pedagogical objectives.

Personal narratives of alienation or subordination present additional challenges when used in the domain of critical legal writing. Being a member of the legal professoriat, even if one is a member of several traditionally oppressed groups, means having a significant amount of social and cultural power and privilege. Personal accounts of humiliation, bias, or deprivation told from within the academy may sound to some like whining, or may be perceived as excessive involvement with the self rather than with the real needs of the Outsider communities. Hopefully, linguistic diversity will be recognized as enhancing the dialogue within the academy by bringing in new voices and fresh perspectives. For this reason, incorporating Spanish words, sayings, literature, and wisdom can have positive ramifications for those in the academy and in the profession and for those to whom we render legal services. I argue that the codeswitching that characterizes bilinguality (and Lionnet's

[1989] *métissage*) is analogous to the codeswitching involved in translating client stories into legal language (Montoya 1994).

CONCLUSION

New discursive formats, including the use of Latina autobiography in legal scholarship, enable us to reinvent ourselves. We can reject the dualistic patriarchal masks that we shrank behind and seize instead our multiple, contradictory, and ambiguous identities. As we reinvent ourselves, we import words and concepts into English and into academic discourse from formerly prohibited languages and taboo knowledge. The disruption of hegemonic tranquillity, the ambiguity of discursive variability, the cacophony of polyglot voices, the chaos of radical pluralism, are the desired by-products of transculturation, of mestizaje (Harris 1990). The pursuit of mestizaje, with its emphasis on our histories, our ancestries, and our past experiences, can give us renewed appreciation for who we are as well as a clearer sense of who we can become.

Our conceptual trenzas, our rebraided ideas, even though they may appear unneat or greñudas to others, suggest new opportunities for unmasking the subordinating effects of legal discourse. Our rebraided ideas, the trenzas of our multicultural lives, offer personally validating interpretations for the máscaras we choose to wear. My masks are what they are: in Santayana's (1967:131–132) words, merely "arrested expressions and echoes of feelings," the cuticles that protect my heart.

Gracias a mi mamá, Josephine Chávez, Gloria Anzaldúa, y muchas otras.

NOTES

1. A version of this essay appeared simultaneously in *Chicano-Latino Law Review* 15 (Spring 1994), 1–37 and *Harvard Women's Law Review* 17, 185–220. This work is dedicated to my husband, my parents, my sister, and my two daughters.
2. I use "Outsiders" to include people of color, women, gays, lesbians, and the poor—members of groups who have been discriminated against historically.
3. From "Mother, may I?" in *Planet, with Mother, May I?* © 1993 by Alma Villanueva.
4. Leslie G. Espinoza (1990:1885–1886) refers to her own "elaborate disguise of acculturation" and observes that other Outsiders "clothe themselves in the domi-

nant discourse of the legal academy and dress [themselves] in the attire of rigor and merit."

5. From "Exilio," by Gioconda Belli, in González & Treece (1992).

6. *People v. Josephine Chávez,* 176 P.2d 92 (Cal. App. 1947).

7. Shortly thereafter, I was nominated and elected section representative to the student government of Harvard Law School. I attributed the election results entirely to my outburst in Criminal Law. Like most other students, I was in search of markers and signs to determine how others viewed me. There were few such signs, and most were ambiguous.

8. The difference attributable to culture and not to denotative meaning between the word "shame" in English and the word *vergüenza* in Spanish is evident to me from the fact that my parents never spoke about shame; they did talk about vergüenza and about this person or that one being *sinvergüenza,* a dreaded condition.

9. Espinoza (1990:1885–1886) writes about exclusion from the dominant discourse: "It is painful to feel excluded and disturbing to perceive the world differently from those whose discourse dominates. . . . To explore that difference, to acknowledge it, is to be vulnerable."

10. From "Poem for the young white man who asked me how I, an intelligent, well-read person, could believe in the war between races," in *Emplumada,* by Lorna Dee Cervantes, © 1981 by Lorna Dee Cervantes. Reprinted by permission of the University of Pittsburgh Press.

11. For other examples of autobiographical legal scholarship by Latinas, see Espinoza (1990) and Hernández (1994).

12. From *Borderlands/La Frontera: The New Mestiza,* © 1987 by Gloria Anzaldúa.

13. When we attempt to understand the full range of connotations of our racial terminologies, we are forced to reexamine the unconscious linguistic roots of racial prejudice and to face the fact that language predetermines perception. This is why a word like *métis* or *mestizo* is most useful: it derives etymologically from the Latin *mixtus* [mixed], and its primary meaning refers to cloth made of two different fibers, usually cotton for the warp and flax for the woof. It is a neutral term, with no animal or sexual implication. It is not grounded in biological misnomers and has no moral judgments attached to it. It evacuates all connotation of "pedigreed" ascendance, unlike words such as "octoroon" and "half-breed."

REFERENCES

Anzaldúa, G. (1987). *Borderlands/La Frontera: The New Mestiza.* San Francisco:. Aunt Lute Books.

Banks, T. L. (1990). Gender bias in the classroom. *Southern Illinois University Law Journal* 14, 527–543.

Bell, D. (1987). *And We Are Not Saved: The Elusive Quest for Racial Justice.* New York: Basic Books.

——. (1993). *Faces from the Bottom of the Well: The Permanence of Racism.* New York: Basic Books.

Belli, G. (1992). "Exilio." In M. González & D. Treece (eds.), *The Gathering of Voices: The Twentieth Century Poetry of Latin America* (p. 345). New York: Verso.

Cervantes, L. D. (1981). "Poem for the young white man who asked me how I, an intelligent, well-read person, could believe in the war between races." In L. D. Cervantes (ed.), *Emplumada.* Pittsburgh: University of Pittsburgh Press.

Cover, R. (1983). The Supreme Court, 1982 term—Foreword: Nomos and narrative. *Harvard Law Review* 97, 4–68.

Culp, J., Jr. (1991). Autobiography and legal scholarship and teaching: Finding the me in the legal academy. *Virginia Law Review* 77, 539–559.

——. (1992). You can take them to water but you can't make them drink: Black legal scholarship and white legal scholars. *University of Illinois Law Review* 4, 1021–1041.

Delgado, R. (1989). Storytelling for oppositionists and others: A plea for narrative. *Michigan Law Review* 87, 2411–2441.

Delgado, R., & J. Stefancic. (1993). Critical race theory: An annotated bibliography. *Virginia Law Review* 79, 461–516.

Elkins, J. R. (1978). The legal persona: An essay on the professional mask. *Virginia Law Review* 64, 735–762.

Erie Railroad Co. v. Tompkins. (1938). 304 U.S. 64.

Espinoza, L. G. (1990). Masks and other disguises: Exposing legal academia. *Harvard Law Review* 103, 1878–1886.

Fajer, M. A. (1992). Can two real men eat quiche together? Storytelling, gender-role stereotypes, and legal protection for lesbians and gay men. *University of Miami Law Review* 46, 511–651.

Finley, L. M. (1989). Breaking women's silence in law: The dilemma of the gendered nature of legal reasoning. *Notre Dame Law Review* 64, 886–910.

Goffman, E. (1959). *The Presentation of the Self in Everyday Life.* Garden City, NY: Doubleday.

Gómez, D. F. (1973). *Somos Chicanos: Strangers in Our Own Land.* Boston: Beacon Press.

González, M., & D. Treece (eds.). (1992). *The Gathering of Voices: The Twentieth Century Poetry of Latin America.* New York: Verso.

Harris, A. (1990). Women of color in legal education: Representing La Mestiza. *Berkeley Women's Law Journal* 6, 107–112.

Helvering v. Horst. (1940). 311 U.S. 112.

Hernández, B. E. (1994). Building bridges—Latinas and Latinos at the crossroads:

Realities, rhetoric, and replacement. *Columbia Human Rights Law Review* 25, 369–433.

Hernández-Chávez, E. (1995). Native language loss and its implications for revitalization of Spanish in Chicano communities. In A. S. López (ed.), *Latino Language and Education: Communication and the Dream Deferred,* Volume 5 (pp. 58–74). New York: Garland.

Lawrence, C. R. (1992). The word and the river: Pedagogy as scholarship and struggle. *Southern California Law Review* 65, 2231–2298.

Lionnet, F. (ed.) (1989). *Autobiographical Voices: Race, Gender, Self-Portraiture.* Ithaca, NY: Cornell University Press.

Matsuda, M. J. (1987). Looking to the bottom: Critical legal studies and reparations. *Harvard Civil Rights-Civil Liberties Law Review* 22, 323–399.

Minow, M. (1987). The Supreme Court 1986 term—Foreword: Justice engendered. *Harvard Law Review* 101, 10–95.

Montoya, M. (1994). Law and language(s): Image, integration, and innovation. *La Raza Law Journal* 7, 147–153.

Morejón, N. (1989). Nación y mestizaje en Nicolas Guillen. In F. Lionnet (ed.), *Autobiographical Voices: Race, Gender, Self-Portraiture* (pp. 15–16). Ithaca, NY: Cornell University Press.

Noonan, J. T., Jr. (1976). *Persons and Masks of the Law: Cardozo, Holmes, Jefferson and Wythe as Makers of the Masks.* New York: Farrar, Straus, & Giroux.

People v. Josephine Chávez. (1947). 176 P.2d 92 (Cal.App. 1947).

Piatt, B. (1990). *Only English?: Law and Language Policy in the United States.* Albuquerque: University of New Mexico Press.

Rajan, G. (1992). Subversive-subaltern identity: Indira Gandhi as the speaking subject. In S. Smith & J. Watson (eds.), *De/Colonizing the Subject: The Politics of Gender in Women's Autobiography* (pp. 196–222). Minneapolis: University of Minnesota Press.

Reich, S. (1976). California Psychological Inventory: Profile of a sample of first year law students. *Psychological Reports* 39, 871–874.

Rosaldo, R. (1989). *Culture and Truth: The Remaking of Social Analysis.* Boston: Beacon Press.

Sánchez, M. E. (ed.). (1985). *Contemporary Chicana Poetry: Critical Approaches to an Emerging Literature.* Berkeley: University of California Press.

Santayana, G. (1967). *Soliloquies in England and Later Soliloquies.* New Introduction by Ralph Ross. Ann Arbor: University of Michigan Press.

Scales, A. C. (1990). Surviving legal de-education: An outsider's guide. *Vermont Law Review* 15, 139–164.

Scales-Trent, J. (1992). Sameness and difference in a law school classroom: Working at the crossroads. *Yale Journal of Law & Feminism* 4, 415–438.

Villanueva, A. (1993). "Mother, may I?" In A. Villanueva, *Planet, with Mother, May I?* (pp. 85–123). Tempe, AZ: Bilingual Press.

Weigert, A., et al. (1986). *Society and Identity: Toward a Sociological Psychology.* New York: Cambridge University Press.

Wildman, S. M. (1989). The classroom climate: Encouraging student involvement. *Berkeley Women's Law Journal* 4, 326–334.

Williams, P. J. (1991). *The Alchemy of Race and Rights: Diary of a Law Professor.* Cambridge, MA: Harvard University Press.

About the Contributors

Charlene Villaseñor Black received her Ph.D. in art history at the University of Michigan at Ann Arbor and is an assistant professor at the University of New Mexico. She teaches Spanish and Latin American art and is currently expanding her dissertation, "Saints and Social Welfare in Golden Age Spain: The Imagery of the Cult of Saint Joseph," into a manuscript for a book on saints' cults in Spain and the Americas. Her research focuses on the intersections of political, gender, and racial ideologies in religious art.

D. Letticia Galindo holds a Ph.D. in applied linguistics from the University of Texas at Austin. She is an associate professor in the Department of Languages & Literatures and an associate research professor at the Hispanic Research Center at Arizona State University. She is also an affiliated faculty member of Women's Studies. Her research interests include women's language use, language contact phenomena, language attitudes, and linguistic descriptions of Spanish and English varieties, including caló and Chicano English. She was an invited speaker at the third annual Berkeley Women & Language Conference, where she presented a paper entitled "Capturing Chicana Voices: An Interdisciplinary Approach." Her publications include "Dispelling the Male-Only Myth: Chicanas and Caló," "A Sociolinguistic Description of Linguistic Self-Expression, Innovation, and Power among Chicanas in Texas and New Mexico" (written with M. D. Gonzales), and "Crossing Borders/Cruzando Fronteras: The Transmission of Chicana Voices across Disciplines" (forthcoming).

María Dolores Gonzales earned a Ph.D. in Spanish linguistics from the University of New Mexico. Currently she is the program manager at the Southwest Hispanic Research Institute at the University of New Mexico. Her primary research interest is language and gender. In 1992 she presented a paper at the Berkeley Women & Language Conference, "A Sociolinguistic Description of Linguistic Self-Expression, Innovation, and Power among Chicanas in Texas and New Mexico," which was published in *Locating Power: Proceedings of the Second Berkeley Women & Language Conference* (1993). Her most recent publication is a book chapter, "Sometimes Spanish and Sometimes English: Language Use among Rural, New Mexican Chicanas," in *Gender Articulated: Language and the Socially Constructed Self* (1995). She is currently researching interviewing styles and techniques used in the Chicana/o community. In addition to her academic research, she is a published poet and essayist.

Erlinda Gonzales-Berry is chair of the Ethnic Studies department at Oregon

State University. She is editor of *Pasó por aquí: Critical Essays on the New Mexico Literary Tradition 1542–1989,* and coeditor of *Las mujeres hablan* and *Recovering the U.S. Latino Literary Heritage.* She is also author of numerous articles on Chicana/o literature and culture and of a novel, *Paletitas de guayaba.*

Ida M. Luján is a resident of Santa Fe, New Mexico. She has a J.D. from Baylor University School of Law and has practiced law in New Mexico since 1982 in the areas of employment, administrative law, and general civil law. She currently provides consulting services, such as conducting sexual harassment and mediation training seminars and drafting sexual harassment, grievance, and investigative procedures, to governmental and nonprofit organizations and educational institutions.

Christine Marín is a native Arizonan and curator/archivist for the Hayden Library's Chicano Collection at Arizona State University. She is a Ph.D. candidate in the Department of History and an adjunct faculty associate in Women's Studies, where she has taught courses on the history of Mexican-American women. Her journal articles and book reviews reflect her expertise on various themes in Mexican-American and Chicano history. She participates in the Speaker Services Program for the Arizona Humanities Council, which presented her with its 1995 Distinguished Scholar Award.

Jacqueline M. Martínez is an assistant professor of communication and Women's Studies at Purdue University. Her research focuses on the relationship between the constraints of dominant discourses and the possibilities of human agency in the constructions of race, class, and sexuality. Her current work includes a phenomenological essay, "Radical Ambiguities and the Chicana Lesbian: Body Topographies on Contested Lands." She is coauthor, with Andrew Smith, of "Signifying Harassment: Communication, Ambiguity, and Power," in *Human Studies* 18 (1995).

Norma Mendoza-Denton received her Ph.D. in linguistics from Stanford University and is an assistant professor in the Department of Spanish and Portuguese and the Department of Linguistics at Ohio State University. Her current research is on language, style, and identity among Latina gangs.

Margaret E. Montoya is an associate professor of law at the University of New Mexico School of Law. She is a graduate of San Diego State University and Harvard Law School. She is currently working on a book on Latinas and legal identities. Her research focuses on feminist and Outsider legal discourses, language suppression, and reclamation. She is currently using interdisciplinary and bilingual scholarship to analyze cross-cultural collaborations. She is also working on a project using border metaphors to explore hybrid identities.

Aurora E. Orozco was born in Nuevo León, Mexico, and immigrated to Mercedes, Texas, when she was six years old. She is a community activist, writer, historian, and poet. She writes of the struggles she and her family endured while she was growing up in Texas, being discriminated against for speaking Spanish, and her determination to educate her children, who are all university graduates and successful professionals. She has been an active speaker on behalf of the Chicana/o community and has spoken to groups at the University of Texas at Austin, University of Texas at San Antonio, Laredo State University, and Our Lady of the Lake University in San Antonio.

INDEX

academic achievement, 51, 54

accommodation, 24, 30; in social activities, 31–34

acculturation, 195. *See also* assimilation

acequia systems, 6; and gender, 101–5; in northern New Mexico, 98, 99–100; operation of, 100–101

adolescents, and *pachuquismo,* 177–78

age, 24, 31–32

Aguascalientes (Mexico), 85

Agustín, José, 129

Alarcón, Norma, 79

Albuquerque (N.Mex.), 23, 27, 155–56

Alcoff, Linda, 66

Alegría, María Fernanda, 129

Alejandra, 49

altars, 151

Alvarez, George, 181

American G.I. Forum, 114–15

Americanization, 14–15, 21, 44

Ana, 45

Anaya, Rudolfo, 124

Anglo Americans: in Globe-Miami area, 85, 87, 89, 90; and Mexican Americans, 71, 78; in New Mexico, 14–15; in Texas, 109–10, 111, 115, 116

Annia, 49–50

Anzaldúa, Gloria, 6, 64, 135, 175

Arizona State University, 91–92; and Chicano Movement, 93–94; Chicano Research (Studies) Collection, 6, 95–97; and Mexican American Students Organization, 94–95

art, 7, 135; aerosol, 155–56; of Elena Baca, 137–44; of María Baca, 160–67; Catholic themes in, 134, 136–37, 167–68; collaborative, 154–55; of Lydia Madrid, 144–49; of Delilah Montoya, 149–54, 156–60

Ashcroft, Bill, 125

assimilation, 60, 66, 72, 78, 195–96

Athena's veil, 127

Atocha Dream (Baca), 138–40, 141

Austin (Tex.), 176, 177, 178, 183

authenticity, 124

autobiography, 203–4, 207

Axford, H. William, 94, 95, 96

Aztecs, 145–46

Baca, Agnes, 140–41

Baca, Elena, 149, 167–68; *Atocha Dream,* 138–40, 141; *Milagros* series, 141–44; *Portrait of My Grandmother,* 137–38

Baca, Elena (grandmother), 137, 138–39, 140, 142, 143, 144

Baca, Juan, 137, 140, 141–42

Baca, María, 149, 160, 168; "Dream #1," 166–67; *God Grant Me the Serenity,* 161–62; *Puentes/Bridges,* 161, 162–64; *Responding to Life's Forces,* 165–66; *Sweet Dreams of You,* 166

Baca, Miguelito (Michelo), 137, 140, 142–43

Baca Zinn, M., 64

"Bamba, La," 89–90

Barrera, Martha: "Café con Leche," 78

Baylor Law School, 103

Bexley, Laurie: "Even Unintentional Racism Hurts," 50

bilingualism, 25, 26, 91–92, 114, 115, 118–19; and gang identity, 44–45; and language choice, 178–79; and voice, 123–24

Bishop (Tex.), 107–8

Blacks, 116, 117

boarding school, 21

boats, 147

border culture, 30–31, 36n. 2

Brice (N.Mex.), 86

bridal shower: codeswitching at, 34–35; respect and accommodation at, 32–34

Brito, Aristeo, 124

Buchel Bank, 117

cábula, 186–87, 189, 190

"Café con Leche" (Barrera), 78

California, 5, 6; Chicano/a culture in, 40–41; discrimination in, 71–72; high school in, 39–40; middle-class upbringing in, 73–77

California State University at Northridge, 60

California State University (CSU) system, 48, 49

caló, 7, 114, 125, 178, 180, 181; female use of, 182–83, 186–91; terminology of, 183–84

calques, 125

Camp Pine (Ariz.), 87

Camp Verde (Ariz.), 87

cantineras, 18, 183

Caras viejas y vino nuevo (Morales), 123–24

Carolina, 178, 184–85, 186–87, 188

Carrancistas, 107

Castellanos, Rosario, 129

Castillo, Ana, 79

Catholic Church, 14, 25, 108–9

Catholicism, 7; iconography of, 135–36, 170–71n. 18; Spanish, 137–44; syncretism in, 154–55; visual imagery of, 134–35, 146, 147–48, 149, 151–54, 156–60, 161–64, 166, 167–68

CCC. See Civilian Conservation Corps

Cerralvo (Nuevo León), 106–7

Cézanne, Paul, 161

Chávez, Josephine, 198, 199, 200, 201

Chicana Lesbians: The Girls Our Mothers Warned Us About (Trujillo), 77

Chicanas/os, 3, 40, 42, 64; and Catholic imagery, 134–35; ethnic consciousness as, 59–61; in gangs, 43, 44–45; identity as, 6, 62, 63, 67, 93–94; lesbian, 77–78; and narrative voice, 129–30; silencing of, 4–5; spirituality of, 150–54

Chicano Art: Resistance and Affirmation, 1965–1985, 136

Chicano Movement: and Arizona State University, 93–95; and art, 149–50, 168; documenting, 95–96

Chicano Neoindigenism, Madrid's art as, 145–49

Chicano Spanish, 7, 40–41

Chicano Students Association, 60

Chicano Studies (ASU), 95–96

Chihuahua, 86

Chimayó, 140

cholas/cholos, 178, 182–83. See also pachucas/pachucos

Christ: as artistic theme, 137–38, 140, 141, 148; imagery of, 151, 152, 153, 158, 167

Cinco de Mayo, 109

Cisneros, Sandra, 124, 126; *House on Mango Street,* 123

Civilian Conservation Corps (CCC), 87

Cixous, Helene, 132

class, and knowledge, 201, 202

classism, 64, 71

Coatlicue, 148, 170n. 10

codeswitching, 5, 7, 36n. 4, 96, 124, 125–26, 179–80; in Córdova, 16, 19, 20, 26, 27, 31; in Hispano community, 29–30; purpose of, 185–86; at social activities, 34–35

collaboration, 155–56

colonialism, 80; in artistic themes, 137–44, 149, 156, 159–60, 167–68; and history, 78–79

comisiones, 99, 104–5

communities, 36–37n. 5, 196; interaction in and among, 24–26, 29–30; and public domain, 27–28

compadrazgo, 25, 37n. 6

Compañeras: Latina Lesbians (Ramos), 77

compliments, expletives as, 189

Concerned Citizens for Education, 119

Condi, Marise, 124

consejos para la novia, 34–35

Corazón Segrado/The Sacred Heart, El (Montoya), 154–56, 157(fig.)

Córdova (N.Mex.), 15; community interaction in, 24–28; cultural brokers in, 35–36; data collection in, 16–17; education in, 20–21; employment in, 22–24; families and generations in, 17–18; family size in, 21–22; language use in, 19–20; and noncommunity interaction, 28–35; social networks in, 13–14

Cota-Cárdenas, Margarita, 129

Coyote (N.Mex.), 100

CSU. *See* California State University system

Cubism, 161

Cuero (Tex.), 115; discrimination in, 116–17, 118–19

cultural brokers, 22, 35–36

culture: Chicano/a, 40–41; diversity of, 45–46; masking, 200–201; Mexican American, 69–72, 74, 75–77, 88–89, 117, 118

Cummings, Laura, 182

cursing, 180; and gender, 181–82; purposes of, 188–89

Daule School, 117

Davis, C., 107

deportations, 114

Depression, 86–87, 111–12

derogation, 175–76

Desen/Mascarando Silencio/Un/Masking Silence (Montoya), 196–97

Dewitt County (Tex.), 115

discrimination, 6, 69; against Mexican Americans, 70–72, 86; in Texas, 113, 114, 115–17, 118–19

disenfranchisement, 182–83

division of labor, 100

domain: and language use, 18, 19–20, 24–25; public, 27–28

"Dream #1" (M. Baca), 166–67

drugs, 184, 185

earth, 151

East Austin (Tex.), 177, 178, 183

education, 72, 106; at Arizona State University, 91–93; in Cuero, 116–17; in Globe-Miami schools, 86, 88, 89–91; and identity, 54–55; importance of, 119–20; and language attitudes, 51–54; in Mercedes, 109–11; in New Mexico, 14–15, 20–21; in Texas, 115, 118

El Paso (Tex.), 177, 182, 183

employment, of Cordovans, 22–24

English, 23, 88; Chicano, 40, 44–45; in Córdova, 19, 24, 26–27; education in, 15, 20, 21, 109–10; fluency in, 46–50, 54; and noncommunity interaction, 28–32; Standard, 41–42; use of, 123–24, 179

English as a Second Language (ESL), 5, 41, 47, 48, 49

Española, 22, 26

Estrada, Roberto, 113

Estrada Phillips, Lorenzo, 106, 107

ethnicity, 62, 64, 67; and English fluency, 46–47; in Globe, 87–88; and language, 24, 26–27, 65–66; and modes of consciousness, 59–61, 79–80

ethnography, 16, 39–40

"Even Unintentional Racism Hurts" (Bexley), 50

expletives, 189; and gender, 181–82; as taboo language, 180–81

Familia, La (Montoya), 156

Familias Unidas, 118

families, familia, 72, 106, 200; artistic portrayal of, 137–44, 169n. 5; in Córdova, 17–18; sizes of, 21–22

farmwork, 107–8

femininity, 127, 165–66, 175–76

feminism, 65, 141, 154

feminist theory, 62, 63–64

FEP. See Fluent English Proficient

fiestas patrias, las, 109

Fluent English Proficient (FEP), 47–48, 50

funerals, 109

gangs, 178; Latina youth, 39, 42–45; terminology of, 183–85

Gaspar de Alba, Alicia, 136

gender, 100, 127, 203; and acequia tradition, 6, 101–4; as artistic theme, 156, 168; and expletives, 181–82; and language use, 131–32, 175–77, 182–83, 189–91; and voice, 128–30

generations, 18, 25–26, 154

Globe (Ariz.), 85, 86; Euclid Avenue in, 87–88; high school in, 89–91

God Grant Me the Serenity (M. Baca), 161–62

God's Gift (Montoya), 156

Goldman, Shifra, 136

Gonzales, María, 107

Gonzales, Miguel, 113

Gonzales Toscano, Gertrudis, 106, 107

Gonzalez, Deena, 78

Gonzalez, S., 64

grammar, art as, 147

Greco, El, 161

Greñas: Un/Braiding Latina Narratives (Montoya), 205

Griffith, Gareth, 125

Guadalupana. See Virgin of Guadalupe

"Gulf Dreams" (Pérez), 77

Harvard Law School, 202–3, 208n. 7

Hayden Library, 92, 94, 95–97

Head Start, 21

Helvering v. Horst, 201

Henderson, Mr., 117

heterosexuality: and identity, 62–63; and privilege, 68–69

high school: ethnographic fieldwork at, 39–40; Globe, 89–90; Standard English in, 41–42

Hill Street School (Globe, Ariz.), 88, 89

Hispano community: codeswitching in, 29–30

history, 78–79, 144
Holy Child of Atocha, 140, 141
Holy Family, 156, 158
Holy Week, 151
Hoover, Herbert, 111
House on Mango Street (Cisneros), 123
Houston (Tex.), 176, 178, 184
humor, 131–32

iconography, icons: Catholic, 134–36,
    153, 168; religious, 161–64; Sacred
    Heart as, 154–55; Spanish colonial,
    137–44
identity, 6, 36–37n. 5, 39, 70, 168;
    artistic themes of, 140–41, 165–66;
    Chicano/a, 93–94, 154–55, 168; and
    education, 54–55; ethnic, 64–65,
    66–67; gang, 43–45; and language,
    16, 21, 24, 26–27, 41, 51–54, 65–66,
    126; lesbian, 61–64; and modes of
    consciousness, 59–61, 79–80; and
    privilege, 67–68
ideology, and gang structure, 43, 44–
    45
illness, as artistic theme, 140, 141–43
imagery, 156; Catholic, 134–44; Native
    American, 145–49
immigrants, 6–7, 39, 42; in Arizona,
    85, 86; in Texas, 107–14
indigenous peoples. *See* Native Ameri-
    cans
Inspiration Consolidated Copper Com-
    pany, 86
Inspiration Hill, 87
Iragaray, Luce, 127
Iron Cap Mine, 86
Islas, Arturo, 124

jacales, 106–7
Jaenicke, Ethel, 90
Jay's Credit Clothing, 91

Jemez Mountains, 100
Jesús' Carburetor Repair (Montoya),
    156
Jim Crow laws, 115–16
Juanita, 178, 181, 184–85, 186–87, 188
Jung, Carl Gustav, 164

knots, symbolism of, 146–47
knowledge, 154, 199, 200, 201–2
known-knowing, 60, 61

labor, 24
labyrinths, 146
language attitudes, and identity, 51–54
language choice, 178–80, 189–91
language hybridity, 26, 36
La Raza Unida, 118
Latina-Daughtertalk, 199–200
Latinas/os, 3, 39, 64, 112; and English
    fluency classification, 49–50; and
    law, 198–99; in law school, 197–
    98; in legal profession, 195–96; in
    northern California, 5, 40; and Stan-
    dard English, 41–42
law: contextualization of, 198–99, 200;
    and *mestizaje,* 205–7; and story-
    telling, 204–5
law school, 197–98, 203; knowledge
    in, 199, 201–2; masking in, 200–201
League of United Latin American Citi-
    zens (LULAC), 112, 115, 117
legal profession, 195–96, 207–8n. 4
legal scholarship: and *mestizaje,* 205–
    7; storytelling in, 204–5
LEP. *See* Limited English Proficient
lesbian(s): Chicana, 77–78, 136; iden-
    tity as, 61–64, 65, 79; as marginal-
    ized identity, 67–68; and privilege,
    68–69
Limited English Proficient (LEP), 47,
    48, 49

literature, gendered, 128, 129
López, Yolanda, 136–37, 149
Lordes, Audre, 64
Los Alamos (N.Mex.), 22–23
Los Angeles (Calif.), 177
LULAC. *See* League of United Latin American Citizens

Mackin, Jerry, 119
Madrid, Lydia, 144, 149, 168; *Navigation: Reading the Water,* 145; *Ocean: A según lo hagan,* 145, 147; *Señor del Monte/mūXandohu,* 147–48; *Trailblazing: Reading the Ground,* 145; *Wood: A según te lo digan,* 145–47
Maldonando, Dr., 113
Malinche, La (Doña Marina), 79, 129–30, 171n. 19; artistic images of, 156–57, 158(fig.)
Mano Poderosa, 158
Marcelo, 114
marginalization, 4, 67–68, 69
Marín, Alejandro Trujillo, 86, 87
Marín, Eulalia Rentería, 86–87
Marín, Lupe Trujillo, 85, 87
Marín, Natalia Trujillo, 85–86, 88
Martínez, Octavio, 70–72
Martínez, Octavio Tergo, 70
Marxism, 135
Máscaras: Un/Masking the Self (Montoya), 194
masking, 194; bicultural, 200–201; in legal profession, 196–97, 207–8n. 4; outsider, 195–96
MASO. *See* Mexican American Students Organization
Matachín, El, 157–59
Matachines fiesta, 156–58
mayordomos, 99, 104–5
McAllen (Tex.), 70–71

MECHA. *See* Movimiento Estudiantil Chicano de Aztlán
Memi, Albert, 125
Mercedes (Tex.), 107, 108, 115; during Depression, 111–12; education in, 109–11; employment in, 112–13; during World War II, 113–14
Mesa de Poleo, 100
Mesoamerica, artistic themes from, 135, 145–46, 147–49, 168, 170n. 11
mestizaje, 208n. 13; in art, 154–55, 160, 168; in law, 205–7
mestizas/os, 6, 79, 204
Mexican Africans, 106
Mexican Americans, 60, 78; cultural heritage of, 69–72, 73–74, 75–77, 88–89, 118; and Depression, 86–87; discrimination against, 70–71, 113, 114, 115–16; ethnic identity of, 65–66; pride of, 89–90, 112, 117, 120
Mexican American Students Organization (MASO), 94–96
Mexican Mafia, 42
Mexican Muralist Movement, 135
Mexicans, 42, 43; and Depression, 111–12; in Globe-Miami area, 86–87; identity as, 16, 39; in Texas, 107–14
Mexican Social Realism, 135
Miami (Ariz.), 85, 86–87
Miami Copper Company, 86
middle class, in California, 73–77
Migra, La, 114
migrants, 6–7, 85, 86
Milagros series (Baca), themes in, 141–44
mining and miners, 85, 86
mining companies, 85, 106, 107
modes of consciousness, 80–81nn. 4, 6; and ethnic identity, 59–61, 62, 79–80

Montemayor Gonzales, Gabriela, 106
Montoya, Delilah, 160, 168; *El Corazón Segrado/The Sacred Heart,* 154–56, 157(fig.); *La Familia,* 156; *God's Gift,* 156; influences on, 149–50; *Jesús' Carburetor Repair,* 156; *La Malinche,* 156–57, 158(fig.); *El Matachín,* 157–59; *La Muerte and Infinity,* 156, 157(fig.); *Saints and Sinners,* 150–54
Moors, artistic portrayal of, 157–59
moradas, 150, 151
Moraga, Cherríe, 6, 64, 124
Morales, Alejandro: *Caras viejas y vino nuevo,* 123–24
mortality, 156
Mothertalk, 199
Movimiento Estudiantil Chicano de Aztlán (MECHA), 6, 96
Muerte and Infinity, La (Montoya), 156, 157(fig.)
murals, 155–56, 157(fig.), 170n. 11

narration: and gender, 128–30; and voice, 126–28
Native Americans, 21, 81–82n. 12; and artistic themes, 145–48, 162–64, 168; as artists, 160–61; self-realization of, 164–65, 166
Navigation: Reading the Water (Madrid), 145
New Mexican Spanish, 7, 14
New Mexico (Nuevo México), 3, 4, 6, 137, 168; Americanization in, 14–15; Catholicism in, 150–54; public education in, 20–21; social networks in, 13–14; water management in, 98–105; women's language use in, 5, 16–17
Norteñas, 39; identity and ideology of, 43–45

North Ward School (Mercedes, Tex.), 109, 110–11
Nuestra Familia, 42
Nuestra Señora de la Merced, 108–9

Ocean: A según lo hagan (Madrid), 145, 147
orature, 124
Orozco, Cynthia, 119
Orozco, María Teresa, 116
Orozco, Primitivo, 115
Ortega, Adolfo, 186
Otomí, 148
Our Lord of the Mountain, 148
Outsiders, 17, 195–96, 205

pachucas/pachucos, 7, 114, 176, 177–78, 199; language use of, 182–83, 186–88
pachuquismo, 177
Paletitas de guayaba (Gonzales-Berry), 7, 126; voice in, 127–30, 131
panthers, as theme, 165–66
parciantes, 99
paths, symbolic representations of, 146–47
peer groups, 42, 44
penitentes (Los Hermanos Penitentes), 170n. 12; as artistic theme, 150–54
people of color, 3, 195
People of the State of California v. Josephine Chávez, The, 197–98
Pérez, Emma, 6; "Gulf Dreams," 77
Pérez García, Hector, 114
Phoenix (Ariz.), 91
Picasso, Pablo, 161
pictorial language, 7, 134, 135
pintas, 7, 176, 184–85, 186–87
piojos, 86, 116
placas, 156

Portrait of My Grandmother (Baca), 137–38
portraits, 136; Elena Baca's, 137–40
poverty, 70, 72, 75–76, 109; and law, 198–99
power relations, 62
pregnancy, unwanted, 197, 198–200
prisoners, 178; language of, 184–85, 186–87
privilege, 127; and heterosexuality, 68–69; and identity, 67–68
Public Education Act (1891), 20
Puentes/Bridges (M. Baca), 161, 162–64
putas, 182, 183

Quetzalcoatl, 147, 148

race, 203; as artistic theme, 157, 158–59
racism, 64, 65, 66, 81n. 8, 88, 90, 92, 160; internalized, 71, 77, 78, 80; in Texas, 115–16, 117, 118–19
relajes, 184–85
religion, syncretism in, 154–55, 159. *See also* Catholicism
Rentería, Francisco, 86
Rentería, Natalia Chacon, 86
resistance, 15, 28
respect: and accommodation, 32–34; and language, 24, 31–32
Responding to Life's Forces (M. Baca), 165–66
Rich, Adrienne, 68
Río Grande Valley, 6–7, 111
role-playing, 196–97
Roosevelt, Franklin D., 112
Ruiz, Vicki, 78

Sacred Heart, 146, 154–55
Sad Eyes, 45

saints, imagery of, 135–36, 140, 168
Saints and Sinners (Montoya), imagery in, 150–54
San Antonio (Tex.), 107
Sánchez, Mary, 119
Sandoval, Juan, 151, 154
San Fernando Valley, 73
Sangre de Cristo Mountains, 100
San José *(morada),* 151
Santa Fe (N.Mex.), 22
Santa Fe National Forest, 100
Santo Niño de Atocha, 140, 141
San Ysidro (N.Mex.), 150
Sebastiana, Doña, 156
segregation, 86, 87, 116
self-realization, 164–65
Señor del Monte/mūXandohu (Madrid), 147–48
"Serenity Prayer," 161–62
Servín, Manuel Patricio, 94, 95, 96
Seven Acts of Mercy, 153
sex and sexuality, 65, 79, 199–200
sickness, as artistic theme, 140–41
silences and silencing, 175–76, 200, 202, 203; of Chicano Spanish, 4–5; and cultural heritage, 69, 70, 76–78; in narrative, 126–27
Silicon Valley, 42
silicosis, 86
Simi Valley, 70, 81n. 11
Sims, Dr., 119
SJHS. *See* Sor Juana High School
snitches, 184–85
social allegiance, 41
social contact, 24, 25
socialization, and language use, 175–77
social networks: and language, 24, 25–26; in New Mexico, 13–14
social structure, 15, 18
solidarity, 24, 27, 28

Sor Juana, 128

Sor Juana High School (SJHS), 42; demographics of, 45–46; English fluency classification at, 46–50; ethnographic fieldwork at, 39–40; gangs at, 43–45; language attitudes at, 51–54

Soto, Gary, 124

Southern Illinois University, 64

Spanish, 23, 44, 110, 206; and bilingualism, 119–20; Chicano, 4–5, 40–41; code altering in, 125–26; in Córdova, 30–31; and ethnic identity, 65–66, 73–74; and noncommunity member interaction, 28–29; popular, 178–79; in private domain, 24–25; respect and use of, 18, 19–20, 21, 27, 31–32, 91–92, 123, 124, 175

Spanish Colonial Arts Society, 168

Spanish Conquest, 147

speech communities, 13, 15, 31; interaction among, 29–30; silencing in, 4–5; and social context, 27–28, 35

spirituality, Chicano, 150–54

Stations of the Cross, representations of, 151–53

storytelling, and legal discourse, 204–5

suffering, as artistic theme, 137–38, 140, 141–43

Sureñas, 39, 42; identity and ideology of, 43–45; language attitudes of, 51–54

Sweet Dreams of You (M. Baca), 166

symbolism, 171n. 19; artistic, 146–47; Catholic, 137–44; gang, 43–44

syncretism: gender and race, 156–57; religious, 154–55, 159

taboo language, 7, 175; cursing as, 188–89; definition of, 180–81; female use of, 176–77

testimonios, 5–6

Texans for the Educational Advancement of Mexican Americans, 118

Texas, 3, 4, 6–7, 185; American G.I. Forum in, 114–15; Depression in, 111–12; discrimination in, 70–71, 116–17; immigrants in, 107–11; Jim Crow laws in, 115–16; Mexican Americans in, 65–66; *pachuca* culture in, 177–78; silencing in, 175–76; during World War II, 113–14

Thalia, language attitudes of, 51–54

Tiffin, Helen, 125

Tin Tan, 114

Titian, 161

Torreón (Coahuila), 85

Toscano, Ignacia, 107

Toscano, Juan, 106

Trailblazing: Reading the Ground (Madrid), 145

Treaty of Guadalupe Hidalgo, 14

Trenzas: Braiding Latina Narratives (Montoya), 203

Tucson (Ariz.), 182, 183, 186

Tyrone (N.Mex.), 86

UC. *See* University of California system

United Farm Workers, 95

University of California at Los Angeles (UCLA), 71

University of California (UC) system, 48, 49

University of New Mexico, 21

unknowing-knowing, 60, 61, 80n. 3

upward mobility, 23–24

Valens, Richie, 89

Velázquez, Diego, 161

Veronica, 153

Vigil, Evangelina, 176–77

violence, 161–62

Virgin Mary, 153

Virgin of Guadalupe, 136; iconography of, 134–35, 158, 161, 163–64, 166; imagery of, 167, 168

visual language, 7, 134, 135

voice: and bilingualism, 123–25; and gender, 128–30; and narration, 126–28; silencing, 175–76

water management, in northern New Mexico, 98–105

weddings, 27–28, 109

White, Mrs., 110

Wood: A según te lo digan (Madrid), 145–47

World War II, 113–14

Yaquis, 148

Zacatecas, 140

Zavella, P., 64